Errol A. Mullings

THE
BARRICADING
YOKE
OF
UNFORGIVENESS

Editions Dedicaces

THE BARRICADING YOKE OF UNFORGIVENESS

Copyright © 2015 by Editions Dedicaces LLC

All rights reserved. No part of this book may be used or reproduced in any form whatsoever without written permission except in the case of brief quotations embodied in critical articles or reviews.

Published by:
    Editions Dedicaces LLC
    12759 NE Whitaker Way, Suite D833
    Portland, Oregon, 97230
    www.dedicaces.us

Library of Congress Cataloging-in-Publication Data
    Mullings, Errol A.
    I Got Out Alive! / by Errol A. Mullings.
    p. cm.
    ISBN-13: 978-1-77076-556-6 (alk. paper)
    ISBN-10: 1-77076-556-5 (alk. paper)

Errol A. Mullings

THE BARRICADING YOKE *OF* UNFORGIVENESS

Contents

Chapter One The Burdens of Pain..1
Chapter Two Understanding Gives Clarity............................12
Chapter Three Misguided Reasoning..24
Chapter Four Relationships..31
Chapter Five Satanic Deceptive Disruptions........................42
Chapter Six Importance of Time..51
Chapter Seven The Beginning...59
Chapter Eight Problems in Paradise...68
Chapter Nine God is Always Authentic...................................76
Chapter Ten The Cycle of Life...81
Chapter Eleven Life's Curve Balls..89
Chapter Twelve Damaging Children...98
Chapter Thirteen Jehovah's Priceless Jewels.......................109
Chapter Fourteen Ancestral Blunders....................................117
Chapter Fifteen Always Trust God..126
Chapter Sixteen Second Generation Barriers....................135
Chapter Seventeen Children Need Stability.......................143
Chapter Eighteen Choices..151
Chapter Nineteen Unresolved Issues Relocate with Us........157
Chapter Twenty Greed..167
Chapter Twenty-One God Always Gives Second Chances.....175
Chapter Twenty-Two Family Responsibilities....................180
Chapter Twenty-Three Always Remain Focused...............191
Chapter Twenty-Four Casualties..200
Chapter Twenty-Five Never Give Up......................................210

Chapter Twenty-Six Triumphing Over Adversatives...............224

Chapter Twenty-Seven Revenge Is Never Sweet...................232

Chapter Twenty-Eight Cleansing..238

Chapter Twenty-Nine New Beginnings...................................252

Chapter Thirty Sin Will Mutilate Great Rulers........................258

Chapter Thirty-One Obsession Can Destroy..........................265

Chapter Thirty-Two Uncertainty Births Insecurity..................271

Chapter Thirty-Three We killed the Messenger.....................280

Chapter One
The Burdens of Pain

Pain will never be a peacetime advocate. It is our unfriendly central command center. It delivers discomfort with grueling efficiency and precision. But pain is a necessary inconvenience. It is an urgent alert that some obstruction has entered our system. Nobody likes to deal with this potential crisis.

Our first response understandably will be tension and anxiety. Any ailment will automatically be treated as an enemy. But we should investigate the reasons for any disturbance. And we should always prioritize immediate action. This should minimize major concerns.

Initial painful conditions are routinely categorized as physical health related issues. Most will promptly respond to discomfort associated to a physical illness. No one likes to be confined because of an illness. Everyone hates living in misery. But enduring difficult challenges are the sad realities of living. The cycle of life makes this abundantly clear.

Most ailments are routinely considered treatable maladies. But some sickness can be life threatening. A thorough examination should always be a mandatory requirement. Treatment should then be administered in accordance with the diagnosis. Progress should be monitored closely for effectiveness.

Staying healthy is an inbred desire for of all human beings. For many, this is the focal point of their existence. Some will exhaust countless time and effort, to demonstrate and showcase the epitome of perfect health. But our physical health and well being, is only part of our unique and our intricate makeup.

Human beings tend to keenly observe the rules of the literal and visual. Most will readily respond to things that can be seen and touched. This is because we can easily relate to them. Concentrating and focusing and the obvious, is routinely easy and reliable for many.

It is customary to ignore, bi-pass, or misinterpret anything that cannot be literally seen and touched. It is not unusual to become apprehensive and intimidated, regarding situations that cannot be immediately understood. But all disturbances originate from within. Any discomfort will create uneasiness.

Life is constantly exposing us to pleasures and hurt. We will automatically absorb most situations that we are exposed to. Plusses and minuses will always get digested at conscious and subconscious levels. All interferences will eventually get stored in our memory bank. This is what living and learning is all about.

Pain does not discriminate. Physical or emotional hurt carry the same stresses and concerns. These bombardments can have a profound impact on our heart and mind. But we will respond vastly differently to a physical crisis versus a psychological disorder.

There are also times when a mental disturbance can mimic a physical ailment. This is why many experience difficulty understanding, and dealing with severe discomfort affecting their internal infra structure.

Persistent sneezing, a runny nose, or an abnormal temperature, are first indicators that a virus has entered our system. We generally will respond promptly to avoid future complications. Most will seek medication to eliminate any infections. Some will take precautionary measures to boost their immune system. But everyone will do whatever is required to get well.

We should always pay keen attention to discomfort of any magnitude. We should address all disturbances at ground level. We should never vacilate. Problems will not automatically fix themselves. The longer we wait, the more complicated issues can become. This can put tremendous strain on our emotions. This will create deep unrest within us.

We should respond with the same urgency to an internal distress alert, as we would to a problematic physical condition. The heart will alert the mind when it is experiencing duress. Some experience a quick jolt in the stomach, when an unexpected occurrence sounds an alarm buzzer. Oftentimes our heart will begin to flutter. Sometimes our body will quiver and shake in shock.

Human beings look forward to predictability and stability in their lives. Coping mechanisms are rarely equipped to interpret guessing games. Uncertainty under any condition will create anxiety and confusion. These factors will usually birth irritation and tension. Visible signs of discord will become apparent, when unrest begins to take form and shape.

Emotional and mental balance is extremely vital, to our overall health and well being. Instability of our heart and mind will severely restrict our ability to function effectively. But negative and positive forces are closely intertwined. Problematic conditions will arise when persistent hindrances become the dominant factor. Repetitive adversities will impede healthy growth.

"A brother (or sister) offended is harder to be won than a strong city: and their contentions are like the bars of a castle." Proverbs 18 verse 19.

There are those who will deliberately or inadvertently commit offenses against others. And there are those who are left to deal with the aftermath of these offences. Those bent on harming others, rarely consider the damage that they are inflicting on another person. But the recipient(s) will become outraged and feel victimized.

There is virtually nothing more disturbing, than having to respond to an unexpected negative encounter. Our initial reaction is routinely dismay and surprise. Torrential terrifying electric like shockwaves could begin to unnerve us. We could experience chills and goose bumps, at the thought of having to address an unwelcomed intrusion.

We can become highly resentful when forced to deal with hurtful situations. One explosive confrontation can imprison communication and dialogue. Even routine misunderstandings could erupt into serious brawls. This could create a contentious environment. Fortified bars could soon be erected in preparation for violent confrontations. But we can end up imprisoning ourselves.

Emotional upheavals will surface when our mental sanctuary is disturbed. An invasion of our person can leave us feeling disrespected and violated. Many will react with contempt and outrage. Sometimes our sanity could suffer a severe blow. Sometimes we can feel like we are being savagely dismembered from deep within. And we could experience hurt to the core of our being.

We will become highly resentful when our mind is provoked. Resentment is the driving force that propels heated exchanges. It is the birth place for a conflict. Conflict is the forerunner responsible for a multitude of ills. It is equipped with multiple tentacles and poisonous venoms. This routinely can create a dangerous and volatile atmosphere.

A showdown is in the making when hostility begins to populate a contentious environment. A collision with rage can immediately activate our hostility button. Self containment is difficult when we are out of control. This is because hostility will summon strife to join forces. War is on the horizon when conflict, hostility, and strife band together.

Unresolved issues lie at the core of most emotional imbalances. Sometimes these disturbances can be painfully challenging to pinpoint accurately. But the associated stresses can pinnacle to mental disorders. Intense anguish can cause some to become withdrawn and introverted. Other destructive interferences could further deteriorate our internal organs.

We can easily become sidetracked when embroiled in controversy. We can lose focus. We could begin to strategize unconventional methods to get even, when pain becomes unbearable. These drastic measures may or may not guarantee temporary satisfaction.

Strife is the sum total of all negative influences combined. It is an extremely dangerous barrier. It has the potential of being a hurricane like destructive force. Strife is the founder of malicious intents. Malice and anger are co-dependents. These demonic combinations can convert mild mannered people in hardened warriors.

Anger will never surface unannounced. There has to be a reason that will magnify an emotional crisis. Any unexpected disturbance will trigger an immediate response. We will respond aggressively when we perceive that we are besieged with problems. We will retaliate forcefully and decisively. A vexed mind will take no prisoners.

Only the severely wounded heart can truly understand its own misery. Sorrow and remorse can viciously slice and dice our spirit. Intense heartaches can feel like raw and open sores. This is always a brutal experience. There are times when healing can be slow and tedious. Sometimes the after effects can leave permanent scars.

It is virtually impossible to contain an angry soul. A badly damaged mind is hard to mend. We will bleed longer when bitterness saturates our being. Stubbornness can sometimes make repairs extremely difficult. This is because our mind can compel our brain to band together. The body will be forced to comply with the dictates of the mind and brain.

Prolonged mental imprisonment can cause long term psychological damage. The fundamental reason for focusing and examining the topic of unforgiveness, is to illustrate this fact. Monumental burdens can imprison and heavily yoke our heart. We will feel trapped and barricaded when unrelenting fury is consuming us from deep within. The yoke of unforgiveness is a vicious and brutal barrier.

Unforgiveness will never suddenly impregnate our mind. There is always a reason why many eventually embrace this hardened mindset. A germ of unrest will be the first virus to get lodged within our soul. The incubation period can become dangerously progressive. This infection can rapidly poison our entire system.Insensitive actions and indifference can lay the foundation for vicious clashes. Heated confrontations can lead to bitter and nasty arguments. Flaring tempers will ignite torrential fireballs of fury. Dragged out verbal fights will usually end in furious standoffs. The proverbial line in the sand will now be drawn.

There is nowhere else to go but down, when anger reaches boiling point. A feud is on the horizon when fury becomes a raging wildfire. Barbed barriers will eventually be erected to guarantee that hatred remain alive. Long term hatred and strife are two of the founding cornerstones of unforgiveness.

Feuds will hurt everyone. Hate is an insurmountable burden to be saddled with. Those seeking the "why" answers will hurt even more. Those struggling with the yoke of unforgiveness will experience greater torment and torture. Some could resign themselves into accepting these unhealthy conditions as the status quo.No one will ever escape all the pitfalls of life. Nobody can honestly confirm that they have never experienced bitter conflicts. We will face trials and tribulations as long as we live and breathe. But persistent hindrances can cripple our ability to effectively manage our affairs. They can kill our dreams.

We are encouraged constantly to rid ourselves of friction. We are frequently told to ignore ill treatment. Oftentimes we are bombarded with requests to forgive injustice. We are sometimes told that this path will rid our soul of demonic contaminants. There are times when we are admonished that these are our only options. We can interpret these statements to be severe chastisements.

Well wishers can be brimming with enthusiasm. Many will sincerely attempt to comfort and console us. Some will comment that "this too will pass." Others will tell us that our feelings are not logical or practical. We could become very resentful. This would be like being thrown in a patch of poison ivy. We could end up feeling victimized for being victimized.

Skilfully crafted personal observations might be appropriate. Practical advice could be on target. But tattered emotions are hard to reassemble. Good intentions usually will fall on deaf ears when we are hurting. It is virtually impossible to be logical, when we cannot control the angry tidal waves of wrath. An enraged mind will never listen to reason.

We could begin to plot irrational strategies to minimize our rage. We could resort to extreme measures. We could reason this approach justified for damaged rendered. We could conclude our behaviour to be justified. We could automatically begin to endorse unforgiveness as a viable option.

The reluctance to forgive is a heartbreaking condition. And this resistance has saturated the minds of many. Anger has tormented many souls for countless generations. There is no shortage of discussion on this topic. Many books and articles have been written on this subject. Mental health facilities are sometimes overflowing with hurting people. Yet many view forgiving as a distant option. It is relatively easy to verbalize the word "forgive," when an incident pertains to someone else. But when a tragedy befalls us, forgiveness is usually never in our vocabulary. The choices that compel many to cling to unforgiveness are usually multi layered. And it is oftentimes extremely complicated. The route to forgiving can be equally as complex. They both follow the same guidelines and heartaches.

There is not a perfect person residing on planet earth. We will make mistakes as long as we live. Mistakes are always problematic. And some can be extremely costly. Some catastrophic disasters are non reversible. We can pay a high price for recklessly speeding down the wrong choice highway.

Most devastating events are rarely premeditated. But we cannot turn back the hands of time when we indulge in unhealthy choices. The consequences of our actions can be severe. Very few will forgive when others create tragedies in their lives. Weeping and wailing will be of little consolation, when serious damage has been inflicted.

We will feel humiliated when unhealthy choices cause us shame and grief. Wrongful actions can bring us to open disgrace. We will be consumed with remorse when unbearable pain turns to anguish. But wrong choice decisions can taint us for life.

Vexation can short circuit our stress hormones. Anger upgraded to rage can be compared to the devastation from a nuclear bomb. Wrath is no respecter of persons. It can demolish and destroy. This is why the vengeful mind is always bent on keeping barriers intact.

Our mind can be very persuasive in confusing, and quarantining our heart. Our mind is an expert in swaying our brain to join forces. This is why hate is such a very powerful emotion. Blind fury could encourage us to resort to drastic measures. This hardened mindset can create more chaos within us.

Our mind is constantly exploring methods, to avoid dealing with the necessity to forgive. But we are now at risk for other negative related consequences. A mind bent on retaliation is a recipe for disaster. We could become a casualty because of irrational thinking.Each individual is uniquely different as their fingerprints. Most people will express displeasure in accordance with their tolerance level. But anger will put anyone in crisis mode. We will rigorously defend our "air space," if we concluded that an invasion is imminent. Anger management is ineffective when we are on a rampage. Even the professionals could become casualties.

The Bible says: "But the tongue can no man (or woman) tame; it is an unruly evil, full of deadly poison." James 3 verse 8.

It is difficult to remain rational when problems become our unwelcomed companion. Our tongue is usually our first line of defense. It is also our unreliable weapon of choice. Many will verbally lash out to express the pain of displeasure. Most people will take solace by vehemently venting outrage. These efforts sometimes will bring some measure of satisfaction.

The tongue is a mighty warrior. Many regard the tongue as their closest hostile friend. But our tongue can be our worst enemy. Our tongue sometimes can gallop faster than we can think. The unruly tongue is a skilled architect. It is responsible for custom designing and dispensing mayhem.

Situations can get very ugly when our jaws and tongue collide. An enraged tongue is mightier than a sharp sword. The innocent could get caught in the cross fire of the bulldozing tongue. It could mutilate saints. Even Satan and his demons will run for cover from the blazing tongue. The viperous tongue will never be a peace negotiator. However, sometimes the need to vent and rant is necessary. But not everyone will turn to the bullying tongue to mow down the opposition. Satan can encourage some to focus on more sneaky underhanded methods.

Some people can resort to subtle and cunning ways to inflict hurt. Haughty attitudes can inflict more long term carnage than the hostile yapping lips. Some people will casually demonstrate a total lack of respect for the feelings of others. The after effects from emotional abuse can be extremely difficult to shake loose.

Demeaning attitudes have terminated many close relationships. We will feel insulted when we are treated with indifference. No one likes to feel inferior. This could rattle our self esteem. Being taken for granted can be a belittling experience. Arrogant behaviors have severed many intimate bonds.

Love ought to be the glue that cements togetherness. Mutual affection will always propel us way beyond our accustomed comfort zone. Positive influences will nurture our spirit and soul. But it can be a horrible feeling being pushed to the sidelines. Constantly suffering humiliation can birth bitter resentment. We all have breaking points. Emotional instability could exceed our self control level. Desperation could cloud our judgment. But irrational approaches will encourage failure. Sometimes we could benefit from outside intervention. This could be instrumental in loosening the chains of bondage. But some people are veteran procrastinators.

Our heart will never steer us in the wrong direction. But most people rely solely on the dictates of their mind in times of conflicts. Our mind will rarely tell us to pause and reflect. Oftentimes we will explore every conceivable angle to justify our actions. This is why so many will pursue ineffective human rationale, looking for justification and satisfaction.

Many will embark on a dedicated expedition. Their goal would be to discredit the validity of a Higher Power. Some will arbitrarily review what issues merit observation for forgiving. Some will hastily decide whose violations must remain intact. Even when their lives are crumbling around them, they will refuse to be swayed.

The multitude will reflect on God primarily during moments of despair. There is usually a hasty insincere attempt to communicate with Him. The focus is usually on quick fix solutions. Some will reason that all the perceived offences are too severe to warrant forgiving.

Many will bluntly tell God to rain down vengeance. Some will instruct God to custom design the appropriate punishment to fit the injustice. But God will not respond to vindictive and outrageous demands. Some might even turn against their Maker in frustration.

In times of trouble, we tend to cling to the resources of our intellect. Struggling with an unforgiving mind is like swimming in choppy uncharted waters. We could drown. Disaster will strike us if we are bent on just listening to the carnal self.

There are no magic potions that will automatically undo unforgiveness. Sometimes we will experience more pain. This can be devastating. But it part of the process. And it is well worth the effort.

Sometimes we will have to come face to face with a spiritual awakening. This should encourage us to lay our burdens at the feet of Jesus. He is the only One well equipped to heal all wounds. We all need His guidance to dismantle, and uproot multi fanged barriers in our lives. His greatest desire is for us to reach out and touch Him. But we first need to be open and honest before Him.

He can instantly mend our shattered heart and enraged mind. He will understand when we dialogue with Him. Ambivalence to interact truthfully with God, will always grieve His Spirit. Only He can purify our heart and cleanse our mind. But many are too naively stubborn to request assistance. Some are too proud to yield to the Almighty for guidance.

It is easy to be influenced by unhealthy conditions. Unforgiveness is a staunch and determined foe. It loves to cater to the dictates of the flesh. But God expects us to persevere amidst conflicts. Otherwise the bed of affliction will always keep us confined. Peace treaties can be affordable and reliable. But we will first need to get rid of those evil unforgiving companions. For too long they had been our close confidants. This could be a daunting task. Most will refuse to go quietly. Some might even stage a mutiny. But we will need to expel them to be successful.

Chapter Two
Understanding Gives Clarity

THE HUMAN MIND can be likened to a never ending jig saw puzzle. It is intricate and complex. It is virtually impossible to understand it with pin point accuracy. This mystery could be compared to unequivocally confirming the non existence of God. All research thus far has proven inconclusive and subjective. The mystery of things that cannot be literally seen can forever remain hidden.

Our mind is our processing center. It is our decision making fortress. We have a lot of movement within our minds. We have the power to reason. We have the right to make choices. We have the authority to activate our choices. We have the liberty make decisions based on our conclusion.

Experiments are always being conducted, attempting to unravel the vast mysteries of the mind. But it is customary not to investigate, past the visible physical structure of our heart. We can view our heart via the aid of diagnostic machines. We can clearly observe our heart surgically. Oftentimes we can successfully repair malfunctions. But there is a lot more to our heart than its physical structure.

There is an invisible sacred compartment located deep within our heart. This is our spirit. And it is linked directly with the Spirit of God. Our spirit and our visible heart are permanently intertwined. God designed them to operate in unity. Our spirit might get battered and bruised. But God is constantly healing it to reflect His undefiled purity and integrity. The Spirit of God controls all areas of our spirit. He consistently encourages our spirit to live in peace and harmony. Satan loves to plants seeds of discord in our souls. Problems will never originate from our spirit. Our soul is an experienced trouble maker. It habitually gravitates to the dictates of the world. We are our heart and mind combined. The Spirit of God closely monitors the condition of our heart. Satan loves to bully his way into our minds. Satan is a frequent visitor to our mind. The devil and his crew are always saturating our mind with vile ideas.

Our heart should be compared to the peace loving relative. Our mind should be likened to the disruptive sibling. Friction is commonplace between heart and mind. Heart and mind relationship can become strenuous when hurdles begin to bombard. Sometimes we could collapse under the excess strain.

Lucifer's greatest desire is to dominate our heart. He will go to great lengths to gain control. The devil will never be successful. But he can forcefully influence our mind. And we could easily become Satan's pawns. All our reprehensible thoughts originate from our mind. That rocking chair embedded in our mind labelled "unforgiveness," belongs to Lucifer.

Our body is the visible us. It is also God's temple. Our body displays us to the world. This will allow everyone to analyze and evaluate us. We will either demonstrate harmony or discord. Our countenance will radiate tranquility, or reflect discomfort.

We are made in the image and likeness of God. We became a living soul when He breathed His breath in us. God is three in one. There is God the Father. He is the Supreme Creator of heaven and earth.

There is God the Son. The Son obeys the will of His Father. He oversees the vast universe that His Father designed. Jesus is always interceding on our behalf when we blunder. He even visited earth in person.

There is God the Holy Spirit. The Holy Spirit is our permanent companion. He lives in all believers. He closely monitors all our activities. He is also our comforter and guide. We are also three in one. We have a spirit. It is our direct link to the Spirit of God. We refer to our spirit as our heart. We have a soul. This is our mind. Our mind is supposed to work in harmony with our heart. But this rarely happens.

We have a body. This is our outer casing. Our body is our delivery person. It takes orders from our heart and mind. We are routinely judged by our body language.

The Spirit of the Triune God is impartial. He made human to reflect His glory and Supernatural powers. In other words, we were designed to be an extension of the Supreme God. But we frequently disappoint and grieve our God of the universe. The three in one God always operate in unity harmony and solidarity. The three in one human habitually function in discord, disarray, and disunity.

We need to understand and digest some simple yet important facts: God expects us to trust and obey Him. God diligently monitors the condition of our heart to eradicate impurities. Our mind will not become contaminated when we obey the Spirit of God's directives. It is never Jehovah's intention for arguments and strife, to become our daily bread. Satan fed us this bitter morsel.

It is God who instilled within us the knowledge, to decipher right and wrong. It is God who infused in us the power to reason wisely. It is God who granted us the ability to make and execute healthy choices. We stray miserably when we begin to act on what is right and pleasing to our mind.

Honesty is God's fundamental requirement for all humanity. It is the foundation of our sincere commune with Him. Our heavenly Father will teach us how to appropriately dialogue with Him, when we approach His Throne of Grace. His Spirit will guide us to the correct passage of scripture, as it relates to our situation.

The Bible encourages us to ask for guidance, whenever we come before God's Holy Throne. Psalms 19 verse 14 is a vivid reminder of this need and necessity: "Let the words of my mouth, (our mouths) and the meditation of my heart, (our hearts), be acceptable in thy sight, O Lord, my strength, (our strength) and my (our) redeemer."

It is regrettable that so many play games with this powerful prayer. Some recite this important prayer at the conclusion of "devotion". There are those who insincerely mumble these wise words when exhausted, and hastily exiting His Home. Others may utter these words as polite gestures to God. Some will take things to the extreme by paying God lip service.

We should never recite these words as mere Godly protocol. This prayer should be our direct link to the Spirit of God. We should verbalize this verse of scripture at the start of every new day. These words of wisdom should be permanently riveted deep within our heart and mind. We should always prioritize the urgency of this much needed prayer.

We should never perceive these important words as a burdensome task. They should never be internalized as mere utterances. They should be our desperate pleas to connect directly with the heart of our Maker. We all need to utilize His guidelines. This is not paying God ritualistic homage. We should never treat God's instructions with a casual attitude. We should always focus on the power of His wisdom. God's principles will align us to be in oneness with Him. He will reign in our unbridled tongue to conform to His will. Sincerity will penetrate our heart.

During these serene moments, our entire being will be united in oneness with Him. God will release His power within us. We should now be prepared to face adversities. The Almighty will then install His strength within us. We should now be equipped to combat demonic forces. We will stand firm when His Spirit is guiding us.

God will fortify and shield us during our stormy periods. But Satan loves injecting a downside to Godly principles. He will bombard us relentlessly with trials and tribulations. But we should never give in to his demands. We will grow stronger when we learn to persevere.

Perfection will always be absent without perseverance. The more we practice, the closer to perfection we will become. We will understand the importance of honestly dialoguing with God. We have nothing to lose by disciplining ourselves, in spirit and in truth.

We will gain abundant insight when our heart is contrite. Negative influences will be swept aside during these precious moments. Satanic interfering spirits will have to flee. Hostility will be nonexistent when we are truly focused on God.

But no one can remain steadfast in prayer forever. Eventually we will temporarily end our commune with God. We will say "amen." Then we will arise to face this harsh and cruel world. And Satan will be lurking to harass and antagonize us.

The devil always eavesdrops when we communicate with God. His major objective is to disrupt our prayer life. He is dutifully ready to annoy us with distractions. With great urgency, he will attempt to manipulate our mind. This could confuse our brain.

He will tell us that God is too busy to listen to every prayer. He could delude us into believing that meditation is a redundant ritual. He will suggest that we need not report everything to God. Satan will try to persuade us that holding on to grudges are appropriate and legitimate.

Lucifer is always persistent in his efforts to sabotage us. This is his method of operation. But we should have a permanent escape route. We should always run to God for refuge. This should be our first line of defence. God's check valve will keep us evenly adjusted.

Jesus spoke directly with His (our) Father:"I pray not that that thou shouldest take them out of the world, but that thou shouldest keep them from evil." John 17 verse 15

"They are not of the world, even as I am not of the world." John 17 verse 16 Our Savior was formally presenting His inner circle to His Father. But the validity of His prayer is applicable in our current society. Jesus' Words are available to all residents on planet earth. We all have ears. But many refuse to hear. Understanding is difficult when we are not listening.

The Spirit of God created this earth. He put in place everything on this planet. But He is not of this earth. God is the Supreme Ruler of heaven and earth. He is a Spirit. We ought to worship Him in spirit and in truth. There is no other way to honor the Spirit of the living God.

We always need to reverently assemble ourselves before our unseen God. We should speak to Him on a regular basis. But our spirit should be free of contaminants. This is the only method that can interlock our spirit with God's Spirit. We should not be influenced by evil thoughts.

We will not conform to worldly standards when we are in the Spirit realm. Everything with earthly affiliations will be put on hold. Even our thoughts will not drift to worldly expectations. In these spirit filled moments, our entire being will assuredly not be of this world. But Jesus requested of His Father that we be kept in this world. Evil will take flight when God takes control of our spirit. But we live in this world. And Satan lives in this world. Satan is the prince of darkness. He is the best dressed and most dangerous predator. The devil is the greatest illusionist this world will ever know. This prince of darkness is the most influential demonic power on earth.

Peculiar things happen when evil and good collide. Unrighteousness will always search for opportunities to destroy righteousness. No earthling is perfect. Every human being will disobey the revealed will of God, sometime during any given day. Satan can dupe heavenly minded believers, as easily as earthly minded people. This is why we should always remain sincerely committed and focused before God.

Jesus was not inferring that His Father relieve the disciples, of their earthly responsibilities. Neither was He requesting His Father to remove them from earth. He was petitioning God to guide them in their daily activities.

We need to be alive and vibrant to work in the Father's vineyard. But it is difficult to concentrate when we are constantly distracted by evil. As long as humankind inhabit God' earth, some excel by demonstrating Godly principles. And some will deliberately capitalize on evil indulges.

We either labour for God, or we work for Satan. We have no earthly purpose when we are dead. Everything stops when we exhaust our last breath. Our good works are completed when we die. Our evil deeds accompany us to the grave.

The sun shines on good people and wicked people. Rain falls on the just and the unjust. We the people are all here because God designed us. Some will remain loyal to Him until the earth reclaims us. Some will rebel against the Ultimate Ruler until the worms eat them in the grave.

And the Lord said: "My Spirit shall not always strive with man (or woman,) for that he (she) also is flesh: (Genesis 6 verse 3 part 1)

Impatience and stubbornness are breeding grounds for disobedience. We cannot expect the Spirit of God indwell and strive within us, by clinging to earthly principles. Lest we forget, Satan never takes a vacation. His menacing presence is always hovering over us.

No one is impeccably focused and grounded in Godly principles twenty four seven. We can easily regress after pouring out our heart and soul before God. Many could become frustrated with God for not responding promptly to a special request.

God is always meticulous and precise in everything that He does. Our Heavenly Father will always listen to us when we request help and guidance. Then He will grant to us what is best for us. But our rebellious nature could hinder our blessings.

Human beings are always craving for instant gratification. Many of us could quickly return to our habitual ways of mismanaging our affairs. An unforgiving mind is an important example. And wrong thoughts and deeds could continue to flourish.Good and evil will never join hands. The choices we make will determine the outcome of our actions. Doubt is communication's worst enemy. Listening to the wrong voice will always be problematic. There are times when the wrong voice will come knocking in our heart and mind.

This world appears to be spiraling out of control. Earth will always be a fierce battleground between honesty and corruption. The hearts of many have waxed cold. A multitude of minds have become deviously polluted.

Selfishness has taken up permanent residence in many. Wickedness appears to be thriving. Evil spirited individuals are creating wide spread misery. Good people are falling victim to bad things. Sometimes it is difficult to extract a few well intentioned individuals.

Kindness oftentimes is frowned on. Some people interpret a caring attitude, as a sign of weakness. Upright people are having a difficult time coping. Honest people appear to be in the minority. Some have resigned themselves to the ills of this planet. It is sad when decent people have to cringe in fear.

Depression appears to be gaining momentum. And it is saturating the land. Many are becoming introverted and dejected. It is awful when people begin claiming responsibility for circumstances beyond their control. It is even worse when many have to live daily, with issues that were forced on them.

Torment could drive many to adopt a life of isolation. Living in isolation could feel like incarceration. Functioning in perpetual misery can progress to a mental breakdown. It is always frightening when human beings begin to embrace devastation.

It is horrific when some turn against themselves. There can be no peace when problems are in control. Some could retreat to that dark world of agony. This would make recovery more difficult. Many could attempt to take a leave of absence from life. This could have a ripple effect on those close to us.

Everyone would be burdened for us. Some could even begin to redefine their value system. It is always painful to watch a loved one deteriorate. It can be a sickening feeling being powerless to help. It is difficult to console when bitterness becomes the domineering force.

An enraged mind can quickly become a dangerous assassin. Our mind could coerce our body to retaliate on behalf of a grieving loved one. We would now feel justified to declare war. The rationality would be to totally obliterate those who had overstepped their boundaries. But wars will always produce casualties. Conflicts are always painful for everyone. We could become the worst casualty.Jesus says: "There is nothing from without a man (or woman,) that entering him (or her) can defile him; (or her) but the things which come out of him, (or her) those are they that defile the man." (or the woman) Mark 7 verse 15

Jesus also says: "All these evil things come from within, and defile the man (or the woman.) Mark 7 verse 23

We travel everywhere with our thoughts. We are responsible for our thoughts. We have ownership of our thoughts. They could be good. Or they could be diabolically evil. We abuse and defile others when we wantonly execute our evil thoughts. Physical abuse can literally kill us. Verbal abuse can severely mentally paralyze us.

We communicate by gestures, words, and actions. Our character normally is defined by how we present ourselves. Wrong choice thoughts can result in wrong choice outcomes. Crass words will routinely annoy us. Recklessly placed words can easily solidify tension. Irresponsible actions can cause catastrophic damage. Angry responses will enforce this reality.

Jesus says: "A new commandment I give unto you, that ye love one another, as I have loved you, that ye also love one another." John 13 verse 34.

It is always an awesome moment when we feel the presence of God. Totally submerged in His anointing, is a serene experience like no other. We will begin to reflect the love of Christ. Our heart and mind will unite on one accord.

Like Isaiah, He will immediately purify our tongue. He will also skilfully rearrange our vocabulary. He will condition our heart and mind to reflect His love. Peace will begin to radiate within us. We will begin to feel blessed.

People we intermingle with should also feel blessed. Our words of encouragement should feel like the taste of honey. A kind sentence should be priceless in boosting someone's self confidence. Heaven and earth will rejoice when we demonstrate compassion.Encouraging comments should elevate the self esteem of many. Soothing words should nurture and mold countless characters. A genuine gesture should be a motivator to achieve positive accomplishments. Kindness should smother unkindness. The possibilities for performing unselfish service should be literally endless.

Jesus will tell us: "Well done thou good and faithful servant." The Spirit God will build a hedge of protection around us. He will dispatch His angels to encamp round about us. All angry voices from hell will be muzzled and silenced.

We will be reminded of Jesus' next statement: "By this shall all men (women) know that ye are my disciples, if ye love one to another." John 13 verse 35.

We all need to be consistently reminding ourselves, that all humanity is interconnected in one way or other. Everyone is accountable to someone else. This is God's law of the universe. Life is never a one way misadventure. We will encounter problems when we embark on a one way venture. Even the most brilliant minds, are limited to what they can effectively accomplish solely by themselves.

We are all brothers and sisters. This means that we should always treat each other with respect. We should be mindful that no one is a permanent citizen on planet earth. We are all temporary residents on this land. We are many. But we are all one. We all need each other to survive. These are the binding facts.

It was never God's intention to encourage, or promote exclusive self reliance. He made this abundantly clear when He grouped every living organism in pairs. Humankind is the only specie that has consistently resisted the need and necessity to function as a collective group.

Humans are the only life form that God designed with superior intelligence. He infused within us the ability to make and execute healthy choices. But many abuse this freedom of choice. Some will resort to extreme measures to convince others, of the importance of total self dependence. Many will invent creative ways, to justify outrageous beliefs focusing on self sufficiency.

Many attempt to live the myth that "God will only help those who can help themselves." We stray from the leading of the Holy Spirit, when we begin to practice self dependence. We can easily abandon Godly principles when we begin to embrace this fallacy. Living under the curse of unforgiveness is not helping our self.

There are those who religiously live by the inflexible code of self preservation. Turning the other cheek is never a first responder if anyone overstepped their boundaries. "An eye for an eye and a tooth for a tooth," will predominately be the first weapon of choice.

Many will respond with deadly force if anyone crossed the "do not trespass" sign. But will the end justify the means, after we plucked out the eye and mercilessly yanked out all the teeth? We should never start believing that we are all masters of our own fate. This is a blatant lie. This is our super ego in overdrive. This attitude will fall short under even minute scrutiny. We could eventually crumble living this fiction.

"The buck stops here" mentality is a quote directly from Satan's textbook. No one is an island. People always need people. There is nothing more rewarding than being able to depend on positive influences, for comfort and support. There is an abundance of strength when people are united.

Chapter Three
Misguided Reasoning

We breathe and live because of the grace and mercy of the Sprit of God. Life is a precious gift from the Creator of the universe. We transition from slumber to consciousness at the discretion of our Maker. Each waking moment should be cherished and treasured.

Living should never be taken for granted. Each dawn should represent a new chapter in our life. We should greet each morning with a song in our heart. The start of a new day should always be filled with hope and gratitude. We should to be excited.

Every sunrise is a blessing from God. This represents a new beginning. Yesterday is gone into eternity. Tomorrow is not promised to us. We should always live today to the fullest. We should continue fulfilling our dreams and destiny.

Many of us will thank God for the privilege of waking up. We will also bow in humility for the gift of life. Some of us will prayerfully engage in sincere devotion before our Maker. This will strengthen and uplift us. We should be revitalized to again meet this cruel world.

Most in society still wake up taking each day for granted. Some of us will hastily jump out of bed. We will madly rush around performing our morning routines. Then we will dash through the door to resume another hectic work day. Whatever happens during the next few hours, we will roll with the flow.

Demonic minded people also wake up like everyone. The difference is that their evil mindedness, accompany them to another rising sun. They too go through their morning routine. But they drag their wicked thoughts with them.

Their main focus is usually plotting devious schemes. Their objective is to disrupt the lives of decent folks. Until the setting of the sun, and past the rising of the moon, they roam the land. Their priority is to torment the lives of unsuspecting people.

Sadly, many begin every day feeling sick and distraught. A lot of us dread having to face what is supposed to be a brand new life. Oftentimes the horrible yesterday, will be the terrible today. Grief will come calling as soon as we open our eyes. For many, hurt has found a new day to torment.

No one should wake each morning in a confused and miserable condition. This has to be the most horrifying experience for any human being. Oftentimes remorse keeps some of us literally confined in bed. Numerous times we could fantasize going permanently to sleep. This could severely affect our family life.

Life should never be littered with chaos and confusion. Our Maker did not design us to live in misery. Evil people sometimes exposed us to grave harm. Sometimes unhealthy environments badly damaged us. Embracing sinful practices put many of us in this predicament. There are times when we suffer the consequences, because of the mistakes of others. Sometimes our wounds are self inflicted.

Intense pain can cripple our mind. This could severely disrupt our reasoning ability. Some could reason they should never have been born. Some of us could curse our parents. Some could wish they had been aborted at conception. But these are thoughts of the flesh. They are highlights from Satan's manual. We did not wish ourselves into existence. We should never arbitrarily choose a coffin over life.

Some of us could chart other irrational courses. Humans are always seeking alternatives to camouflage pain and suffering. Some could tilt towards total self reliance. But experimenting with self indulgence could further complicate all of our woes.

Help is always a spiritual phone call away. His direct line is never busy. All we have to do is make that call. But many of us will refuse to call God's help center. What can we lose by just making that call?

It is beyond horrific when anyone hits rock bottom. Misery is one lonely and sad road to travel. Emptiness will inhibit us from enjoying a good laugh. A dismal outlook on life, will always keep us confined. We could sabotage ourselves, from experiencing the joys of gainful employment. Even taken for granted social interaction, could feel like a gruesome chore.Irrational thoughts cannot battle the demons of horrible days and nights. Attempting to shut the world out is even worse. These desperate measures will only magnify our plight. We should get connected to Godly supportive groups. We should be introduced to spiritual help lines. This is called fellowship. There is abundant joy in banding together on one accord.

Human beings are always yearning for positive interaction. We all need comfort and peace. We should never deliberately suppress this need. Isolation will never be the solution to our hurt. We could be tackling a dangerous slippery slope. And the pit falls are literally endless. Nothing can replace the human connection.

We embark on a precarious pilgrimage by outsourcing our feelings. An alternate lifestyle will also involve a group of people. They could be living with similar circumstances such as us. We could be swapping worse for worst. Sadly, some get attracted to this presumed less intrusive lifestyle.

Some could get addicted to a "new and improved" living arrangement. Forging intimate bonds with potential harmful activities can create bigger problems. Our world could collapse with a loud bang. It is always a bad idea to turn to Satan's world for comfort.

The deceptive secular society is always on the prowl. The world of the flesh is always appeasing to the eye. Materialistic invitations are always very persuasive. We could quickly discard our ethical and moral value system.It is very dangerous to play games with God. We leave ourselves wide open for Satan to inject poisonous venoms in our system. He could delude into believing we were ingesting syrup. The devil loves when we second guess God. This gives Lucifer the opportunity to skillfully begin to contaminate us.

Satan's first ploy is to dismantle our faith. Then he will push our reliance on God to the sidelines. This is when a multitude of us could stray miserably off course. We could rapidly find ourselves heavily entangled in negative behaviors.

The devil's mandate is always to replace morality with immorality. We could begin to adopt abnormal behaviors. We could start acting aloof and uncaring. We could begin drifting further toward worldly pleasures. But this would be a disguise for our unhappiness.We could easily align ourselves with the wrong crowd. We could begin to drink from their cisterns. We could eagerly begin to embrace these shallow associates. We could easily adopt their irresponsible way of life.

Sometimes we would be distressed by their maltreatment of the less fortunate. But we could hesitantly justify their self centeredness in our mind. This different lifestyle could appear highly appeasing. We eventually could give them our verbal approval. We could end up endorsing them whole heartedly.

Our spirit will desperately advise us to turn back. But we disregard this vital message. Instead we burn our warning flag. Aligning ourselves with negative behaviours can be very expensive. Bad things will befall us when we flirt with demons.

Straying from a God based foundation is dangerous. We will suffer severe consequences. We will get lost by the wayside. We will confuse our right turns with our wrong turns. We can badly scar our integrity. We can forfeit our rights as reliable citizens. Our code of honor could become null and void.

We could compromise our dignity. It could be difficult to function effectively. We could be thrown off balance in all aspects of our life. Our decent values should always be cherished. It is stupid to abandon proper codes of conduct. We could end in a free fall for being disobedient.

We will become bankrupt by aligning ourselves with Satan's crowd. But some form alliances with the prince of darkness. Some purchase front row seats with the devil. Some will bunk down with him. This is so mind boggling. We will suffer humiliation and embarrassment. Then we will crumple.

It is a bad idea to join forces with evil doers. We should steer clear of those who abuse the less fortunate. We should always cling to things that are just and upright. We should never permit Satan to convert us. He will warp our minds. Abominable dedicated Satan disciples should be left alone.

It is high treason to sacrifice Godly principles for earthly pleasures. This is a death sentence sin. God will severely punish us when we recklessly yield to our flesh. We should know when to draw the line. Failure to stop will bring us down.

We can never lie to our Maker. We will be tongue tied before the One who loans us breath. We can blame no one when we deliberately disobey God. We will be flushed out in the open. God will expose us bare and naked. Our fellow human beings could scoff at us.

Wrong choices will assuredly bring grief. Living under severe restrictions is always difficult. We could start hating ourselves. We could also start detesting our horrible "friends." We could even deplore them. But it would be maximized stupidity focusing our displaced anger on society.

We should never recluse ourselves from our errors. It was our bad choice to mingle with the wrong crowd. It was our reckless decision to cling to self pleasers. We poured the gasoline on ourselves. We lit the match. And the heathens watched us burn. Everyone cheered as we were incinerated.

We will self destruct when we embrace unethical habits. We should never tamper with emotional dynamite. We could lose limbs. We could also be killed by the explosion. Our ashes would be personally scattered by Satan. We should never gravitate to the hypnotic materialistic world. We could get lost in the wilderness of despair. We should never give Lucifer the key to our soul. He will build duplicates. Then he will distribute them to his dedicated followers. We could be bombarded with multiple horrible visits. But we are human. And human beings sometimes make horrible mistakes.

The bible says: "If we say we have not sinned, we make him a liar, and his word is not in us". 1John 1 verse 10

The bible also says: "As it is written, There is none righteous, no, not one". Romans 3 verse 10.

Every human being is sin nature prone. Some like to be called honest crooks. We will take. But we will leave you with a little something. Some of us are crooked crooks. We will take everything. Then we will laugh in your face. These actions make us all unrighteous people. But there is not a flawless person in the universe.

Some of us veer miserably of course by making irrational decisions. Some of us block hurt by shunning God and humanity. Some created severe heartaches by succumbing to alternative lifestyles. Some got involved with the wrong crowd. These mistakes almost cost some limb and life.

We are aware that we ought to live an upright life. But bitterness can harden our heart, and poison our mind. Wrong choice reasoning is always problematic. Some of us will pinnacle to disaster. But that still small voice is always whispering not to jump. Repentance is literally one sincere prayer away. Life dictates that positive bonding brings superb results. We isolate ourselves when we recluse ourselves from the pleasures of living. Pain and pleasure are not always peace loving neighbours. But triumphs and failures are intricate components of the human pilgrimage.

It is distressing the games some will play to solidify unforgiveness. Physical ailments will plague us when we stockpile hurt and anger. Many tend to evade reality when problems overwhelm. But we will never experience healthy growth alienated in a cocoon.

Chapter Four
Relationships

Our age is always behind us. We are never asked how young we are. Our age is associated our past. We all have a past. We travel everywhere with our past. Our past is a permanent part of us. But life affords us a multitude of second chances.

Some of us have been able to refurbish our tattered past. Some of us have triumphed over monumental stumbling blocks. Some have pried loose from damaging childhood experiences. Many have rebounded to enjoy a fairly balanced lifestyle.

It is disheartening when so many fall victim, by yielding to wrong choice reasoning. Many suffer because of surrendering to harmful decisions. Some still continue to repeat hurtful failures. Wrong motives will create huge problems cementing meaningful interactions.

Love is a soothing and overpowering emotion. Human beings are forever craving for happiness and intimacy. These are universal inbred needs. They are also compelling overwhelming desires. There is always a thirst for meaningful interconnectedness.

These cravings are from the depths of our hearts. They are an intricate part of our general makeup. These feelings are real and vivid. They are always striving to thrive and come alive within us. Sometimes these aspirations can produce intense hurt.

The greatest contentment is peace of heart and mind. We all need love. We all need to be loved. There is always that yearning to lead meaningful and productive lives. The need to maintain a balanced lifestyle is always present. This persistent inner drive never diminishes. Sometimes our candle might become dim. But that flicker never dies.

Human beings are always exploring ways to live internal wholeness. We are always searching for security and peace of mind. Humanity has been on this determined expedition for countless ages. Some of us are successful. Some fail by giving up too soon.

Love is important. But exercising wisdom is the key. Knowledge and wisdom should work in harmony. This should lay the framework for the priceless gift of understanding. Aspirations to embrace true love will forever be tangible and attainable goals. But we should trust God to direct our footsteps. Like Jeremiah, our lives were pre-destined before we entered our mother's womb.

It is usually an exciting adventure when couples first meet. It is electrifying when positive chemistry begins to saturate the atmosphere. This routinely will send our adrenalin soaring to unpredictable heights. Most couples get goose bumps during these precious moments. In short duration we could make exciting announcements to our family and friends.

Falling in love should be a resounding exotic experience. The intensity of that first intimate encounter could bring earth and heaven to a standstill. But fluttering hearts will eventually subside. This will be replaced by reality. A healthy relationship is in the making, if love and affection emerge triumphant.

Some couples have been acquainted with each other since youth. Some could comment frequently of having been childhood sweethearts. Over the years they grew, matured, and fell in love. Most of these spouses have a well balanced relationship. Honest communication and dialogue is the key to their relationship.

If they are blessed with children, together they enjoy the joys and sorrows of parenthood. Stressful periods are a reality in any committed relationship. They thoroughly understand that there will be times of intense crisis. And they will genuinely support each other during difficult periods. This is because they know that they can always depend on each other.

Many couples however, struggle with comfort and security. They do not have one lifelong partner. A lot of us have been badly damaged by unhealthy intermingling. Some of us have built a dividing wall between us and intimacy. Many of us have placed ice packs over our hearts.

Human beings are always consistently experimenting with new approaches, to experience lasting happiness. But repetitive hurt can plunge anyone in emotional limbo. Some travel through life lugging gruesome burdens. Many suffer because of broken promises, and shattered dreams. Sometimes bitterness can become the only reliable confidant.

A starting over relationship can be anxiety prone. Our previous living condition had become intolerable. Irreconcilable differences caused us be on the verge of a fresh restart. So we now begin to experiment with someone new. But we should first shed our old garments.

Surrendering to multiple wrong choices caused us great sorrow. Many of us could still be vehemently blaming ourselves. Oftentimes we will need to honestly examine ourselves. Sometimes we will have to flush ourselves out of hiding. Then we need to forgive ourselves. This is the only path to move forward.

Sometimes forgiving our previous partners could be equally daunting. But we must also be prepared to forgive them. This will cleanse us of all unforgiving hostilities. This is called healing. We all need to heal. Only then will we be prepared to meet the challenges of a new relationship.

We should never leave gaping loop holes from previous relationships. We should sever all emotional loose ends. Failure to address these issues would be grossly dishonest to our new partner, and to our self. This mindset will inevitably interfere with positive bonding. We could be setting our self up for future problems.

It is important for couples to be totally honest to each other. Healthy communication and meaningful dialogue is the foundation for any relationship. It is unhealthy when unresolved conflicts accompany us into a new relationship. This could be problematic for the spouse who had completely resolved past heartaches. Uneasiness could sneak into the union.   Genuine affection should be shared by both parties. Mutual respect and total honesty, should to be considered mandatory. These are impenetrable bonds that will last into eternity. Strong commitments will hold relationships together during stormy periods. These are the indisputable litmus tests that govern all intimate relationships. A rift will become evident if these key elements are lacking.

A dysfunctional relationship is equivalent to being fed deadly poison. Unrequited love is literally drifting aimlessly through time. A tumultuous environment can feel like living in exile. Being shoved to the sidelines, can be a gut wrenching painful experience.

The affected spouse will feel marginalized and alienated. Sadness and bitterness will replace happiness. Undercurrents of resentment will generate large scale hostility. There is virtually nothing left when love and affectionate intimacy fade. Over time a break up will be inevitable.

There is always a reason for withholding passionate intimacy. Sometimes a voice from our past could begin to call. Some spouses could run towards that voice. Some could amorously reconnect with that voice from the past. Many could still be committing mental infidelity.

Most will embark on relentless crusades to confirm visible infidelity. But unfaithfulness of the mind is equally volatile.

Our secret thoughts could flourish unchecked indefinitely. Living a lie can become very complicated. Our body would be present during pretend intimate periods. But someone else would control our emotions. This is cruel and inhumane in any relationship.

Some spouses are experts in deceptive practices. Some will play manipulative games with the word "LOVE." Some could mislead their partners for years. Relationships can come to a standstill because of two levels of love. There is a vast difference between merely loving, and being in love.

Being in love originates from the depths of our heart. Doubt will never seep into the relationship. Infidelity of any type is nonexistent when couples are faithfully in love. Literal or fantasy unfaithfulness will never become an issue. The other type of love is solely mind propelled. Surface level love will eventually fade.

Deception at any level is dangerously disruptive. This will birth tension in any union. Doubt and suspicion are closely intertwined. A course could begin to be charted for severe complications. Everything is scheduled for the cemetery when mistrust enters an intimate bond.

There are times when children are involved. They are also an intricate part of our past. They could accompany us into our new start. Oftentimes both couples will have children from previous relationships. Our offspring could be excited for us and themselves. But they could also be bringing with them unresolved bad memories.Clear lines of communication should be established during the "courtship" period. Otherwise multiple conflicts will become apparent. Structured guidelines should be agreed on by both partners. Severe disruptions could seriously damage this new beginning when a framework is lacking.

Offspring visits with biological parent should never become a point of contention. But times should be carefully structured. Visiting arrangements should never interfere with the new relationship. This will eliminate the invitation of doubt to become a stumbling block. Step parents should feel comfortable with these procedures. They should harbour no mixed feelings.

It is easier to accept a breakup when both parties, lose interest in each other. Humans generally enter into intimacy with the best of intentions. But repetitive strife will kill any relationship. Most could wish that things could have been different. But many have to sever ties when unresolved issues dominate. Sometimes mixed feeling could still be lingering. But both couples realize that love and affection died. So a permanent break now becomes a reality. Some will take time out to rest and revitalize. Then they will move on. There should be no future interferences. A fresh course can then be charted with relative ease.

It is vastly different when emotional ties are not permanently disconnected. One spouse will be left drifting. The abrupt severing of intimate ties can be earth shattering for the dumped partner. Oftentimes warning signs are glaring and obvious. But some could remain oblivious to them. Hoping for better tomorrows can be a futile pipe dream.

Coping with hurt differ from individual to individual. But sudden departure from a relationship, can feel like the death of a loved one. If children are involved, they could suffer the brunt of the breakup. Offspring abandonment tends to more prevalent with males. This is always very disturbing.

Sudden permanent separations are always difficult to deal with. A lot of men will become angry when their mate abruptly terminates a dysfunctional relationship. Some men will withdraw from their offspring when his partner leaves. Constantly being reminded of the relationship breakup, could prove extremely painful. This can push some men into isolation.

Sometimes the woman will justify the split in her mind. But she could feel responsible for her "ex" losing interest in their offspring. She could secretly blame herself for the disruption her leaving had created. Unresolved issues could deeply disturb her. She could become preoccupied with these concerns. She could become guilt ridden.

She could drift into other relationships to erase bad memories. But she would just be changing living locations. True happiness would elude her. Commitment issues would haunt her. Confusion could make her believe she was being unfaithful to herself. She could eventually erect a barrier between herself and sincere intimacy. This would create a serious disconnect with her new partner.He could begin to feel like an outsider. Loneliness could eventually begin to torment him. This is because both previous partners still carried sexual feelings for each other. These unresolved feelings could remain dormant for decades. One chance encounter could re-ignite a spark that never died. The gut wrenching casualty will be the current partner.

Sometimes warring spouses will resort to dangerous extreme measures. Many will stubbornly refuse to abandon previous dysfunctions. Quite often they will drag their fights into a new relationship. Some will use their children as pawns to enforce leverage. Either sex could be guilty of this deplorable behaviour.

Previous unresolved intimate relationships will always pose a huge problem. Over time this could put severe strain on the new spouse and the offspring. A new legal marriage could now be in effect. This would only further complicate matters.

The ripple effects can cause unimaginable devastation. Those affected the most will be the innocent and the vulnerable. Those craving for love and affection will bear the brunt of the hurt. Emotional detachment is a serious and painful issue. This will eventually become a point of contention. Hurt could escalate into volatile confrontations.

Some spouses are great pretenders. But living round the clock under clouds of lies and deception, will gradually become unbearable. Hidden motives will eventually get flushed to the surface. Lack of interest in intimacy by the fraudulent spouse, will become blatantly obvious. A showdown is in the making when suspicion becomes questions demanding answers.

The insincere partner could become demeaning and insulting when confronted. Bewilderment is usually the reaction of many unsuspecting mates. Some could become hostile to the hurting spouse. They could be accused of expecting too much from the relationship. Some could casually inform the confused spouse that affection was not a priority to them.

Some could draw the line between love and affection. These words could feel like a bullet to the head. How is one possible without the other? Scripture and reality vehemently debunks this statement. This will immediately open the door for more distrust to seep in. Many disgruntled partners could begin exploring other options to meet their needs.

Infidelity in a relationship is usually not a deliberate malicious act. There is normally a reason why intimate partners become disloyal. Most will stray because of discontentment and disenchantment. Loneliness is a primary reason that will push some to investigate alternatives. This could be seeking comfort in the arms of someone else.

Extra marital affairs are always devastating. Betrayal is never an easy burden to bear. Initial reactions are always outrage and indignation. It is never easy to forgive, when the fidelity of a marriage has been violated. Breach of trust issues are always difficult to reconcile.

Some spouses invite heartaches on themselves. Meeting the needs of each other must always be a priority. We invite a third party in our union, when we begin to neglect each other. Serious breaches rarely occur without planning and preparation.

There are always warning signs before illicit activities are exposed. There are always "tell tale" signals before the suspicion of cheating becomes a reality. But alarm bells are oftentimes ignored. Many couples fall in the trap of complacency.

Some could still be preoccupied with issues from the past. This is always bad.

Some could bemoan wasted time invested to make "things work." Others could be furious about pouring their heart and soul the union. The offended party could verbalize that everything was lost. They could mourn that their life had been ruined. It is difficult when our "soul mate" abandons us. We will shed hot bitter tears. But not all breakups are totally one sided.

It requires effort and commitment to remain loyal in an intimate relationship. There has to be steadfast dedicated determination by both couples. They should pour their heart and soul into making their marriage work. Unity ought to be the most important factor in a relationship.

We will face numerous trials and tribulations. But our journey should be a joint venture effort. It is paramount that together, we address our spiritual and emotional needs. Meeting the physical needs of each other, are also extremely important.

Responsibly taking care of our family is high priority. But all couples need time out solely for themselves. Partners need alone intimate moments to revitalize themselves. Without these sometimes structured periods, marriages tend to drift apart.

The man was made for the woman and vice versa. This was mandated by God. It is also the indisputable law of the universe. God bonded couples together to interact in love and harmony. He kept the uniqueness of our individual personalities intact. He designed us differently to balance and counter balance each other. But some of us abuse this privilege.

Individuality ought to encourage a healthy atmosphere in a relationship. Positive differences of opinion should build stronger bonds. Opposing views should be meaningful and productive. Agreeing to disagree, should amicably conclude a disagreement.

Couples should never compete against each other. Eventually this could create bitter resentment. But some people can be insanely controlling. Some could adopt repressive methods to camouflage clandestine agendas. Some could stoop low to mask their own insecurities. Devious minds cannot understand honesty and simplicity. They are always scheming and plotting.

Trickery and manipulation are dangerous tools. Some will exert brute force to dominate. Intimidation can force some to say "yes." But bullying tactics will eventually backfire and become ineffective. Tyranny will always deteriorate relationships. The brutal hand of injustice could savagely turn against many covert operators.

Freedom of expression should be the guideline for meaningful discussions. The focus and outcome should be goal oriented. There also should be a platform for robust exchange of thoughts. But routine misunderstandings can suddenly become complex, and complicated issues. Then all gains will be lost.

Inflexibility is a leading cause of communication breakdown. Some will focus exclusively on pursuing personal agendas. Many will concentrate solely on subduing and winning. Resistance could be met with swift retaliation. This routinely will lead to heated clashes. Feelings could be hurt. Relationships could be damaged.

An intimate relationship breakup is always devastating. It is irrelevant who caused the breakup. Both couples will hurt when dreams are shattered. What went wrong, are questions frequently asked. There are usually more questions than answers. Eventually each spouse could blame the other for the breakup.

Overwhelming grief can be compared to dying. We will mourn when we feel that our world is collapsing. Many of us could grieve beyond the boundaries of our tolerance level. Our breath could begin to suffocate us. Life could suddenly become inconsequential. The will to live could appear bleak for many.

It is never easy dealing with deceit. No explanation can justify a breach of trust. We will be overcome with rage when our spouse betrays us. Rationality will become a foreign word when raw hurt is burning us alive. We will breathe hell fire fury when we are violated. We will dig our heels in. Plotting revenge can demolish all boundaries.

Our "as long as we both shall live" vow should be sacred. We could feel justified to retaliate with vengeance when this is defiled. But we will make mistakes by yielding to this temptation. The pathway to revenge will only intensify our pain. This mindset will further tighten the stranglehold of unforgiveness.

Chapter Five
Satanic Deceptive Disruptions

These are unprecedented tough times. A vast percentage is overtly dedicated to that prized job. Some could use the job as an excuse, to avoid dealing with the realities of life. Some can substitute work for personal relationships. Some can erroneously conclude that hard work is the only asset to success.

Many of us cherish our rigorous work habits. We highly value our job. Our most intimate relationship is our work. We are very possessive of this vocation. We do everything to preserve it. We wholeheartedly protect this forsaking everything for way of life.

We are happily married to our employment. This is the most important entity in our life. There were times when we had stooped low. We had frequently compromised our moral and ethical values. Sometimes we had tarnished our personal integrity. We perceived this as an insurance policy for job security.Then one morning our world collapsed. Our most prestigious position got eliminated. We were abruptly terminated. There was no prior warning. We were coldly informed that our services were no longer needed. In an instant we were now an outcast. We suddenly became a non entity.

Shock could overwhelm many of us like a tidal wave. We would be stunned beyond belief. Some of us could collapse. Then reality would set in. We are now unemployed. We could suddenly feel totally dehumanized. Embarrassment and bitterness could quickly consume us. Unmanageable hurt can be compared to being wrapped a fiery blanket. Shame can feel like being roasted in an oven. Our dignity could be incinerated. Our pride and self esteem could lie in ruins. We could suddenly feel we had sunk lower than low. Seething rage could emerge when we assessed the carnage.

The volatility of the economic climate is extremely frightening for many. This can mislead some to behave inappropriately, for the sake of employment stability. Some can become very callous and self centered in their quest to succeed. Some will resort to unscrupulous methods just to survive. But it is downright degrading for anyone to be disrespected.

Nobody should to be subjected to unfair treatment. It is very hard not entertain angry feelings, when we are treated with impunity. It is demoralizing, to be mistreated with below human dignity. But injustice could easily befall any of us.

There are times when we will err seriously in judgement. But we should never conclude that one defeat defines us. We should always fight back when we have been knocked down. We should make a serious resolve. We should take the high road to recovery. We should make every effort to hold our head high. We should always aim to move ahead in dignity. Swallowing our pride could prove difficult. Some of us experience monumental difficulties. Our relationship with God could suffer severe disruptions. It is difficult to function when our self confidence is trampled on. We could become apathetic in our daily routines. The lists of psychic distresses are literally endless.

There will be times when we are at our lowest ebb. We will experience many challenges during these "free fall" turbulent moments. We will have to make tough choices when surrounded by problems. We can cave in and give up. Or we can push harder to get up.

Jesus says: "I will not leave you comfortless; I will come to you." John 14 verse 18

World tribulations are always exploring ways to wear us down. Many could get trapped in this horrible dragnet. Many will begin to re-evaluate life after a terrible collapse. Some will attempt to revamp and re-define priorities. Many will only ask God for help after all humanistic crutches fail.

Some can get viciously caught up in society's stigma. Most worldly indoctrination enforces that God is past tense. And many believe this lie. Some behave as if yielding to God is inferior. Some will aggressively rationalize this as an act of weakness. And there are those who get highly offended, that a majority of us steadfastly believe in an unseen God.

Many of these individuals will argue vigorously that our faith is a myth. Do they secretly envy us? Can they instill lasting peace within us? Are they intimidated by the powers of the Super Natural? Are they jealous that God's Spirit offers us bold confidence? Can they give round the clock comfort, when we wrestle with depression?

Will they always be near when we are blanketed in darkness? Are they always going to be available during times of peril? Do they always have answers during periods of uncontrollable torment? Some might try their best. Eventually the will get exhausted. But Jesus will readily comfort and console us. He is always by our side.

Jesus says:"If ye shall ask anything in my name, I will do." John 14 verse 14

Jesus is our Divine intercessor. This is a universal fact. When we petition His help, He will never ignore us. Our calamities will immediately evaporate when Jesus shows up. The materialistic world will be dumbfounded. Unbelievers are always baffled by the mysteries of Jehovah.

It is childlike simple. Our invisible God will immediately console us. He will put His light back in our lives. His presence will become a reality. We will now have nothing to fear. Does it really matter what other people may say or think? Does the skepticism of humans really matter during these precious moments?

Some of our friends will call us lucky. The naysayers will be puzzled. The critics will be baffled and mystified by our new turn around lifestyle. They could secretly begin yearning to be like us. But we will be overjoyed that God rescued us. We will be humbled when Jesus begins to take charge. He will completely restructure us. He will show us a different approach. We will joyfully embrace this new era.

It is never an easy task dismantling multiple layers of resentment. Permitting the Sprit of God to rearrange us can result in internal power struggles. But we should never stubbornly use anger and bitterness as weapons. It can be a nightmare being compacted with multi yokes of un-forgiveness.

We should steer clear of strife and hate. This will only prolong our pain. We make our beds in hell by refusing to let go. We will be besieged with problems. We will live in torment. We will function in chaos. Our recovery road will be unnecessarily burdensome. This can severely scar us.

Blocking hurt is self defeating. We cannot mask bitterness indefinitely. It will leak to somewhere else. Detouring severe emotional turbulences is equally bad. Avoidance will only make issues more complex. We can never sleep away our heartaches.

Trying to ignore problems will lead to greater distresses. Sometimes flash backs can haunt us. Eventually we could need a showdown, to align matters into proper sequence. Sometimes this will be the only pathway to resolve disputes. Life will not always be peaches and cream.

The thorn bushes of life will prick us severely sometimes. We will suffer scratches and cuts as we meander on this earth. Jesus never said to take up His cross and follow Him. He instructed us to pick up OUR cross and follow Him. Believers oftentimes misinterpret our Lord's statement.

Jesus stated: "Blessed are they which are persecuted for righteousness' sake: for theirs is the kingdom of heaven." Matthew 5 verse 10

Most earthly leaders will sacrifice others to promote their cause. They will argue that they need to stay alive to plan and to strategize. Jesus did the opposite. He put Himself in the line of fire between God and the population. He offered Himself as a living sacrifice. This was to save humanity from total destruction. He died to set us free.

Satan is greatly displeased when we stop listening to him. He will huddle with his demons when we begin to follow Jesus. He will assemble an army. Then the devil will unleash fire and brimstone wrath on us. Satan will attack us as he did unto Job.

Lucifer will embark on a relentlessly vicious campaign against us. He will be persistent in his attempts to humiliate us. He will try to destroy our livelihood. The devil will rush to put our finances in shambles. He will push to create turmoil in our household.

He will orchestrate strife to destabilize our intimate relationships. He will explore new methods to plague us with health issues. He will incite our family and friends to turn against us. The snake will attack our loved ones just to punish us.

Surrounded by evil is always a frightening experience. Confronting hardships is stressful and devastating. Enduring persecution will never be pain free experiences. The multitude will resort to extreme measures to avoid excruciating heartaches. But believers will triumph over adversities and injustices. This is the reality when we begin to represent the King of kings. Jesus paved the way for us. He demonstrated the high standards that we ought to live by. Sometimes we will have to endure suffering. But rewards are always abundant when we persevere under pressure. A clear focus and an unrelenting determination will give courage and stamina. These strengths will encourage us to stay committed. It is easier to cope when we know who is holding our hand. Jesus slowly suffocated to death. The Lamb of God absorbed all the sins of the world. He endured torture to offer humankind a second chance for redemption. Jesus gave His Father's children a fresh re-start. His death was to offer to the world a brand new makeover.

His sacrifice gives us the opportunity to clean up our act. Atonement for sins means a complete change. It does not mean a continuation of amoral activities. We should sever all ties with unhealthy habits. But some still misinterpret the core essence of Jesus' sacrifice.We cannot flippantly demand forgiveness, after deliberately engaging in carnality. This is grossly irresponsible. It is also disrespectful to God. A fresh start does not mean habitually repeating sinful indulgences. We will suffer dire consequences if we fail to take heed. But many refuse to learn from past blunders.Most of the population is in denial. They behave as though they have forgotten the ultimate price that Jesus paid for our sins. Increasingly many are becoming lovers of themselves. They trivialize the principles and expectations of God. But they will get their bitter reward.

Believers do not have the option of straddling the fence. We would be playing dangerous games with God. We have two choices: We can continue to flirt with temporary trappings of the world. Or we can proudly uphold the banner of Christ.

Some will attempt to rip and desecrate our banner. But we must never permit anyone to destroy it. We should always focus on what Jesus taught us: "Let your light so shine before men, (and women) that they may see your good works, and glorify your Father which is in heaven." Matthew 5 verse 16

Palms 23 verse 4 begins:"Yea, though I walk through the valley of the shadow of death, I will fear no evil:"

Our determined walk with Christ will always infuriate the devil. Satan will become aggressive and dangerous. There are times when evil can hit us faster than a bolt of lightning. We can suddenly be surrounded by danger from every angle. We will become dazed and disoriented. Goose bumps could send shivers vibrating throughout our body. Our knees could begin to buckle uncontrollably.

   We would suddenly be overcome with fright and fear. Some could collapse and become unconscious. Then Satan will personally descend on us. He will be equipped with every conceivable weapon. And he will aim straight for our heart and soul. He will unleash torrential disaster on us. He will attempt to completely destroy us. Any serious injury will momentarily cripple our reasoning abilities.

   Losing a loved one can literally feel like walking in the shadow of death. There is no greater pain than the finality of death. Sorrow and remorse will savagely rip us apart during these horrific moments. Hot bitter tears will flow from us like the billows of raging oceans. The jagged fangs of agony will bury us deep in the bowels of despair.

   Unimaginable terror is more intense and mortifying when an offspring suddenly dies. This is always a beyond comprehension blow. Our children are supposed to bury us. It should never be the other way around. Some parents never rebound from this devastating experience.The Psalms conclude:" for Thy rod and thy staff they comfort me."

   Shepherds use their rod to prod the sheep. They rely on their rod and staff to guide and control the sheep. This should prevent them from staying and getting lost from the flock. They also use these devices to ward off predators. Good shepherds tend diligently to their flock. They will rigorously defend and protect the sheep in their care. Jesus is our good Shepherd. He is our eternal shepherd.

   Our Saviour tells us in John 10 verse 11: "I am the good shepherd: the good shepherd giveth his life for his sheep."

   The wolf Satan is always relentlessly on the prowl to conquer and destroy. Without God's protection, the evil one will slither into our midst and scatter and devour us. Our good Shepherd Jesus gave His life defending and protecting us.

   God never said He would use His rod and staff to chastise and punish us. He never said that He would belittle and humiliate us. But He gives this assurance: He will use His rod and staff to comfort us. He will strengthen us during our feeble and weak periods.

Dealing with a personal tragedy is horrendous for anyone. Satan will mislead us into blaming God for this devastation. The devil will beguile some of us into believing that God is angry with us. Many could stop communing with God when life is instantaneously disrupted. But this attitude will further compound our plight.

Satan never gives advance warning when he attacks. Sometimes adversities will be lurking and waiting in line to ambush us. Nobody is immune to the fiery darts from hell. There will be periods when our faith is pushed to the brink. But surrendering to Satan's guillotine blade will never bring relief.

Some of us could be tormented with guilt for not being more vigilant. "If only I had done this or that," are comments frequently uttered when a tragedy occur. Some of us could verbalize that God had blinked, and Satan had pounced. Many will ask God for answers without even knowing what questions to ask. But we should never give Satan credit for creating havoc in our lives.

We should forcefully plead the blood of Jesus against Satan. God makes the final decision on all matters. God is always near to guide us during difficulty. He will never leave us. Neither will He ever forsake us. These are the assurances that we can rely on.

We can never gain understanding by seeking answers to unknown questions. Only God has all the answers. And He may never reveal them to us. But He will show us how to endure in spite of our grief. Closure may never become a reality. But God will teach us how to cope.

Some horrible memories will never completely fade away. But God will give us peace in the midst of the storm. This is a promise worth holding on to. Life and living are universal facts. Death and dying are also indisputable realities.

We mourn and bury our dead. But being alive should make us rejoice.

There will be periods when we will grieve nonstop. It is not abnormal to verbalize about eventually reconnecting with our loved ones. There will be times when we will vehemently complain how unfair life is. And we will become scared and saddened even more. But we should continue to keep their love alive in our hearts. These cherished memories should console and comfort us.

Chapter Six
Importance of Time

The pendulum of a clock traditionally swings from side to side. The pendulum is always visible in larger clock. It is a vital component. The swaying of the pendulum will inform us if the machine is functioning. We always need to check the hour and minute hands. The need to verify the accuracy of the clock is very important.

The invisible interior compartments are the propelling forces that drive the pendulum. The visible and invisible parts should function in synchronized harmony. This accurate co-ordination will assure us that the unit is in precise working order. Even a small malfunction will throw the entire machine off balance.

Some clocks are equipped with motion sensors. Some have voice activated devices. These are intricately installed configurations. These contraptions are designed for our benefit. They alert us when an hour is forever gone. Another alarm will sound in sixty minutes.The minute hand functions in a less conspicuous manner. But it is equally important. We are constantly being reminded when precious minutes leave this hemisphere. It also alerts us that new unblemished minutes are about to descend on us. Expired hours and minutes will never return in our lifetime.

Second hands are important accessories. They should be co-ordinated with the hour and minute hands. The unit will cease to function if they become inoperable. Monitoring time would come to a standstill. Severe inconveniences could occur. Time keeping machines should be professionally serviced. And they should be constantly monitored for effectiveness and precision.

The swinging pendulum clock is usually a decorative home accessory. Most people relate more readily to the wrist or pocket watch. Our portable timepiece functions as effectively as the larger clocks. They are just as reliable. And they are promptly assessable. We can multi task with a time keeping device on our person.

Clocks or watches are essential and necessary. They are constantly fine tuning our daily and nightly activities. Some of us habitually neglect to carefully monitor our watch's performance. Some take for granted that the correct time, will always be available on demand. It is never a good idea to treat time in a casual manner.

We the people can be compared to the stationary clock. We are also like the portable timepiece. Our spirit and soul could be compared to the invisible structures of clocks and watches. They follow the same basic pattern. Our body can be likened to swinging pendulum. This represent the visible us.

The world cannot see our spirit and soul. But our body is always in plain sight. Opinions are formed by the manner in which we conduct ourselves. This analogy demonstrates the reality that society is consistently watching us. And we are always being scrutinized. Earthlings can be brutal in hunting for flaws to smear us with.

It is important that our heart and mind operate in solidarity. Then our outer self will behave likewise. Self unity is unique and special. A contented self is a satisfied self. We should always cherish and embrace the precious moments, when we are completely at peace. We will now begin to function in perfect harmony. And God will be pleased.

But our spirit could be burdened. And our soul could be in disarray. Then our body would send out conflicting messages. This would demonstrate a visible display of disunity. There is no greater misery than inner turmoil. The world never stops observing us. Negative perceptions tend to stick.

The pendulum of the universe is always tirelessly moving. Jehovah is the original designer of all time keeping machines. The Triune God closely monitors all time in heaven and on earth. He stores expired earthly time in His heavenly data bank. He freely distributes day time and night time to all humanity. It is at God's discretion to grant or deny tomorrow's time.Some people genuinely believe they own time. How factual is this statement? Ownership means total control. Can we ever accurately predict that our current time table will never be interrupted? Can we stop time? Can we retrieve lost time? Can we fast forward time? Do we have control over the next second of our life?

Things freely given are oftentimes lavishly wasted. The gift of time is no exception. Some abuse the allotted time that God has loaned us. Some behave as if their time on earth will never end. Some misuse precious time by plotting evil. Some waste valuable time by holding on to grudges.

All aspects of living revolve around time. The clock started ticking the moment we entered earth. God gives us time to utilize life productively. Responsible use of time gives a positive sense of accomplishment. There is no greater lamentation than time frivolously wasted.

Human beings are forever complaining about lost time. Irritation and negativity come alive when careful planning suffers disruption. Many will become impatient if fine tuned timing, encountered major stumbling blocks. Some could get furious if poor planning resulted in ruined deadlines.

Time will wait for no one. We should always respect time. We should never take time for granted. Severe consequences could be imposed when time is disrespected. Employments have been terminated for failure to obey the importance of time. Many lives can be disrupted because of lackadaisical attitudes.

The world is always in a rush to meet secular obligations. Many exhaust precious effort and time chasing the wrong set of values. Misguided logic can erode the real essence and purpose of life. God and family should never be shelved because of displaced priorities. Worldly timetables should not take precedence over God and family time.

Youth is typically the period when we delude ourselves. Many erroneously reason that time will always be available. We rarely think that we age every day. Living for the carefree moment is a preoccupation of many. Serious blunders can occur by functioning in this fantasy bubble. Time becomes more valuable as we get older. Some could secretly wish that they had put time on an installment plan. There are times when some could yearn to push back the hands of time. Some could grieve over wasted years and missed opportunities. Regret will be our tormentor when we disobey the rules of time. We need time to effectively monitor all our activities. Otherwise we walk in darkness. We will function as one tightly blindfolded. But time will still be an ever present reality. Time will never cease to alert us to the necessities of life.

Fleeting time will not always be on our side. We should never vacillate with our allotted time. We should never reason that time will always be in abundance. This is a lame excuse. Our time will eventually expire. We will never escape the grave.

We misappropriate time by putting God on our "back-burner." Some misuse time as an excuse to put God on a waiting list. Some could reason that there will always be time to try "the God thing." This is a serious mistake. Precious time could turn against us.

Our clock will not tick forever. At some point our pendulum will stop functioning. Then it will be cross over time. And everything will change. Time will now have no beginning or end. This is called eternity. Eternity is forever. We will either enjoy everlasting peace. Or we will endure endless torment.

There are no time clocks to punch in heaven. God's headquarters of the universe is a time free zone. Clocks and watches will never accompany us into the heavenly realm. It is a place where joy and happiness will never cease. God's kingdom is free of hostility and strife.

Hurt and bitterness will be replaced by praise and worship. Giving glory and honour is always in abundance in heaven. God sits on His righteous throne in His kingdom. His Son Jesus sits at His right hand. Humankind can never comprehend the vastness of the heavenly realm.

There was a time when Satan lived in God's headquarters.. He was a permanent resident. He was an important member of God's team. He likely belonged to God's inner circle. But he was not satisfied to work for God. Satan misused time to introduce evil mindedness in heaven.

Satan tried to exalt himself above God. The devil devised his personal a timetable. He organized a coup against God. He failed. He was expelled for treason. He was exiled to earth. (Isaiah 14 verses 12-13) The devil brought his evil intentions to earth. And he has showered humanity with terror since then.- God puts all human beings on a time share plan. We ought to wisely divide time between God and family. Satan invented the manipulation of time. This is his method to keep us confined. He tightly bandages the eyes of the young. He hoodwinks the old. This will enable him to destroy anyone at will.

Satan is the arch enemy supreme. He is a dangerous parasite. The devil has an insatiable appetite. He always travels with his visible and invisible, specially selected demons. He is always orchestrating horror. He is always using time as a weapon against us.

He delights in confusing, and tormenting us the people. His job is to create wide scale disruption. He will throw the super fit in our midst in a crazed frenzy. He takes pride in targeting God's set apart people. He could warp the mind of the most dedicated believer.

Satan loves no one. He detests all the people. He will use his followers to spy against God's people. He will turn against his own when he deems it appropriate. Then he will double cross them. He will then utterly demolish them after they have fulfilled his objective.

Lucifer is not an entity. He is real. And he is a serial killer. We should never be flippant when we discuss him. He is dangerous. And he is cunning. We should never stray from God. We should never start dabbling in dirty antics. This will only lead to disastrous consequences.

Jesus says:" And fear not them which will kill the body, but are not able to kill the soul: but rather fear him which is able to destroy both soul and body in hell." Matthew 10 verse 28.

We should pay close attention to our Savior's words. He loaned us life. We should never forget this fact. Humankind can destroy our body. In an instant we could breathe our last breath. We will then be summoned permanently into eternity.

Eternity will be heaven or hell. Living by God's principles, will put us safely in His presence. Living by our rules, will doom us in hell. God will redeem our soul if we obeyed His guidelines. Our soul will burn in hell if we worship the devil.- God grants us time to freely make choices. But it is God who permits or allows all things round the clock. Our name will be called at the end of our journey. It will be kingdom time if God is pleased with the condition of our heart and mind. He will then reclaim our spirit and soul to Himself.

Lucifer is always dangling his hook to snag our soul. He is delighted when we abuse freedom of choice. But only we can permit Satan to sink his fangs into us. A life of carnality will shorten our lifespan. We will permanently reside in hell when we die in sin.

Satan is mass murdering snake. And he is always restlessly slithering around. The devil will silently wait for any opportunity to strike. He is delighted when we momentary stray off course. Then he will pump his venoms in us when we least expect. But God has the snake bite antidote.

Satan stands at the helm of all bad things. This enemy is a formidable foe. And he is an extremely powerful force. His portfolio is packed with every conceivable evil. All wicked inroads on the planet lead to the devil's doorsteps.

Scripture makes no mention regarding Satan being stripped of his powers, when he was kicked out of heaven. He landed on earth with all his demonic influences still intact. Satan still yearns to be superior to God. The devil would bully his way back into heaven if he could. He still fantasises about sitting on God's throne. But he knows this will never happen.

Lucifer was an underling then. And he will forever remain an underling. We the people must never underestimate the enemy's prowess. We must never minimize his skilful deceptions. Satan will always outwit us unless God's Spirit is indwelling us. We are powerless against the devil without the covering of Jesus' blood.

Some preach that Satan is a weakling. Some proclaim that Lucifer has no power. Jesus says that these statements are inaccurate. This enlightenment is in sharp contrast to many beliefs. It debunks the casual attitudes of countless believers. Let us revisit Matthew 10 verse 28. "But rather fear him which is able to destroy both soul and body in hell."

God is always present to protect His own. He will always dispatch His guardian angels to watch over us. Jesus left us a comforter in the person of His Holy Spirit. He permanently resides within us. He will never leave us nor forsake us. These are the undeniable truths. This is the lifetime guarantee we have from the Triune God.

Chapter Seven
The Beginning

IN THE BEGINNING God created the heaven and the earth. We are not told when the beginning was. God's Holy Book only informs us that the earth was void and without form. And that darkness was upon the face of the deep. God's Spirit then moved upon the face of the waters. (Genesis 1 verses 1-2)

God meticulously and supernaturally began re-assembling His universe. And He made no mistakes. Everything was perfect. His foundational structures were clear and precise. The Spirit of God put life in everything on this earth. God infused in all His creations, the ability to reproduce and replenish. Male and female He created last. He assigned to them more detailed responsibilities. He instructed them to subdue, and have dominion over every living and moving being on His planet.

God's reconstruction process is plain and simple. There is nothing complicated in the way God re-organized planet earth. He hand crafted a new world to perfection. And everything pleased Him. God rested on day seven after He had completed His work.

God then encountered a situation. He had withheld rainfall from the earth. Essential irrigation was lacking. Only a mist went up from the earth, to water the face of the ground. Plus there was no man to till the ground. (Genesis 2 verse 5 part B, and verse6.)

Adam was God's first hand crafted male. He was made from the dust of the earth. God then breathed His breath into this human. And man became a living soul. The Lord God then planted a garden for His new living breathing human. This garden was on the east side of Eden. God put Adam in charge of the garden. (Genesis 2 verses 7-8.)

God then laid out Adam's job description. God's directives were very specific. Eat anything from any tree. But do not eat from the tree of good and evil. God reinforced this command with a death penalty order. Everything apparently went smoothly for a season.

In spite of living in paradise, God's image and likeness was probably lonely. He had no other human to communicate and dialogue with. God observed that there was a void in this man's life. He recognized that that this human being needed companionship.

God eventually put Adam in a deep sleep. He extracted a rib from him. And Jehovah made a female companion for His first custom designed male. God then introduced them to each other. The woman was now the man's wife and helpmate.

Eve was God's first hand crafted female. Husband and wife lived blissfully in the garden Eden. They roamed the land freely. They were naked and unashamed. Then well dressed Satan disguised as a serpent paid Eve a visit.

The devil immediately began manipulating Eve. He forcefully reasoned with her mind. He impregnated her thoughts. He cunningly coerced her. Then he lied to her. Satan told Eve God was selfish and stingy. She believed him. He said that God wanted her to remain uneducated and unenlightened. Again she believed him.

He suggested that he was more genuine than God. His told her that his methods were more practical. They were also more logical than those of her Maker. He convinced her. He offered to assist her. Resolving the stingy God issue in her favor was his proposal.

The serpent's speech sounded genuine. But initially Eve resisted the serpent's power play. The sneaky snake continued to smoothly tantalize he mind. He seductively stirred up her imagination. He used what we now term reverse psychology on her.

Serpent Satan finally persuaded Eve of his sincerity. She began to trust him. She then made a decision. She activated her Maker's permanently infused right to choose. She exercised this right in the wrong direction. She now started to envy her Maker.

Eve was the first human to challenge God's authority. She formed an alliance with the serpent. She succumbed to jealousy and greed. Demon serpent then offered Eve a fruit from the off limits tree.

Eve eagerly ate the forbidden fruit. She displayed the fruit to her husband Adam. He could not resist her offer. He yielded to temptation. He also ate the fruit.

Eve deactivated her right choice decision making principles. She activated her wrong choice disaster mindset. Eve presented Adam a very appealing offer. He accepted and partook of this offer. He immediately crashed his right action choice. He plowed headlong in the wrong direction.

Satan cunningly tricked Eve. He badly polluted her mind. She then willfully defiled her husband. God's first couple orchestrated a mutiny. They moved against the One who gave them life. They failed miserably.

Satan deputized the serpent. The serpent performed his dirty work. And he did this in one swift seductive demonic encounter. He deliberately contaminated God's perfect plan for humanity. Purity and innocence was eliminated from earth forever.

God's pampered couple suddenly realized what they had done. They discovered that they were naked and exposed. They covered themselves with fig leaves. They attempted to hide their nakedness from their Maker. They were still in hiding when Jehovah paid them a visit. They heard the voice of

God walking in the garden in the cool of the day. God enquired of Adam as to Adam's whereabouts.

And he said:" I heard thy voice in the garden, and I was afraid, because I was naked; and I hid myself." Genesis 3 verse 10.

And He said:"Who told thee thou wast naked? Hast thou eaten of the tree, whereof I commanded thee that thou shouldest not eat?" Genesis 3 verse 11.

And the man said, "The woman whom thou gavest to be with me, she gave me of the tree, and I did eat." Genesis 3 verse 12.

And the Lord God said unto the woman, "What is it that thou hast done?" And the woman said, "The serpent beguiled me, and I did eat." Genesis 3 verse 13.

God had decreed a command to Adam. He had forbidden him to eat from the tree of the knowledge of good, and of evil. The bible makes no mention of Eve when God gave Adam instructions. Eve was not yet made when Adam received God's directives.

God called Adam into accountability for disobedience. Adam tried to absolve himself from his responsibility. He blamed his mate and partner. She blamed the serpent for tricking her. Everyone blamed someone else. They all attempted to deflect their individual acts of disobedience.

Adam made an irreversible blunder. He disregarded explicit orders under the threat of death. Adam resorted to lowest form of cowardly behavior. He sidestepped his obligations. He blamed his wife instead. God then sewed clothes to cover their nakedness. And He banished them from the garden.

God always demands high standards from for His earthly leaders. He customarily will communicate in His still small voice. God's directives are always crystal clear. Oftentimes He will only speak once. We should never arbitrarily disclose everything that the Spirit reveals to us immediately. His Spirit will impress on us how to effectively relay His proclamations.

He will wisely guide and instruct us to the where and when. Sometimes He will tell us to instantly deliver His message. There are times when He will put us on hold. God will then tell us to await further instructions.

Oftentimes we execute unwise choices. We could stray from His directives. We could ignore His instructions. We could fall in the trap of naivety and stupidity. We could become needlessly zealous. Self importance could warp our mind. Our indiscretions will always cause His Spirit grief.

We always need to exercise Godly wise discretion. Sometimes we just need to shut our mouth and keep our ears open. Talking prematurely will give Satan a reason to infiltrate. Naivety and stupidity can create huge problems. Indiscretion could be misinterpreted as self righteous arrogant aloofness.

We always need to pay close attention when the Spirit is speaking. And we need to listen keenly. God never issues confusing messages to us. But at times we interpret what we want to hear. This is when Satan's voice will lead us astray.

It is a vagrant sin when purity is defiled. Spiritual crimes are always extremely damaging. They have long lasting consequential and detrimental climaxes. Diluting or defiling Godly ordinances is dangerous. It is an abominable affront to His dignity.

Participating in sinful activities is a blatant disregard for Godly principles. And it is no joking matter. Punishment will always be severe. God is a loving and a nurturing Father. He is slow to anger and plenteous in mercy. But He will not tolerate disobedience.

God's first chosen couple were recklessly disobedient. They suffered severely. They received harsh life changing consequences. All human beings still suffer because of that first sin. We all have to live with Adam and Eve's first blatant and barefaced transgression.

Humankind inherited polluted genes from God's delinquent children. Daily we are reminded of their first fall from grace. The ramification of their first revolt is ever present. They will abide with us as long as we reside on this earth.

We do not have to keep on repeating the mistakes of our first ancestors. God has exposed us to alternatives to live by. All we have to do is read His instructions, and follow His guidelines. But we must first ask for knowledge. He will teach us how to manage every situation.

We should never sidestep our God mandated obligations. We should never ignore, or shun our responsibilities. We will suffer hardships by disregarding His expectations. We will be held accountable. God expects right moral and ethical choices. Otherwise we will experience hurt in great proportions.

Some of us have a hard time dealing with damaging issues. Many of us will dodge accountability when confronted. Some of us could begin lashing out. Many will deny ownership of a messy malfunction. Casting blame is always the easy way out.

Blaming is immaturity at peak level. It also could be viewed as a sign of weakness. But it is still a cowardly act. This is a reality for many human beings on planet earth. All the people have the potential of being tainted by this character defect.

We all will mess up at some stage in our life. Then many of us will resort to claiming immunity. Some will conveniently blame the serpent, Eve, and Adam for everything. There are also times when many will blame heaven and earth when they exercise poor judgement.

Making wrong choices are human handicaps. But we should be willing to confront our mistakes. Illicit enticements of this world are always tempting. But we could get badly damaged by partaking. Temporary pleasures can tilt us towards wrong choice reasoning. But we will be penalized for our wrong choice decisions.

There are times when blame could be interpreted as an accusation. We could feel unjustly targeted. Some could even view blaming as a blatant lie. Tempers will flare if we were left no option to defend our self. We can create a volcanic atmosphere when we disavow our participation. People can get badly hurt when anger begins to devour.

God always demands straightforward accountability from us. He expects us to be totally honest to ourselves. We lie to ourselves when we cast blame to ease our guilt. Eventually everything will backfire on us. We could be reduced to wallow in disgrace.

Adam was God's first young world leader. But he sidestepped his mandated instructions. He just could not resist the urges of his flesh. Adam participated in a rebellion against his Maker.The Supreme Judge found Adam guilty of insubordination. Adam placed himself on death row. He should have known better. Everyone will suffer until eternity because Adam just could not say "NO".

Every human being will reach the age of accountability. This is when we possess the ability to differentiate between right and wrong. This is a very important milestone. We are now expected to begin behaving in a responsible manner. But expectation and harsh exposure to life's challenges differ dramatically.

Not everyone is mature enough to manage responsibilities. This can place us at risk to be influenced by negative circumstances. Knowing better does not automatically mean that we will do better. Harmful activities can easily tarnish us when we lack insight.

Experimentation without knowledge can be very dangerous. Many get badly hurt by stubbornly refusing to follow wise instructions. Experience is the oldest and wisest teacher. It will instruct us how to bi-pass obstacles. We could suffer immense pain when we refuse to listen and digest.

God made Adam and Eve completely physically developed. They were fully grown adults with the mentality of infants. God was their only guidance, and support system. But

He implanted within them the knowledge to decipher between right and wrong.

Adam and Eve had not yet been exposed to the negative elements of life. This inexperienced couple was being groomed to rely solely on God. This was their only expectation. Then Satan descended on them. They succumbed to the first anti God temptation. We all know what transpired next.

Adam and Eve were the Lord's first prototype. They were chosen and anointed by their Maker. They were Jehovah's personal representatives. They were God's first hand crafted role models. But they were still in training. Adam and Eve disobeyed the only instruction they were told to obey. They just could not wait. They charted their own agenda. Immediate gratification became their downfall. They fell from Grace to disgrace. And this "must have" mentality is still pushing the population on a downward spiral.

God's instructions do not need interpretation. They are comprehensively simple. Follow His guidelines and do well. Abundant blessings are always bestowed on those who wait patiently. God will administer swift judgement for impatience resulting in disobedience.

Human weakness has slaughtered many. It can be insanely compelling to instantly gravitate to things that are pleasing to the eye. Not every ravenous eye contact is nourishing for the spirit soul and body. But Satan is still busy inoculating the general public. He is still aggressively inciting the people to mutiny against God. The devil has a long line of converts. He also has a huge waiting list of recruits.

God freely entrusted His world to humankind. We are the recipients of His generosity. Everything on earth is a priceless gift from God. Each moment we are reminded of these gifts. Every day and night we live these gifts. God expects us to wisely enjoy His blessings and gifts.

We call God's planet our homeland. We have gotten accustomed to enjoying His paradise. Many forget to thank Him. Some refuse to acknowledge the Sovereignty of God.

Many abuse Jehovah's bountiful gifts. There are times when we take everything for granted. There are times when we plunder the land. There are times when we hurt and antagonize each other.

Chapter Eight
Problems in Paradise

GOD RENDERED LIFE changing punishment to His delinquent couple. But He granted Adam and Eve a stay of execution. He also issued to them a pardon. God then gave them a second chance. And He extended to them a new beginning.

Adam and Eve were permanently tainted. So God had to restructure their lives. But He kept their replenishing and reproductive organs intact. God then activated their biological clocks. This enabled them to start family planning.

The bible does not enlighten us as to when Eve got pregnant. It simply informs us that she conceived. She brought her first son into this world. She named him Cain. Again she conceived. And another son was born. She named him Abel.

God's first family was now moving forward in earnest. The children grew and matured. Eventually they reached the age of accountability. The family unit was probably basically somewhat adjusted at this junction. There is no record of sibling dysfunction during Cain and Abel's formative years.

Cain took on the vocation as tiller of the field. This meant that he became a farmer. Abe became a keeper of the sheep. This meant that he worked as a shepherd.

Cain brought his first fruit offering unto the Lord in due season. This was the first portion of his crop. Abel brought the first of his flock as an offering unto the Lord.

The bible states that the Lord accepted Abel's offering. The bible says that God rejected Cain's offering. The bible gives no reason why God accepted Abel's offering. It makes no mention why God rejected Cain's offering.

We have just been exposed to a very startling fact. First fruit giving to God was a practiced custom from the era of our first ancestors. This requirement was obviously mandated by God. It is doubtful that Cain and Abel would automatically begin to fulfill this obligation. Someone had to have informed them of God's expectations.

This information is an amazing and intriguing eye opener. This revelation is important and insightful. The Father obviously decreed first fruit giving as an obligation and responsibility. This formal practice was obviously an accepted way of life from back then.

Giving back to God is our duty. We are obliged to give back. This includes the first portion of our increase. Freely giving back is not a debatable option. It is not a whimsical afterthought. It is also a wonderful framework for worship.

It is our responsibility to give back. We are required to take our duties seriously. This is an extremely sacred expectation. These instructions should be viewed as mandatory. All human beings should wisely follow these guidelines. But we should always give with a willing heart.

The bible says: "Then the people rejoiced, for that they offered willingly, because with perfect heart they offered willingly to the Lord: and David the king also rejoiced with great joy." 1st Chronicles 29 verse 9.

Jesus says: "Give, and it shall be given unto you; good measure, pressed down, and shaken together, and running over, shall men (or women) give into your bosom. For with the same measure that ye mete withal it shall be measured to you again." Luke 6 verse 38.

Giving and getting go hand in hand. This is not a flippant act of charity. We should always abide by God's expectations. But we should meticulously and consistently examine ourselves at all times. We should focus on our real motivation to give.

We should question our at times non-giving mindset. We also should investigate our cold hearted reluctance to give. God requires the purity of our heart. He is pleased when we give unselfishly. He is always assessing our attitude when we give.

We need to understand the true meaning of giving. And we need to digest it. Giving should be unconditional. We should always be happy to give. We should back up talk with actions. God will reward us when we practice what we preach. He will give back to us in great abundance.

We should always give to the poor and the needy. We should always show compassion to the less fortunate. We should commit ourselves to freely give. It is our duty bound obligation. These are the requirements from on High. It is only fully realized when we put it in proper perspective.

We should never feel intimidated or pressured to give. We will understandably become resentful to forced giving. We can become highly offended under these conditions. We can suddenly be exposed to frustration. We could get angry if giving is a demand.

Bickering will usually be the emotional fallout to forced giving. Being manipulated to give is not giving freely. We should be careful not give under duress. We should never consider giving a burdensome job. Giving back should not be stressful task. Our blessing could be impeded if we murmur.

We should always feel comfortable to give. We should never feel compelled to give. This could cause us to grumble. If our heart is not in the right place; our giving might be in vain. Our gifts might be ineffective. They could be spiritually non-productive. God will not accept gifts from the mind.

There will be no rewards for giving with ulterior motives. We should never give with string attached. This is basically a down payment for future favours. We assuredly will receive no blessing harboring this mindset. Our attitude should be unconditionally wholeheartedly motivated based.

Earth was breathtakingly perfect before the fall of Adam and Eve. It was also contamination and pollution free. Genesis 2 verse 9 tells us: "And out of the ground made the Lord God to grow every tree that is pleasant to the sight, and good for food; the tree of life also in the midst of the garden, and the tree of knowledge of good and evil." Let us also be mindful of what He did in Genesis 2 verse 7. God had to reorganize His original plans after Adam's catastrophic downfall. In Genesis 3 verse 17 God cursed the ground because of Adam's disobedience. In Genesis 3 verse 19 God imposed a hard work until death sentence on Adam.

Cain took on a vocation as a farmer. Was Cain aware that the ground was contaminated? Did Adam inform his son that the ground was cursed? Adam could have been was at fault. Cain could be unaware that he was farming polluted land.

Bad decisions can have damaging ripple effects. Our mistakes can seriously affect our loved ones. They can suffer severely when we withhold detrimental information from them. This could birth hatred against us.

The bible tells us that Cain challenged God. He became angry at God for rejecting his offering. Cain's behavior was grossly inappropriate. His dialogue with his Maker was way out of line. We could conclude that Cain had an attitude problem. God tried to console Cain in spite of his rudeness. God explained that if Cain had done well, he would have been accepted. God also told Cain that if he did not do well, sin would lay at his door. But Cain apparently was not satisfied with God's explanation.

Cain was still furious that God accepted Abel's offering. He became enraged with his brother. He probably blamed Abel for everything. Cain could have worked hard to present God with a perfect gift. He probably felt humiliated being demoted to second place status.

Cain was first born. He could have reasoned that God should have given his gift first place. But his furious conduct short circuited mature rationale. Rage suddenly erupted deep within his bowels. Cain lost his sense of balance. He then abused his right choice ability. He permitted Satan to warp his sense of reasoning. He listened to his carnal mind.

Cain channeled his senses in the wrong direction. He surrendered to his anger. His wrath pushed him to the extreme. He was now totally out of control. Cain then made a very disastrous irreversible decision. He devised a devious plan of action. He took his brother Abel into the field. There he murdered him in cold blood.

God called Cain to accountability. He challenged Cain's despicable and atrocious actions. Cain became arrogant when God confronted him. He acted contemptuously. He blatantly lied to his Master. God meted out related consequences against Cain.

God convicted Cain for his brother's murder. The Supreme Judge told Cain that the earth had opened up, to receive Abel's blood. God informed Cain that the voice of Abel's blood was crying out from the ground. Jehovah then cursed Cain. (Genesis 4 verses 3 to 12.)

Bad things will befall us when we start listing to our irrational mind. Many of us could fall victim to Cain's hideous acts. Devious plotting can easily escalate to out of control conclusions. We are never in a safe zone when our temper begins to flare. We could resort to murdering an innocent person.

Our perceptions can be extremely dangerous. Wrong conceptions will progress to misconceptions. The backlash can be severe when fierce disagreements stalemate into unresolved conflicts. Minor incidents can quickly get blown out of proportion.

We should always bear in mind that unhealthy situations and circumstances, can slaughter anyone at anytime. Being at the wrong place at the wrong time can be problematic. This can be disaster prone. Right place at the wrong time can be equally disastrous. We should be constantly reminding ourselves of these realities.

Sin had polluted the genes of Cain's parents. They were permanently scarred. Cain would have inherited tainted genes from both parents. He could have modeled his life after their impure standards. But he took the wages of sin to another frightening level.

What Cain did was more heinous than his parents' first blunder. Sin had separated his parents from God. But Cain was now a cold blooded murderer on the run. Satan had again meddled with God's righteous plans for humanity.

The devil convinced Cain to behave impulsively. He acted without thinking the consequences through. But murder is irreversible. New generation Cain was now tarnished for life. This was the reality.

The parents must have been traumatized by this horrible tragedy. They had to have been devastated. But the bible makes no mention of their emotional condition. Neither is there reference to their mental state. But they undoubtedly would have been overwhelmed with shock.

Cain's parents probably vehemently blamed themselves. They could have felt that they had failed miserably as parents. They were likely consumed with guilt and shame. But there was nothing they could to reverse this horrible tragedy.

It is always devastating when parents mourn the death of a child. It is even more painful when their loss is the result of murder. These parents had lost both children. One was murdered. The other was exiled for life. It would be difficult to imagine the anguish that they must have experienced.

Adam and Eve probably reflected deeply on their own imperfections. First generation parents had failed God miserably by behaving dishonorably. Second generation Cain took evil intent to the extreme by callously executing his brother. Both generations had committed irreversible transgressions because they listened with Satan. This family had again tremendously grieved to the Spirit of God.

Cain could have been furious that God was not interested in order of birth. He could have felt rejected. He probably resorted to murder to eliminate the opposition. But his devious actions backfired on him.

The first born is usually considered special. Some offspring will deliberately capitalize on this fact. They could use this to their manipulative advantage. They could expect and demand preferential treatment. Some behave as though the world owes them special status. Many could trample on others with this superior mindset.

Many of these individuals firmly believe that everything should revolve around them. They could portray an addictive crave to be at the forefront of everything. Their inflated ego could re-enforce this fallacy. They could become extremely obnoxious and demanding.

Some can become extremely cunning and deceptive. People with dysfunctional personalities can be very selfish. Oftentimes there will be a frantic push to be immediately seen and heard. Many will throw temper tantrum fits if situations did not progress as pre-planned.

Most people will find pushy attitudes offensive and annoying. This could encourage some ego driven persons to resort to bullying tactics to prove a point. An adrenalin rush could push some over the edge. Blind rage could propel them to cause serious injury to others. They could end up destroying the innocent and themselves.

There are many with Cain's mentality roaming the land. Some will sulk if they were reduced to second place. Some can become belligerent if they had to settle for less than best. Some will eliminate the opposition to maintain their status like Cain did.

Many could attempt to cover their tracks as Cain did. They could become hostile when confronted regarding their evil actions. Like Cain, they could resort to lying before God and humanity. But the harsh hands of justice will render severe punishment. Only then will some realize that sometimes the last will be put in first place.

Chapter Nine
God is Always Authentic.

THE WRITER JOHN DECLARES: "In the beginning was the Word, and the Word was with God, and the Word was God." John 1 verse 1

The Bible says: "Thy Word is a lamp unto my feet, and a light unto my path." Psalms 119 verse 105. "The entrance of thy Word giveth light; it giveth understanding to the simple." Psalms 119 verse 130.

Isaiah 55 verse 6 reminds us: "Seek ye the Lord while he may be found, call upon him while he is near."

The authenticity of God is as clear as bright sunny day. The Spirit of God is as real as the air we breathe. God chose and instructed His chosen prophets and leaders. These anointed men and women were ordained and set apart by The Most High God. They documented Jehovah's righteous expectations for all humanity to live by.

Their recorded predictions are tangible proofs that God is real. The Lord's insightful revelations are straightforward and practical. His revealed will is available to all humankind. The Word of God is our instruction manual. It is also our reliable guideline.

Jehovah's directives are uncomplicated. His prescribed principles and expectations are comprehensive and binding. They are applicable under all conditions. His authentic messages will never become outdated. They will live forever. His fathomless wisdom will never be mundane. God should never be considered redundant or irrelevant.

The Word of God Word is readily available to everyone. All human beings should embrace and obey scriptural revelations. This should be for as long as we live. His priceless insight should always be our guiding light. We should all embrace all His teachings. We should internalize and utilize His prescribed principles. We should envision them as our security blanket.

The word of God is holy and undefiled. Priceless words of wisdom are put forth in it. Different faith groups call this bread of life book by different names. But this is the same wisdom principle book. Followers of Christ refer to this book as "The Holy Bible." All humanity should feast on, and digest the contents of the word of God.

This is a one of a kind universal book. This book is our beacon of life. It was written for believers and non believers. Everyone should familiarize themselves with this book. We should pray and meditate before we read this book. We should study this book. Everybody should rely on the divine wisdom contained in this book. Then we should to ask for guidance to understand this book.

We all need to understand the spiritual revelations put forth in this book. This book is the binding revealed will of God. The population should memorize this fact. All humankind should live by the practical realities if this book. The world should interact with this book. This book should be on our must have list. We should always cherish this book. This book is from the One who piloted us to earth.

This book has been persecuted. This book has been banned. This book has been scorned. It has been subjected to public mockery and ridicule. This book has been trampled on. It has been burned. This book was thought to have been destroyed forever.

However, this book has survived. This book has thrived. This is an important and valuable book. This is the most popular book in the world. It still is the worldwide best seller of all times. The need to own this book is more urgent than ever.

We should never downplay God's vital life sustaining principles. It is our spiritual and our emotional lifeline. It gives us mental and psychological strength. We should never flippantly browse over the pages of our bible. We should never seek out verses just to satisfy our fancy.

No one should use this sacred book for manipulative purposes. We should never assimilate skillfully crafted passages. We should never pick verses with the intent of misleading. We should never use the Word to brain wash our brethren. It is a grave travesty if this occurs.We delude ourselves by behaving in this manner. We will lose His blessings when we resort to deceptive practices. We should never distort the real purpose for Jehovah's guidelines. We miss the effectiveness of His revealed will when we dilute His Word. We will stray from Godly principles.

We will not be led by His Holy Spirit. We will end up causing problems for ourselves. We should always cling to His moral and ethical road map. We should never minimize God's instructions. We should never trivialize his messages. We should never discard as irrelevant the nudging of His Holy Spirit. Our God will always be present tense.

Our Father did not commission His Word solely for His chosen prophets. He did not issue them just to His selected leaders. His Word was not compiled only for the people of old. God's word is not an interesting history book. It should never be read as amusing documentations.

God's Word is not irrelevant occurrences from ancient times. His Book should be our current reference manual. The recordings are always relevant. This book is alive. This book is now. It is our torch in our current dark society. The Word of God will lead us to the mercy seat of Christ.

We need it for our yesterdays. We need it for our today. Sometimes we can peek at our tomorrows by believing in this book. Our faith will grow stronger by practicing the true meaning of this book. God's Word has been the same before the generations of our fore parents.

This however, is our 21St century materialistic society. Many reason that this era is the dawn of new beginnings. Some say that we are pioneering new frontiers. Many say that practices of old have become antiquated or obsolete. A lot of so called spiritual leaders have endorsed this recklessly misleading humanistic agenda. Many have deliberately misled and pressured their followers into believing this falsehood.

A lot of people are now confused. Many are questioning the authenticity of the bible. They complain that it was written by humans. Therefore it is subject to human interpretation. Some dedicate countless hours finding faults with God's word. Ignorant people have become highly skeptical about the contents of the bible.Many have begun to doubt the validity of the bible. Some relentlessly demand to be convinced. Some aggressively require proof that there is only one God. Some will embark on a tedious expedition to prove their point. Their goal is to disprove that God alone is the Supreme Ruler of this universe.There is also a powerful group who cohabit this earth. They hate God. They vehemently propagate an anti God agenda. They display a hardened anti Christ mindset. They set themselves apart. They call themselves orators of the truth.

They ridicule our God. They discount our core belief system. They hold in disdain our faith. They make fun of our customs. They love to hurl insults at us. They mock the large multitude in society who believe and rely on God. Many call us weaklings. They treat us with impunity. The truth is never in them.

We verifiably accept the existence of a God. They do not. Sometimes we are acutely bombarded by Satan's disciples. Sometimes we get the sad impression that atheism is on the rise. Some people say that it is thriving in our land.

Most of us earnestly comply with our secular guidelines. We will readily adapt society's standards. We eagerly embrace our earthly principles. But a multitude lack enthusiasm to follow God's life essential instructions. Some are often below grade level energetic. Many are antagonistic and skeptical regarding spiritual guidelines. Many stubbornly will not believe in God.

No one will abide on earth forever. We all must die sometime. We should behave in accordance to this fact. We do not own our breath. We cannot purchase life. We will leave our secular belongings behind when we expire. The armoured truck will never be in a funeral procession. God wisely installed us here. We function as a collective group. We mingle as a fragmented body of people. But God granted us permission to be on His planet. We live in love and harmony because of this fact. We function in disharmony or confusion because of this reality. These are the indisputable truths. Most of us ardently believe that God is the Sovereign Ruler of the universe. We worship Him in spirit and in truth. Some have convinced themselves that there is no Sovereign God. Some believe they control their fate and destiny. But all human beings have to intermingle with each other on this planet.

Chapter Ten
The Cycle of Life

We freely inherited our earthly home. We share living and breathing space with other life forms on this planet. We have the liberty to replenish and reproduce. We cannot ignore or discount this truth. We live this practicality. We will die with this reality.

God oversees and controls everything on His planet. He has a pre-destined agenda for all. He has a pre-purposed plan for everyone. None of us stumbled here. No one was suddenly shoved to earth. Nobody was threatened to come to this land. There is no fee to take up residence in this world.

Life begins at conception. We began our journey to earth in darkness. Our mother's womb was our fortified fortress. We were blanketed in protection. We were physically inseparable. And we were intricately intertwined. We were consistently nurtured in her dark chamber.

We exited the snugness of her womb at an appointed time. The Spirit of God made our safe delivery possible. He guided us from darkness into light. It is God who gave us permission to enter a strange and unfamiliar land.

Our tiny body was received by large hands. Our umbilical cord was immediately cut. We are now literally free from our mother's internal bond. We are now baby citizens on planet earth. But we are still dependent on our mother for all our needs.

Positive nurturing will guarantee a healthy foundation. An unstable environment will have a negative impact on us. None of us entered this world with a pre-installed mean streak. But unhealthy influences could taint and contaminate us, at a very tender age. These are the binding facts. These are the undeniable truths from heaven and earth.

We all enter this world in purity and undefiled innocence. We came to earth reflecting the heart of God. Our debut could be pleasant. Or things could be frightening. Our environment could radiate joy and happiness. But our new surroundings could be overflowing with negativity and hostility.

Living and aging begin at birth. We become a legitimate member of the population on arrival. The laws of the universe dictate this fact. This law also applies to awareness and internalizing. We get inducted into an imperfect society at birth. We immediately become exposed to all the elements around us. God installed life skills essential survival kits within us before our first exhale. He then implanted His internal safeguard systems deep within us. He did so for our current and future protection. They became fully operational with intricate monitoring features immediately. No one should ever underestimate the power of an infant's observation center.

God also put invisible cameras in us. They are pin point accurate. They are always precisely timed and fine tuned. We start taking snapshots of everyone and everything, from the moment we enter earth. We record all things in and around our environment. We immediately start storing them. We do this in our obviously tiny memory bank.

We also arrive in our new homeland equipped with powerful antennas. They are uniquely designed and invisible. We begin recording signals the moment we were separated from our mother's womb. We immediately commence to pick up messages. We start deciphering conflicting codes.

God custom designed and infused in us hidden radar detectors. Our radar detectors and antennas work on one accord. We keenly listen to communications. We carefully record dialogue. We store all data for future usage. A new birth is usually very exciting. We focus a lot of attention on this. But we rarely recognize another reality. Our new resident's internal monitoring system is now fully operational. Our earthly journey begins with awareness. We immediately begin observing and internalizing. These functions will terminate when we exit this planet.

God selected some of us for parenthood. It is God who assigned us the responsibility to caringly train up a new generation. In other words, God passed the mantle to us. We should perform our duty reflecting His high standards. But sometimes we forget that we were once the infant.

We are obliged to provide superior care for our children. God mandated this requirement. This is our duty. This is also a universal expectation. We should happily embrace this fact. Above reproach nurturing standards should always be a priority. God has entrusted His gift to us. Society expects us to honor our commitment.

Our offspring's formative years are extremely important. We will be assessed on our dedicated effectiveness. We will be evaluated on our performance. We will be tested for positive consistency. We will be graded by God and society. We should all pass the positive nurturing test.

Society is always scrutinizing parents. Earthlings love to diligently look for human blunders. Parents need to be aware of this fact. We should dutifully uphold high standers for our children. We should to take seriously our parental duties.

We should be caring and vigilant. Our children will adapt to our standards. They will conform to our expectations. We should manage our assigned tasks with passion and compassion. We will be rewarded when our offspring reach the age of accountability. We will have passed. Or we will have failed.

Passing the good parent test is a goal worth striving for. Failing the good parent test is a flaw that society is always on the lookout for. Many could organize witch hunts to defile our characters. Some are quick to label our environment unstable.

Sometimes our characters are put on trial. Sometimes we are dragged through the mud.

Some people are quick to dramatize issues. Many could quickly publicize our parents' errors. We could sometimes be linked with their problems. This could happen quite often. We could be regularly subjected to microscopic observations. We could be constantly under surveillance. Oftentimes our parents' poor choice decisions would be hot topics of discussions.

Human beings can be merciless in imposing brutal negative assumptions. One poor choice decision on our part could encourage a swift guilty verdict. All our good deeds could immediately be deleted. This could stir up vicious rumour mongering. Gossip clubs could become fast and furious. We could be left feeling that we were in the presence of a lynching mob. The world tends to hastily hold fast to inaccurate assumptions. Oftentimes this could encourage the public to impose negative labels on us. Most of the population could conveniently omit to verify facts. Biased assessments will assuredly cause us to grieve. Disassociating ourselves from harmful perceptions could prove difficult.

Sometimes it could be extremely difficult defending ourselves. This is because our formative years were terrible for some of us. We had endured immense pain and suffering. Our basic coping performances were vertically non-existent. We lacked base level communication skills. Oftentimes we just drifted aimlessly through life.

Things could get worse. Many of us were not taught foundational moral and ethical values. We were not given the opportunity to explore a spiritual connection. Oftentimes our emotional balance sheet was completely disorganized. Internal buffer structures were never instilled within us.

Now we are first time parents. And we lack the reservoir of positive infusions. We have nothing to fall back on. But the population expects us to be well adjusted parents. Frustration could overwhelm a lot of us. We could retaliate in anger. We could explode when perfection on demand was expected.

Some of us could get hostile and rebellious. We could resist suggestions from others. Sometimes advice would be genuine and caring. But we could rebuff good intentions from other people. We could regard these gestures as an invasion against us. Unforgiveness could begin to fester if we felt bombarded and trapped.

Proverbs 22 verse 6 states: "Train up the child in the way he (or she) should go, and when he (or she) is old, he (or she) will not depart from it."

This scripture could sound like a harsh expectation from God. We could become scared and resentful for Him exposing us to this reality. We could become angry with God Almighty for placing unrealistic demands on us. Our offspring could immediately begin to be adversely affected.

Training is virtually impossible if we have no well of knowledge to draw from. We can only train effectively when we understand how to teach. We would have nothing to work with if our parents had not taught us meaningful values. We could drift in the rough ocean of life without a paddle. We could tell God that we were the ones in need of training.

Most of us cannot cry out to God during times of crisis. We could be genuinely too petrified to correspond with God. We could continue to grieve nonstop instead. Many could endorse what comes naturally. We could cling tighter to the pangs of sorrow. Some could collapse and wallow in self pity.

Our parents played important roles in our lives. Their influences guided us to this moment. We are here because of them. We are living this period because of them. We learned good and evil from them. We should excel by being exposed to parental positive molding. But we could become deviant because of negative indoctrinations.

We absorb much during our tender years. All learning is part of our general makeup. We will remember what we were taught. Some we will embrace. Some we will ignore or discard. Some we will question. Our conduct will reflect how well we were molded.

We also learn and model our way of life by observing others. We grasp and internalize from the adults and peers we were exposed to. We will absorb how to gentle and tolerant. We will digest how to be mean and rotten. Nobody came to earth with a character defect.

We all reach that first bridge. This is learning right versus wrong principles. The second phase is just as important. This will be accountability and independence. Then we will the write the test called life. Our grades will reflect how well we did.

We all eventually enter the workforce called living. Our performance will reflect how properly we had been trained. Good moral and ethical skills will put us in line for promotions. A spirit filled foundation will help us combat the storms of life.

A shaky infra structure could pit us against the raging storms of this world. The brutal elements could repeatedly toss us to and fro. Our unstable foundation could suffer serious erosions. Sometimes we could find ourselves living under life threatening conditions. There is no perfect person on earth. But many try to live this myth. Everyone will repeatedly veer off course. Sometimes we could get stuck in our pot holes. There are times when we will pedal in the wrong direction. Sometimes we will fail. At times we will fall flat. But a strong support system will help us to weather the perils of life.

God is always watching over us. Maturity should come with Godly infused wisdom. He will instill within us knowledge and understanding. His Spirit will teach us how to navigate through the murky waters of despair. God will always dispatch his representatives to pull us to dry land.

It is never easy being a first time parent. Beginner parenthood will always be a period filled with anxiety. It is irrelevant if we are well adjusted, or if we are struggling with a problematic past. A new life represents a new beginning.

Life will never be just about us anymore. This is because a new citizen is now journeying to earth. And this little one will eventually permanently reside with us. Many of us could have to grow up in a hurry. The condition of our heart will tell the whole story.

"In my distress I cried unto the Lord, and he heard me." Psalms 120 verse1

There is nothing more frightening than being trapped with nowhere to turn. Some mothers struggle with the uncertainness of an unplanned pregnancy. In brokenness and desperation, many will turn to God for comfort. He will never deny the cries of the broken hearted.

God will remove the doubts that can so badly keep us confined. God will instill within us faith and hope. He will provide spirit filled mentors to guide and assist us. The Spirit of God will look way beyond our current woes.It is disgusting to be forced to take possession of rotten goods. These are merchandise that we did not legitimately purchase. But negative influences forced us in accepting them. We ended up stockpiling these dirty and filthy inventories. Nasty habits were force fed us. Mean streak personalities were installed without our consent. We inherited vile and deplorable attitudes at a very tender age.

These are but a few amoral things that we can be exposed to. Some of us tend to keep on hording a lot more. And some of us passionately claim ownership these demons. God did not manufacture explosive tempers in us. We inherited these malfunction in our new homeland.

Oftentimes we drank generations of "bad medicine." And we were powerless to resist. Over time we started purchasing them on our own. We then fed them to our offspring. They also got sick. Countless future generations could continue to ingest harmful medications.

Replacing minuses with pluses is never as easy as the stroke of a pen. It takes prayerful determination and hard work. Some merchandise is packed with hidden defects. Some inheritances are littered with harmful hidden clauses.

The Lord will teach us how to avoid contaminated seeds. He will instruct us to purchase healthy soul foods. He will give us the strength to say "no" to bad inheritances. Everything worthless should be bundled and burned. Our legitimate inheritances will have the stamped approval of Jesus. God will convert our heartrending minuses, into meaningful pluses. All good things are worth fighting for.

Sadly many still keep on going around in circles. This is very unfortunate. Some frequently continue to reopen old wounds. Some stubbornly still cling to inherited burdens. This is in spite of God showing alternatives. It is sad when some refuse to listen and take heed. Many now risk recycling and repeating serious blunders.

Chapter Eleven
Life's Curve Balls

We should never permit our body to control our emotions. We would be charting a precariously dangerous course. Not everything that is pleasing to the eye is good for the spirit and soul. This is especially factual when we get involved in intimate relationships. We can suffer grueling heartaches if we let our flesh control our actions.

An intimate relationship is important. Most enter into relationships with the best of intensions. Some relationships begin with curiosity. Sometimes it is from deep infatuation. At times motives are those of lust and pleasure. There are times when feelings are genuine.

We can easily convince ourselves that we are truly in love. We will be heatedly passionate during these moments. We routinely will consider our intensions to be above reproach. We will reason that our heart is pure and unblemished. But our body could begin to play tricks on our mind.

Our relationship can progress smoothly for a period. Communication could be free flowing. But meaningful dialogue could be restricted. Mature reasoning could be elusive during these moments. Our "honeymoon" period can dim our sight and dull our senses. When lust is reigning supreme, everything else is put on the back burner. The status of our relationship could be rarely discussed. Commitment issues can be completely overlooked. Wholesome goals could be swept aside. Futuristic planning could be conveniently put on hold. Proper guidelines would be absent. No structure would now govern our relationship.

We would now be acting grossly irresponsible. A noncommittal attitude will spell calamity. Problems will do the planning for us. Complications will invariably surface. They can mushroom rather quickly. Disaster will be lurking when sheer pleasure is our only ruler.

Casual sexual relationships usually lack structured guidelines. They are basically extended one night affairs. Passion will always outsmart logic. Quite often many of us will postpone taking precautionary measures. There are times when one partner could deliberately mislead the other.

Complete honesty could be shrouded in mystery. The inevitable could quickly become a reality. We will now pay the full price. A pregnancy could be the proof of our careless practices. This is as factual as night time follows daylight.

Suddenly we are no longer a twosome unit. We are now a threefold entity. A living and a breathing tiny human being now is involved. A baby is on the way to take up occupancy in the land. Some could be ill prepared for this reality. Tension and uneasiness could quickly erupt. Failure to put our flesh on hold can create many distresses. This will also encourage havoc. We could needlessly embrace sorrow. Trauma could rear its ugly head. The pain could become severe.

Consequences will yell "present," when proper planning is absent. We could be steering our emotions into a bottomless pit. We will collide when we ignore built in safeguards. We have a responsibility to God and ourselves. We should always involve Him in our decisions. Otherwise we sidestep our obligations.

Shock is usually the initial reaction surrounding an unplanned pregnancy. But we will have to deal with this fact. Anxiety and fear could suddenly grip us. We could be faced with a grim situation. Remaining focused could be extremely difficult.

This could be a potential nightmare. Our relationship could encounter a major stumbling block. Emotional curve balls will always disrupt our thought process. Many questions would be asked. Many answers would be elusive.

Indifference could immediately override passion. Intimacy could suddenly become deader than a doornail. Resentment and puffed up attitudes could become glaringly apparent. Excuses could become commonplace. Self defensive measures could be quickly invoked.

We could become downright nasty towards each other. We could violently lash out. Blame could rear its ugly head. Emotions could begin to gallop wildly out of control. We could experience difficulty containing them. Hostility can lay the foundation for vicious fights.

This would impair our ability to communicate. Meaningful dialogue is impossible when disappointment turns to grief. Irreconcilable differences could take center stage. Our lopsided arrangement would now be scheduled for burial.

All nonverbal assumptions could become heated points of contention. Nothing would get resolved. Anger and logic is never compatible. But we will eventually have to isolate our personal differences. We will have to put them on hold. Would we be able to courageously examine ourselves? Would we be able to push our emotional shock aside? Could we put our mental traumas on the sideline? Could we now focus on the important pressing issue at hand? Would we be able to concentrate on the inbound child? Would we discuss meeting the current and future needs of this infant?

Our careless actions resulted in this potential problem. But an innocent life is now earth bound. Our focus should be our unborn child and beyond. This could be a crisis prone moment. But we should retain level headedness. We will desperately need to get our priorities straight. It is important that we unconditionally avail ourselves. We will have to make major adjustments and preparations. A new life will now have to be accommodated. This innocent infant will eventually arrive on earth. And this life will forever be linked to us. Until death this child will be a part of us.

Intimate partners tend to needlessly argue. It is difficult to focus when we are upset. But when mistakes occur, we should never try to devour each other. The blame game will only put more pressure on our emotions. This attitude will further alienate us. Honest dialogue is the only path to dislodge any impasse.

Many hold on to hallow expectations. This is very bad. We could get severely hurt. This could make it difficult for us to candidly express our feelings. Our heart can be ripped to shreds when we discover that we had been misled. What we assumed was love, was infatuation and lust.

Many could get caught up in bitterness and anger. Rage could quickly blanket us. An unforgiving spirit could quickly surface. A semi bankrupt state of mind is always disturbing. But these are consequences we will endure by failing to act responsibly.

The call of the flesh will always recklessly entice. Delusions can be earth shattering. It is never easy to cope when our taken for granted relationship hits the skids. But this frequently happens when a relationship is totally one sided. Now we will have to deal with the agony of being rejected.

Most women rely on their intuition and instincts. They rarely will get intimately involved without first checking with their heart. Many rely on their hearts to guide them at the onset of intimate relationship. But the mind can play tricks on the heart.

Some will conduct an intimate assessment based solely on their feelings. Sometimes the eyes will relay to the mind and brain that all is well. These feelings can easily lead us astray. It is always wise to embark on the slow approach. This will avoid future potential complications.

Men normally think on different plateaus than women. They tend to be more aggressive and persistent. Their mind usually will relay to the brain what is pleasant for the eyes.

This can be problematic during initial introductions. Most women will rebuff pushy demands.

Some men consider themselves hunters. They are frequently on the prowl to conquer and ravish. They thrive on short term sexual adventures. Some will abruptly abandon their partner if she became pregnant. Some wholeheartedly believe that their major purpose in life is to impregnate, and move on.

Some men will resort to extreme measures to nullify their parental obligations. Taking responsibility for their actions is rarely a debatable option. Some will aggressively attempt to distant themselves from current and future obligations. Many could casually leave a multitude of fatherless children behind.

Society is swift to pronounce harsh judgment on men who abandon their family. Selfish and irresponsible fathers deserve to be chastised. Communities oftentimes label them as horrible monsters. Most will treat them with disdain. Some will passionately hate them. Absentee fathers are routinely advertised on the wall of shame. Family abandonment is beyond shameful.

It is always rough dealing with the premature abortion of an intimate relationship. This could create severe hardships for most pregnant mothers. First time or experienced mothers could be exposed to similar traumas. Remorse and humiliation could drown them in a sea of sorrow. It is never easy dealing with rejection.

We incur instability in our children when we recklessly fight. We can damage their self esteem when we demean each other. It is sad when warring adults are in full attack posture. Some act though self preservation is the only route that matters. Some people thrive on being selfish. Victory is the only rule that some will observe.

It is hard to be logical when we are in counter attack mode. We rarely consider the needs of our children during these moments. We could end up harming them. This fact holds true if they are earthbound or are already here. Even when we at times call a truce, the damage sometimes already has been done.

Some of us have lived through hell on earth treatments. Many of us have endured brutal punishments from our so called caring adults. Some of us and have emerged battered. Some have been crushed by mal-functioning; and dysfunctional families. Some of us are scarred by personal family crisis. Horrible family relationships can ruin us.

Life can be brutal. Some of us will face these harsh realities. Some parents make wrong choice intimate relationship decisions. Their mistakes can rub off on us. We could needlessly endure pain and suffering. This could inhibit our overall ability to function effectively.

Sometimes history will repeat itself. Some of us could end up repeating our parents' mistakes. We had vowed to avoid their failures at all cost. But many of us fall victim to these same problematic situations. Now we are caught in this same precarious circle.

Some of us will pause and reflect. This re-think is not uncommon. We will take stock. We will evaluate our course of action. Some of us will reassess our mindset. Embarking on the no return warpath would be our last resort.

This is the mature segment within our society. And level headedness is the prevailing rule. The positive welfare of our offspring should be a must. This should outweigh our self agenda. The love for our children should come first. This should include burying our pick axes. The warring issues that mean so much to us should be shelved. The potential damage for our offspring is minimized when we harness our emotions. The necessity to reconstruct our dialogue should now loom large and urgent.

Sometimes it's not easy saying goodbye. Some of us are flexible. We are able to re-adjust our drift away lifestyle. Some of us are even able to reconnect and reunite. A percentage of us eventually reignite the passion. The intimacy of our relationship could grow stronger. Many of us are able to cement our family unit back together again.

Sadly some of us fall through the cracks. Some of us get plowed by the wayside. A large amount of us permanently drift apart. Our children now are forced to suffer because of our mistakes. They could have to endure the dire consequences of our failures.

The burdens of our wrong choices could cling to them for a very long period. The danger exists that they will be tarnished by our negative influences. They are now at risk of repeating our unhealthy role model standards. This could be problematic when it is their turn to reproduce and replenish.

Some of us could become guilt ridden. We will internalize the devastation that our abrupt departure could create. The conscientious in our midst will make sacrifices. We will digest the long term potential damage. Then we will make a decision.

Our spousal relationship could have reached the point of no return. All feelings of intimacy could no longer exist. But we will consider seriously the needs of our children. We will make the necessary adjustments. We will stay in contact with our children. We will remain active in all aspects of their lives.

We are being selfish when hard hearted behaviors take center stage. This is grossly unfair to the family. We will inflict needless burdens on our spouses. It is unconscionable when we neglect or discount their feelings. It is even worse when we permanently remove ourselves, from the lives of our offspring.

It is beyond evil when we are cruel to our spouse. Our partner was once supposed to be our significant other. We should never trample on their vulnerability. We are horrible human beings if we resort to these measures. God will hold us accountable.

Selfish people only think about themselves. Many are usually preoccupied with making hasty exits. Empathy is a foreign word to most of them. They frequently display callousness. Many will leave their other half to suffer all alone. These deplorable individuals demonstrate complete indifference, to the bitter embarrassment that they are exposing their partner to.

It is not our intension to portray all men as villains. Not all men are idiots. They should not all be blamed for everything that is vile. Not all males are guilty of spouse desertion. Many are not responsible for relationship failures. Sometimes they are the victims.

We cannot honestly exonerate all women. Some women are equally guilty of causing a relationship breakup. Some females can behave very dishonorably. She could be the one instigating problems. She could be the unreasonable fault finder. She could be the partner manufacturing arguments. She could be the person creating strife.

Many women have wrecked their relationships. Some can become cold hearted towards their mates. Pregnancy could encourage her to abruptly terminate her relationship. She could leave without even saying goodbye. This would be grossly unfair to her partner. He could be left feeling completely baffled.

Men are not immune to hurt. Many get branded unfairly with negative labels. Oftentimes they are not afforded the opportunity explain the facts. This is grossly unfair. This could be highlighted as reverse discrimination. The mother is the carrier of the child. This puts her in a unique position. But does she have the right to arbitrarily solely decide the future for this child? Is she being fair to her mate? Could she assuredly guarantee that her decision was best for the incoming child?

There is one extremely important exception. This would be abuse on any level. These factors would obviously override everything. All aspects of the relationship will now have to change drastically. And swift action will have to become mandatory.

The welfare of the affected adult and child must be of the highest priority. This has to supersede everything else. They have to be protected at all cost. Sometimes legal actions could have to be levied against the offending spouse.

It is regrettable that domestic violence is still rampant in society. But a half of a whole is better than nothing. Not everything that is broken can be repaired. Some things cannot be restored. Idealistic "what if" is solely wishful thinking. This will never be compatible with reality.

It is always sad to watch any relationship deteriorate. Emotional malfunctions are always difficult to deal with. It is irrelevant who carries more blame. It is unimportant if this is a short term or a long term union. Episodes of hurt will affect the immediate family and the extended family.

An intimate relationship breakup is usually very painful. It is rarely a hot topic of discussion. Precautionary boundaries and guidelines should always be established. Sensitivity should be the key when discussing this problem. Only the two parties concerned really know.

They have the answers to their intimate issues. Only they can relate to what actually transpired behind their closed doors. The intimacy of a personal relationship should be closed to the public. It would be grossly unfair to label one sex. It would be irresponsible to put a stamp of approval on the other.

We should always refrain from passing our personalized value judgment. Our interpretations and conclusions could be on target. Sometimes our perceptions could be totally off base. We should be cautious at all times. We should never jump to hasty conclusions.

Nobody ever wins when we neglect our family responsibilities. Hurt will always be a two way street. We will suffer. Our mate will suffer. Our offspring will be left dangling. They will in time grow up. And they will remember. Sadness and remorse could torment the entire family structure. Irresponsible behavior by either party will always hurt everyone.

Chapter Twelve
Damaging Children

PARENTS WILL RESORT to extreme measures to protect their children. They will run bareheaded through the gates of hell, to shield their offspring from harm and danger. They will violently attack Satan if he interfered. And they would not consider the consequences. The majority of parents will take whatever steps necessary to ensure the continuance of their linage.

Many of us had a tough upbringing. Some came through the ranks of the under privileged. Sometimes our parents could not adequately care for us. Oftentimes we suffered severe hardships. At times we had no positive support system. Unhealthy living environments took a toll on us. Deplorable conditions stirred hostility and anger within us. We detested and hated this restrictive way of life. But we dared not complain. Frequently we went to bed hungry. At times we felt humiliated because of our circumstances. There were times we felt like giving up.

Misery appeared to be our only option. But we never caved in. We yearned for a brighter tomorrow. Positive thoughts became our reliable companion. This preoccupied virtually all our waking hours. This inner drive kept us going. We began to push harder. And we never ceased to pray.

We then made a concentrated effort. This was a hard choice. We were determined to rise above the fray. We made a meaningful calculated decision. Enough was enough. This gave us strength and courage. We submitted to a Higher Power. We yielded to the guidance of this Power. We eventually overcame our grueling hurdles.

God blessed us with a family in due season. Now it is our turn to make a difference. We embarked on a mental and physical journey. Our offspring would never suffer like us. At all cost we would give them a better quality of life. We calmly made a serious commitment. We start loving our children exclusively.

We pour abundant nurturing into them. We protect them fiercely. We do a superb job of policing all their activities. Our goal is simple. Smother them with our influences. We begin shielding them from all life's negative influences.

We vow to be there for them as long as we live. This will be our full time occupation. We are extremely satisfied with our reasoning. We put in practice our choice. We now develop an addictive mindset. We end up overprotecting our offspring.

Parents who practice emotional control can severely damage their young. But there are usually underlying reasons that propel some parents, to excessively cater to their children. Those who participate in this irrational mindset should honestly examine themselves.

Some should embark on a sincere soul searching pilgrimage. They should focus on unearthing the hidden motives behind their determination, to shower their children with unnecessary abundance. Many could be in for a rude awakening.- Most parents could discover that dedication to excesses had nothing with their offspring. A lot could have to concede that this illogical mindset, stemmed from their personal childhood. Many try to recoup the material endowments they missed out on while growing up. Some will live prominence and status through the lenses of their new generation.

There are times when this behaviour will create a rift among spouses. One spouse could adamantly push for moderation. The other spouse could stubbornly decide to pursue their pre-meditated agenda. The mindset of the dominant spouse usually will prevail.

Sadly many parents continue to supply material wants to their young. And the needs of their children for free quality time, is usually discounted as being nonessential. Pampered children quite often lack intimate bonding with their parents. These are a few examples of the downside to overprotection.

Overprotected children are at risk of becoming spiritually and emotionally deficient. We can damage our children when we cater indiscriminately to their wants. We will overcompensate when we over facilitate. We will end up supplying them too much of everything. This will not be healthy for them. Countless psychological disorders can plague them as they grow and mature.

Overcompensation will always create problems. Our offspring's value system will suffer. It will be poorly aligned. We hurt our children by denying them basic learning techniques. Their emotional and mental stability is extremely important. It is paramount that they learn constructive ways to explore life.

Parents should never shield their children from life's realities. This is unrealistic. It is also harmful. They need the freedom to experiment in a healthy environment. Otherwise they can fall victim to a false sense of security. They could also develop a superiority complex. An aloof attitude towards the world could pose problems. The ripple effects can be disastrous.

Parents need to be careful. We always need to exercise extreme caution. We should never embark on the over privileged highway. Mudslides could await us. We could be swallowed by sinkholes. Everyone could suffocate to death.

We should never force feed our offspring. They could eventually choke. We should never deliberately stifle our young. We should never rob them of life's challenges. We should never construct an impenetrable fortress around them. We should always remain level headed. They are our future leaders. They will need to tackle problem solving.

We will not always be around. Adulthood is a road everyone must travel. We will need to equip them for this eventuality. Occasionally they will encounter emotional fender benders. They will eventually confront head on collisions with the world. They could survive. Or the wreck could make them a statistic.We could sacrifice everything for our children. We could do all the thinking for them. We could do all the planning for them. Sooner or later they will break free. They need their independence. They eventually will have to function on their own. We should teach them manageable skills.Our misguided efforts will eventually become meaningless and ineffective. Our pride and joy could turn against us in latent years. They could feel betrayed and confused. They could label us superficial. They could see through our hallow grandeur. They could tell us that we had let them down. Disappointment is always a painful blow.

They could be furious for being led astray. Bitter resentment could rear its ugly head. Our prized possessions could be overcome with rage. They could feel justified to begin hating us. They could blame us for their lack of moral and ethical values.

We will falter when we lack life's solid foundation. A structure built on shale will eventually crumble. Proving a safe environment will guarantee protection. Godly principles should be our focused goal. We fail miserably when we short change our young.

Inexperience at anything can be challenging. Minor issues could devastate our young. They could experience problems interacting with society. Some could have difficulty focusing. This would encourage feelings of inadequacy and insecurity.

Many could encounter difficulties with peer relationships. They could frequently struggle with healthy intimate bonds. Oftentimes their attempts could end in failure. Our offspring could erroneously begin claiming ownership for our mistakes. They could also start lashing out at themselves. Some could begin to feel lethargic and helpless. These symptoms are forerunners to depression.

They could become furious at God and humanity. They could reason that no one had cared to intervene. Our linage could feel powerless. Violent thoughts and actions could surface. Our offspring could develop an unforgiving mindset.

We would be at fault. We had imposed too many unrealistic standards. We were the force behind their spiritual and emotional decay. Our future leaders could unnecessarily burden themselves because of us.

The overprotection of children should never be minimized. This is a serious issue. Parents can easily damage their children. Lives can be ruined. We should honestly acknowledge this fact. Many parents can easily yield to the temptation of overcompensating. But we could be setting our children up for untold failures. Multiple issues could torment them indefinitely.

Our intentions could be as pure as the driven snow. This is irrelevant. And it is unhealthy. Problems will never take a vacation. Fortified blankets will never be permanent. This world is always brutal. Children can get badly damaged for the lack of knowledge.

Child neglect is the opposite. There is usually too little of almost everything. The needs of impoverished children are frequently ignored. Their wants can sound like a foreign language. Many envy privileged children. Some yearn to be like them.

Neglect is damaging. Excessive catering is equally problematic. The rich and the poor should compare mental notes sometime. They would discover some interesting truths. They would realize that their basic needs and desires would be similar. Their yearning to experience no strings attached love would be identical.

Long term complications can affect any group. Internal imbalances will restrict any culture. Although overprotected status is usually reserved for the privileged, the plight of neglected children is of equal importance. In some cases, child abuse has become a global pandemic. Some horror stories are beyond deplorable.

Cruelty is a malicious and deliberate act to inflict maximum pain. Persistent abuse will eventually break the backbone of spirit and soul. These heinous actions are designed to dominate and control. Once the will to resist has been broken, total submission will now become self evident. Control of the mind will guarantee total compliance to the oppressor.

The above statements can apply to any age group or nationality. Anyone can be subjected to cruel and barbaric treatment. But these atrocities are widespread among the young and the vulnerable. A host of children are being systematically violated and abused. Countless children on God's planet are in grave danger.Damaged children are powerless to defend themselves. Daily they function as robots doing whatever is demanded of them. Many attempt to comply under extremely adverse conditions. But their good deeds get trampled on. They are instead rewarded with harsh and demoralizing consequences.

Child endangerment had become alarmingly widespread in some communities. Deprivation and neglect is sometimes a way of life for these hurting children. Their plight is oftentimes minimized because they are oftentimes categorized as a burden to society. The gravity of their situations is distressing and heartbreaking. This is a blatant disregard for human dignity.Not everyone possesses the inner strength, to pull themselves up by their own boot strings. It is not uncommon for some parents to be in dire straits as their offspring. We can only care for another if we can care for ourselves. Deplorable living conditions for parents will mean deplorable living conditions for their offspring. This sub standard environment will have a traumatic impact on the family.

Society expects parents to adequately provide for their children. Sadly not everyone is capable of living up to this expectation. Constantly recycling anger and bitterness can become a nightmare like experience. Many parents desperately need help battling multiple past and present demons. Some turn to substance abuse to numb their pain. Some could abandon their children for the next quick fix.

It is gut wrenchingly when children get penalized, for circumstances beyond their control. Many are left with no other option but to fend for themselves. Most will do whatever is necessary just to survive. Some steal to satisfy hunger. Some seek acceptance by getting involved with gangs. This usually gives them a false sense of security. But they now prime candidates to be exploited and manipulated.

There are some who will "intervene" under the pretense of crisis management. Many lure children into their custody under the guise of offering them love, food, and shelter. Most of these individuals will satisfy the mandated legal requirement, to demonstrate their commitment and sincerity. But their mindset is filthier than an open sewage pit. Many of these counterfeit caregivers have been mistakenly screened and vetted, as being trust worthy citizens. This is because they have been grossly dishonest to the governing agencies. These people are a disgrace to God and humanity. Their behaviors are downright despicable. And they are beyond disgusting.

A multitude of our children are severely affected. Only below grade level people will stoop to hurt children. Some of these rotten folks call themselves prominent law abiders. Some of these evil people profess to be Jesus' disciples. This is appalling and shameful.

Callous exploitation of children is a stigma in any society. Failure to be defenders of our young is downright sickening. We are citizens in bad standing, when we shun our duties to protect them at all cost. Shame shall be our constant companion.

We are terrible people if we fold our arms, and ignore the plight of disadvantaged children. We will have failed our youth. We agree with criminals when we fail to expose evil.

We are co-conspirators when we fail to respond. We ignore our God and society's expectation when we fail to act. Constant misery should torment us. We should be punished for turning a blind eye to suffering children.

No justification can be fabricated for the endangerment of children. No one should ever remain silent and passive. We should always behave as upright and upstanding human beings. We should always be vanguards for our future leaders in training. We should never sidestep our obligations to guard and protect. It is inexcusable when they are ever violently let down.

Ambassadors of Christ should vehemently denounce the maltreatment of children. Society should be quick to mobilize and help. A child's hurt should be our hurt. Our silence could be interpreted as agreement. We could experience problems sleeping. We could have difficulty living with ourselves.

We can excuse ourselves by remaining indifferent. We could rationalize we are not personally affected. We could reason it is none of our concern. But we cannot hide in our untouchable comfort zone forever. This will not ease our guilt. Our inaction should add more torment to our consciences. And we will not escape a guilty verdict.

We will never be immune by remaining neutral to human suffering. We should never detach ourselves from society's horrors. We should never become indifferent to the catastrophes of this cruel world. Abuse on any level is abuse on all levels. Sometimes we should leave our well fortified glass house. We should just look around. We are our brothers and sisters keepers. Be they young or old.

Not everyone will turn blind eyes to the plight of impoverished children. There are many who are working diligently to make their lives and environments more safe and stable. They realize the dire need to be the voices for the voiceless. And they work tirelessly to offer hope and purpose, to a hurting and struggling junior population.

Many dedicated workers' efforts are oftentimes hampered, by a lack of meaningful resources. Bureaucratic streamlining is oftentimes a major stumbling block. Programs that will benefit the poor and needy are routinely red lined. Rarely are they ever highlighted. The end result is that those who are in desperate need of help get roughly shoved to the sidelines.

Power brokers are generally obsessed with minimizing cost and maximizing profits. Many look for opportunities to keep the vulnerable and down trodden marginalized. Some autocrats will conveniently sidestep their responsibility, to make available critical funds to help the under privileged. Some will secretly condone forced child labour. This is why so many children end up in sweat shops.

Child care advocates sometimes face challenging hurdles. The majority are overworked and over stressed. Many are saddled with huge workloads with limited resources. Quite often they have to operate with less than adequate funding. Many frequently get disheartened because of governmental red tape. Some are forced to abandon their good intentions due to policy stonewalling. And the cycle of neglect continues.

Society will react forcefully to physical abuse. There is always a swift public outcry. We will take appropriate actions rectify this problem. But psychological abuse often times gets ignored. Too often this is quietly swept under the emotional rug.

There is no difference between the two levels of abuse. But some categorize them as separate entities. A segment of our population invented this doctrine. They should wake up and smell the stench. No one is above the perils of pain and suffering. These are the facts of life.

All suffering had a starting point. But sometimes many struggle to remember when the nightmares began. So we grunted and bore our pain. We bemoaned our burdens. We coped to the best of our ability. We performed in like manner.

Many of us lamented our hard luck stories. Some journeyed through life in a comatose condition.

The real culprits were our bogus caretakers. They were responsible for protecting us. They failed us horrendously. Their transgressions against us were degrading and cruel. Some inflicted almost irreversible brutality. Some were silent enablers. We pronounced guilty verdicts on all.

Our transgressors violated their spiritual and secular obligations. They ignored society's lawful expectations. They injected bitter poison medicine into our system. We could feel that everyone had abandoned us. Hostility could become our comfort and support. Our anger could become trigger happy. We could claim justification for seeking revenge.

We could plateau to an even more dangerous level. We could become callous and cold hearted. We could graduate to become highly dysfunctional. We could rebel in destructive defiance. We could begin participating in highly amoral activities. We could embrace unethical behaviors. Unforgiveness could get lodged in our soul.

Sometimes we would reflect on our past. We would lament during these ravenous periods. Unspeakable vile and deplorable conditions almost destroyed us. Some could explore illegal methods to seek justice. Many could deliberately break the law to violently punish. But we would be brutalizing ourselves for being a victim. These horrors were forced on us.

Living with severe trauma is always heartbreaking. We will at times detest our miserable life. And we will mourn. These reactions are appropriate and necessary. But we must never surrender to the perils of anger. This would be handing the victory flag to our tormentors.

It is our right to be furious if we are exploited and violated. It is our duty to express outrage. It is our responsibility to seek legal recourse. Crimes against us should never go unpunished. But eventually we will need deep internal cleansing. We should forgive those cruel offenders. Unforgiveness will keep us in limbo. Forgiveness will make healing possible.

Chapter Thirteen
Jehovah's Priceless Jewels

THE BIBLE STATES: "Lo, children are an heritage of the Lord: and the fruit of the womb is His reward." Psalms 127 verse 3.

Our offspring ultimately belongs to God. Children are God's chosen little people. God is the sole proprietor of our children. Children represent the heart of The Almighty. They are His most valued treasure. The Spirit of God rewarded our mothers, to be carriers of His most prized possessions.

Good luck will never guarantee an offspring. But some women could complain that bad luck resulted in a pregnancy. Trial and error efforts can never guarantee a new life. Oftentimes we are rewarded with failure and frustration.

Fertilization clinics are abundant and thriving. And they are extremely expensive. But these methods will never be able to assure positive outcomes. Artificial insemination oftentimes will fail to produce the desired results. Various other experimentations have also proven ineffective over the countless years.

There are various documentations in scripture pertaining to barrenness. Only God has the answers to why some women are unable to conceive. Only He can repair the restrictions that prevent a woman from reaping the rewards of motherhood.

God gifted some doctors with skills to treat many reproductive disorders. But the final decision is at the discretion of the Almighty. It is only God who can breathe life into our mother's womb. Only the Spirit of God can make a successful pregnancy possible. Sometimes we forget that we are here because of God's breath.

Divine influences are behind every new bundle of joy. But some refuse to acknowledge this fact. Many rely on the forces of nature to produce a living breathing human being. God controls nature. It is not the other way around. All living organisms are gifts from God.

Human beings are very possessive of their children. Some will claim sole ownership to their offspring. But God says our children are His heritage. He loaned His precious little people to us. And He expects high standards from us. We ought to love them no less than He loves us. These are our duties and responsibilities.

It pleased God to bestow His highest honor on parents. We demonstrate our commitment to God by treasuring His children. God commands high expectations and standards. He will teach us how to effectively manage our assignments. We will become expert nutritionists. He holds us accountable to execute the highest quality of care for His children.

God appointed us to be worthy caretakers of His children. We should willingly and diligently, execute our role as prudent caregivers. God mandated us to provide a safe and healthy environment for His priceless jewels. God expects us to protect His young from negative exposures and influences.Consistently we should bow in humility before God. We should always thank Him for trusting us to care of His children. We should never forget that it is God who granted us this privilege and favour. We should never cease to pray blessings on our children. God wisely entrusted these innocent lives in our care. Little children are the unblemished representatives of Christ Jesus.

God will appoint us to be His ambassadors when He is pleased with our performance. He will anoint us to reflect His standards in all aspects of child rearing. Our permanent occupation will be to raise and guide His heritage. We should respect and cherish this fact. We should present ourselves worthy before Him. We should never take our duties lightly.

Jesus says: "Suffer the little children to come unto me, and forbid them not: for as such is the kingdom of God." Luke 18 verse 16.

Parents brought infants to Jesus that He might touch them. They obviously knew about the power of Jesus laying hands on individuals. They gathered around Jesus so that He could bless their little ones. They were well aware that only God can truly bless and consecrate children. Jesus' disciples were annoyed when they observed what was happening. They rebuked the crowd for attempting to converse with their Master. They could have reasoned that the people and infants did not merit an audience with our Lord and Savior.

It is doubtful that the religious rich and powerful would have brought their children to Jesus. This elite group hated Jesus passionately. They vehemently rejected everything He represented. The less fortunate were those who eagerly listened to the Son of God.

The Messiah's disciples were still in training. It is possible that some held prejudicial views regarding the disadvantaged. This probably was still embedded within them. Some probably reasoned that the poor were society's outcasts. Some could have exhibited condescending demeanours toward these yearning souls.

Some could have labeled the poor as misfits and low entities. They could have deemed them unimportant. They could have concluded that they were not worthy of the Messiah's blessings. The Son of God knew their thoughts. He sternly rebuked them for their lack of wisdom. The old and the young knew who Jesus was. And Jesus was cognisant of this fact. They realized that He was the One sent to redeem all humankind. Jesus' disciples probably were not yet convinced of this fact.

Jesus also knew that His men did not fully realize the importance of children. They probably viewed them as meddling little brats. But Jesus intervened on behalf of the grownups and the children. Our Saviour admonished his inner circle for being insensitive to their needs.

There could have been emotional carnage had Jesus not intervened. The people could have experienced instant rejection. Their self esteem could have suffered a severe blow. Deep hurt could have gotten lodged in their spirit and soul. They could have departed feeling totally humiliated.

They could have interpreted the disciples' indifference as an indictment against them. This would have reinforced their inferiority complex. The adults would now transfer a low self esteem image unto another generation. This generation likely would grow up feeling like second class citizens.

Jesus quickly put a stop to this potential mayhem. He demonstrated concern and a willingness to listen. The Son of God lovingly interacted with these children. He did so with Godly compassion. They were formally recognized. They were readily accepted by this Great Man. And He did so without being judgemental or prejudicial.

Jesus embraced them with unbiased affection. This would have made them feel important. The Master's special treatment would have elevated their self esteem. Their self confidence would have gotten a well deserved boost. Their inner strengths would have soared to infinite heights.

Human beings are predisposed to jump to hasty conclusions. Sometimes their assessments are based solely on their interpretation of an issue. Quite often their assumptions are grossly incorrect. It can be relatively easy to label and compartmentalize a targeted group. The vulnerable in society tend to suffer needlessly because of this stigmatization.

Non believers and believers can easily get caught up in this bigoted attitude. This ignorant mindset has damaged a large segment of the population. Oftentimes believers begin walking with Christ. But they refuse relinquish their filthy baggage. This garbage should have been burnt at the altar.

Society has divided the population in two basic categories. There are those who are privileged. And there are those who are not. The rich tend to view the poor with disdain. Many rigidly enforce this doctrine. They will go to great lengths to protect their status quo. The religious sect demanded respect and compliance. The disciples likely would have welcomed the prominent and affluent. Infants reflect the authentic embodiment of Christ. Their purity represents the kingdom of God. We the people could learn from the interchange between Jesus and His disciples. We should pay close attention to Jesus' remarks. They should serve as a vivid reminder to us. We should always be careful how we interact with all the people. This means the old and the young. It is important that we always show everyone recognition and respect.

Children are untainted visionaries. Their innocent wisdom can be profound and baffling. The purity of their comments and questions sometimes will puzzle the most brilliant adult minds. This is because they have not yet been corrupted by worldly influences. The keen discerning spirits of children could confound and infuriate many religious intellectuals.

Adults can learn a lot from children. It is important that we always demonstrate a willingness to listen to them. We should give children our undivided attention all the times. They are our eager and yearning young future leaders. We should treat them as such.

The children's encounter with Jesus transpired over two thousand years ago. This is here and now. This is at this moment. This is in our so called enlightened era. How are we treating our children? How would we measure up before God and humanity?

Have we learned anything from the examples that Jesus demonstrated to us? Do we encourage our children to interact with us? Do we savor moments when they vie for our attention? Do we guide them when they are yearning to learn? Do we embrace these precious moments?

Would we develop the uncaring mindset of His disciples? Would we deem our needs more important than those of our offspring? Would we ignore their pleas for attention and affection? Would we not be damaging their self worth? Would we not be injecting negativity into their lives? Would not their self confidence suffer gravely?

Many of us should periodically recluse ourselves, from our daily rat race. We should take time out to reflect on our childhood. How did we respond at our tender age to emotional neglect? How did we feel when we experienced rejection? How did we handle embarrassment? What lasting impact did it have on us?

Jesus says: "Verily I say to you, except ye be converted, and become as little children, ye shall not enter into the kingdom of heaven." Matthew 18 verse 3.

Children cry when they are experiencing discomfort. Don't we cry before God when we are hurting nonstop? Are we not like little children when we experience turbulent times? Do we not sincerely look to Jesus for help?

The Triune God uses examples of innocence. He references the fragility and vulnerability of children. He demonstrates to us a clear necessity. We should always completely submit to His will and wisdom. Only then can He begin to reassemble us on His potter's wheel.

Our little children depend on us wholeheartedly. They trust and rely on us for everything. We should also depend wholeheartedly on our Maker. We should trust and rely on Him for everything. Our children expect us to always respond to them. And also tend to all their needs. We also have this assurance from our God.

Our offspring expect from us security and protection. Our security and protection comes from an invisible God. Our children run to us for shelter from life's bombardments. We too run to God when we are overwhelmed. Sometimes we chase the "monsters," from under our children's bed. We seek refuge with the Almighty when we are wrestling with demons.

When the chips are down, we are no different from our defenceless children. But our inflated super ego is our biggest hurdle. Most will display a fake show of strength to mask vulnerability. God sometimes has to melt our tough exterior before addressing our situations.

God's Spirit will burden us to discard our old habits. We will undergo a change. The change is when we experience a new birth. This will be our re-birth. This is a spiritual birth. We will then be washed in the blood of the Lamb. God will discard our filthy garments when we get cleansed.

We will feel vulnerable when we are born again. We could also feel defenceless. But we are definitely not innocent. Contaminated genes got us here. Saturated rotten malfunctions of this world put us in this plight. Pursuing flesh agendas contributed to our state of helplessness.

The Spirit of God is beyond wise. Sometimes He will freeze us in this state of helplessness. This is necessary. He can now begin His work in us. He has to purge us of our impurities. He has to wash and cleanse us of all unrighteousness. He has to align us on His potter's wheel. Then He will begin to spin that wheel.

Jesus says: "And whoso shall receive one such little child in my name receiveth me." Matthew 18 verse 5.

How can we be mean and cruel to a child, and profess that we love God? What excuse do we give to God if we abuse a child? How can we expect God to tend to our needs if we disregard the needs of a child? How can we expect God treat us with importance if we refuse to acknowledge the importance of a child?

We cannot sincerely embrace a child if our mind is polluted. We need purity of heart to comfort a helpless child. This is demonstrating true discipleship. We should always treat children with love and compassion. These are true reflections of Godly standards.

We need to understand Jesus' message. And we should internalize the true meaning of His explicit statement. We expect from God unconditional love and protection. We are as little children when we bow before Him. He holds us all precious in His sight. We ought to always hold our children precious in our sight.

He entrusted His innocent future generation in our care. We ought to training our children in a God fearing and an upright manner. This is not a frivolous pastime. It is our solemn duly. It is our mandated responsibility before God and all humankind.

Chapter Fourteen
Ancestral Blunders

WE CAN GET SWALLOWED by the complexities of this world. We could easily drown in the ocean of confusion and sorrow. Trials and tribulations of life can at times send us insane. Our hectic daily activities can become nerve wracking. Juggling endless responsibilities can give us nervous breakdowns. We all bemoan at times how unfair life is.

There are times when mysterious issues will confront us. Puzzling emotional ailments could baffle us. We could perceive these challenges as a global first. But our unique situations are never new frontiers. Our current dilemmas are not at all current. And they are definitely not new discoveries.

Trials and triumphs have been around long before our time. Bad choices have created chaos since the beginning of time. Our terrible mistakes are recycled disasters. Our horrible blunders will never be showcased as custom tailored failures. Problematic conditions have been spreading havoc, before our greatest grand parents' era and beyond.

Disobedience has been a major stumbling block, since the era of our biblical ancestors. They habitually made wrong choice decisions. They encountered monumental problems because of their irresponsible actions. Implementing their personal agendas created gigantic obstacles for them. And they suffered severely because they refused obey God.

Sometimes they triumphed remarkably over their circumstances. Sometimes their evil minds became their downfall. Time and time again they strayed. They frequently erred badly in judgment. They got themselves entangled in some dangerous situations. Sometimes their predicaments were beyond distasteful. Some of their behaviours would have been deemed unpardonable offences, even in this society.

The Lord God told Abram: "And I will make of thee a great nation, and I will bless thee, and make thy name great; and thou shalt be a blessing:" Genesis 12 verse 2.

Abram was a just man. Abram was an upright man. He was upstanding. He was a leader in his community. He was well respected within his the social circle and beyond. He was important and influential. He was a very wealthy man.

Abram loved his God. And God loved Abram. Abram obeyed and trusted his God. Abram's God rewarded him abundantly. The Lord God bestowed upon Abram, abundant blessings and prosperity.

Abram was married to Sarai. She was his half sister. The bible documents Sarai as an extremely beautiful woman. But Sarai had a human diagnosed problem. She was barren. She was incapable of carrying out her reproductive role of motherhood.

This condition made it highly unlikely that she would ever conceive. Her husband had no blood heir. He had no son to carry on his linage. There was also another major situation. Sarai's biological clock had stopped. She was way past her child bearing age.

Although Abram was powerful, a vital part of him was missing. He had no one to pass his mantle to. He was heirless. This reality could have deeply disturbed Abram. He probably felt embarrassed at times. It could have been difficult for him interacting with his peers.

Abram likely carried this heavy burden daily. He probably was convinced his linage would become extinct when the earth reclaimed him. He began to make preliminary plans. He contemplated transferring his assets to one of his male servant's offspring.

Abram probably pondered frequently over God's message to him. He may have concluded that he had misinterpreted his Maker's words. He obviously had nothing to start a great nation with. Abram was probably confused and very perplexed. Nation building would be impossible without a blood heir.

A fertile womb gives a woman a sense of security. Motherhood produces a contented feeling of accomplishment. Sarai could have been burdened throughout her reproductive years. She lacked a gift that most women took for granted. She could have felt inferior mingling with her peers. She could have grieved frequently.

Sarai was not about to resign herself to a doomed fate. She chose not to accept her condition. She decided to fight the odds. She was determined change her situation. She made up her mind to fix her problem for her husband. She fixated her sights on achieving motherhood.

Sarai took matters unto herself. She was determined to bring some happiness into her husband's life. Her biological clock had gone to sleep. But there had to be another way to compensate for this. She was not going deny her husband things that she could fix.

She moved forward quickly with an idea. She began focusing her energies into helping her husband. He wanted a blood heir. And he was going to get a blood heir. But a plan had to be implemented.

She then began to execute her plan. Sarai had a handmaid named Hagar. Sarai made an unusual decision. She demanded the services of Hagar's womb. Hagar had no choice but to comply. She had to say "yes."

Sarai approached her husband. She put forward her proposal. She convinced him to take Hagar as a surrogate wife. Abram and Sarai would obtain a child via Hagar's womb. Abram would be guaranteed a blood heir. His linage would continue uninterrupted. They probably intended to exclude Hagar from child rearing responsibilities.

Abram likely thought Sarai's proposal sounded practical. He could have eagerly agreed to his wife's request. He probably was excited about this arrangement. He executed his portion of the agreement. He took Hagar as his temporary wife. And she conceived. She was now carrying the heir of a very prominent man. Hagar's status within the household changed. This could have instilled in her feelings of self importance. She could have reasoned that she was now special. She could have concluded that she was now more privileged. She began displaying a superiority complex toward her mistress.

Sarai was barren. Hagar was fertile. And she had the proof. She was carrying inside of her a living human being. She began to flaunt her new found freedom. Problems erupted in Abram's household. Pregnant Hagar began stirring up trouble. She became arrogant. She was aloof and rude to her mistress.

Hagar's attitude towards her employer was condescending. It was also likely demeaning. This infuriated Sarai. She felt extremely belittled. She was deeply hurt. Sarai responded by getting extremely angry. She consulted with her husband. She told him about her helper's behavior. She rigorously and furiously complained to him.

Abram immediately distanced himself from the problem. He made no attempt to defuse an extremely volatile situation. He was the major beneficiary of this arrangement. But he chose to remain neutral. Abram decided to take the easy way out.

Abram was very blunt and direct with his wife. He told her not to pester him. Hagar was Sarai's maid. Husband told wife to deal with her problematic maid. Sarai took the leadership role. She severely reprimanded Hagar. She undoubtedly reminded Hagar that she was still a servant girl.

Hagar would have been shocked that her mistress had reacted so forcefully. She became upset and humiliated. A furious pregnant Hagar made an irrational decision. She ran away from home. She ended up in the wilderness. Obviously still angry, she was now very frightened.

Abram could have intervened at the onset of the conflict. A volatile situation probably could have been defused. Two women were deadlocked in a heated battle of wills. One was his wife. The other was the mother of his unborn child. This would put Abram in an uncomfortable position. But he could have negotiated a compromise.

Sarai had masterminded this triangle. But Hagar's pregnancy created this crisis. This was an obvious fact. Hagar's attitude was definitely wrong. She was completely out of line. She grossly disrespected her employer. Sarai's anger was legitimate. But Abram could have tried to reason with his wife.Everyone's stress levels could have been minimized. The warring women could have arrived at an understanding. The welfare of the unborn child was at stake. But no one thought this delicate situation through. Hagar's abrupt departure put her pregnancy at risk.God took control of this potential human tragedy. An angel of the Lord visited Hager. He began reasoning with her. The angel highlighted Hagar's faults. He admonished her. She had been insubordinate to her mistress. Her actions were wrong. God's messenger instructed her to return home.

The angel consoled her. He gave her a promise to multiply her seed. This meant future generations of her unborn child. The angel named her unborn child. He instructed her to name the child Ishmael. Hagar obeyed the angel's instructions.

A subdued Hagar returned home. She continued residing with Abram, and Sarai. She was probably still angry. But she had to obey God. Abram was eighty six years old when Ishmael was born. Issues apparently quieted down for a period. Hagar and Ishmael likely lived peacefully in the household. (Please research Genesis 16.)

God paid Abram another visit. And Abram received more startling revelations. God changed Abram's name to Abraham. He also changed his wife's name from Sarai, to Sarah. God then revealed another element of His master plan to Abraham.

And God said: "Sarah thy wife shall bear thee a son indeed; and thou shalt call his name Isaac: and I will establish my covenant with him for an everlasting covenant; and with his seed after him." (Genesis 17 verse 19.)

Abraham was one hundred years old. Sarah was ninety years old. And God told Abraham that his wife would bear him a son. Sarah was amused when she overheard God's conversation with Abraham. This was not surprising considering her situation.

This was obviously exciting news for Abraham. But he could have reacted with mixed feelings. This turn of events could have a drastic impact on Ishmael. This would put first born in a lesser category. Abraham was likely concerned how Ishmael would react. Ishmael would no longer be Abraham's sole heir apparent. The second son Isaac would be the heir to Abraham's estate. Unborn son was designated by God to carry on Abraham's linage. Ishmael could begin to feel like an outsider. It could alter father and first born relationship. This sudden shift would understandably have devastated Hagar.

God fulfilled His promise to Abraham. Sarah conceived. And Isaac was born. Abraham undoubtedly was a very proud man. Isaac was weaned from Sarah's breast at the allotted time. Abraham threw a great feast to celebrate this occasion. Things then turned sour. Sarah observed Ishmael mocking Isaac.

The bible does not elaborate on Ishmael's behavior. It does not say why Ishmael was mocking his half brother Isaac. But Sarah deemed Ishmael's behavior totally inappropriate. She became very angry at Ishmael. She reacted extremely harshly to the incident. Ishmael received a very brutal consequence.

Wherefore she said to Abraham: "Cast out this bondwoman and her son: for the son of this bondwoman shall not be heir with my son, even with Isaac." (Genesis 21 verse 10.)

Sarah was probably looking for an excuse to banish Hagar and Ishmael. She saw a small window of opportunity. Sarah opened this window wider. And she savagely pounced. This abrupt request shocked Abraham. He would have been caught completely off guard.

Sarah's demand left him saddened and burdened. But the Lord consoled Abraham. God instructed him to listen to his wife. God said He would reward Ishmael. He explained the details to Abraham. Ishmael would also become the founder of a great nation.

Abraham wrestled with feelings of remorse. But the final decision came from God. Abraham had no option but to obey. Abraham said goodbye to his second wife and his son early the following morning. He furnished Hagar with bread and a bottle of water. He then expelled Ishmael and Hagar from his household.

Hagar and her son left the father's dwelling place. Mother and son wandered in the wilderness of Beersheba. They languished in isolation for a long time. They endured grave hardships. Conditions were exceedingly tough.

She was overwhelmed with panic. She also reasoned that the pressures would kill her son. But God piloted mother and son through their turbulent seasons. She prevailed because God was with her. (Genesis 21 verses 15 and 16)

God tended to all their needs. God had mercy on this single mother and her son. At the appointed time, the Lord God rewarded Ishmael. He became the founding father of the Ishmaelite nation.

Sarai fast forwarded God's timetable. She solicited the intimate services of her maid. Abram got drafted into this agreement. They dragged Hagar into this emotionally charged situation. An innocent life was brought into the world. These actions were not sanctioned by God.

Hagar had no alternative but to obey her mistress. And she paid a high price. She was rewarded with punishment for her obedience. She was treated grossly unfairly. She suffered shame and humiliation. Then mother and son were exiled to battle the elements.

Selfish adults were in charge. They abused their responsibilities. Hagar was basically a pawn and a puppet. An innocent child suffered horrible consequences. He was forced to live with excruciating wrong choice decisions. His caretakers imposed these problems in his life.

God made a covenant with Abram. Abram probably got impatient when he couldn't see progress. Then wife Sarai strong armed a vulnerable maid. A quick fix solution was presented to Abram. He yielded to the dictates of his flesh. He became a willing accomplice. He should have known better. Like Adam, Abram just could not put his flesh on pause.

Hagar should not be blamed for sleeping with Abram. Sarai made that decision for her. Sarai used her to satisfy her one sided selfish mindset. Times and cultures were different in that era. Hagar was Sarai's maid. She was a slave. A slave always had to follow orders.

Vulnerable people have rights. Their vulnerability should never be trampled on. They should never be abused. They should never be forced into compromising positions. They should never be denied their right to say no.

Sarah was an aggressively strong willed woman. She obtained what she desired regardless of the human toll. She could have compelled her husband to comply with her wishes. We could easily label Sarah as a vicious cold hearted individual.

Husband probably couldn't say NO to his wife. He could have feared her. But both refused to abide by God's time table. They turned to Satan's world for immediate gratification. They embraced the lust of their flesh. Pleasure crumpled to sorrow. Grief will always be in abundance when we disobey God.

There are still similarities between Abraham's period and now. Human behaviors have basically not changed. We are still getting trapped in issues as our ancestors. Many are still addicted to the dictates of the flesh. Relationships of convenience can become very complicated. We could make huge mistakes. We could hurt others badly. Self agendas will always create a mess.

God's wisdom is unfathomable. And He is infinite. Our intellect is limited. Our capabilities are flawed. Human reasoning is irrelevant to God. His master plan will always supersede ours. Nothing has changed in this century. Our culture is only getting worse. But God is still holds our lives in the palm of His hands

Unfair treatment forced Hagar to live like a fugitive. The cruel hands of injustice became a way of life. This could have hardened her heart and poisoned her mind. Rage likely tormented Hagar and her son for many seasons. Forgiveness probably became a daily challenge. But Hagar rose above her infirmities.

Ishmael prospered because of God's promises. But he likely carried hatred in his heart towards his father and his step mother. His anger could have kept on rekindling from generation to generation. Emotional stability could have been problematic for this nation.

Ishmael's tribe was likely very hostile. Angry people will produce a hostile community. An unstable environment can easily produce rebellious dysfunctional adults. And dysfunctions tend to recycle. They will eventually reproduce a negative value system. Ishmael's nation probably closely resembled this group.

Chapter Fifteen
Always Trust God

Long before Genesis 12 verse 2, Abram struggled with belief issues. Lack of trust in God predated the period when wife Sarai strong armed her vulnerable maid Hagar, to produce an heir for her husband. (Genesis 16 verses 1-4.) This debacle could have ruined the lives of Hagar, and Abram's son Ishmael.

Abram found favour in the sight of God at a young age. God removed Abram from his kindred and familiar surroundings. God set Abram apart by relocating him to a new environment. Wife Sarai and Abram's household accompanied Abram to his new home. (Genesis 12 verses1-5)

God informed Abram that all his future generations would inherit this new land. Abram should have felt honoured and pleased. He should have been satisfied with God's promises. Abram's responsibility should have been to completely surrender to the will of his God. Abram should have been contented that God would supply all his needs. His main focus should have been obedience to God.

God expected Abram to adjust and settle in his new homestead. But Abram kept scouting the land. He probably was exploring the beset location to reside. He eventually encountered a problem. There was a famine in the land. Abram made the decision to relocate to Egypt. It is unclear if God sanctioned this move. Abram could have relied on his limited intellect.

Unbelief is the driving force why people encounter difficulties. Poor planning will result in mistakes and frustration. This can lead to desperation and irrational behaviours. Human beings could chart their own course of actions, when situations are not progressing as they envisioned. This will propel them implement their personal agendas.

Trusting and relying exclusively on God, takes unwavering commitment and diligent effort. Impatience is a leading factor that causes some to stray from God's timetable. Taking short cuts to please ourselves can further complicate matters. Problems will arise when we begin to doubt and ignore God's mandated instructions. Disobedience will cause us to err badly in judgment.

Guidelines and instructions are established for specific purposes. They are designed for easy and comprehensive understanding. Valuable information is always highlighted. This will to ensure that everything is put in place for practical application. Trial and error methods will end in disaster. Established protocol should be carefully followed. Deviation can create serious issues.Leaders are expected to govern and lead by example. But sometimes the mind can trick the heart. Problems will arise when those in authority do not adhere to set policies and procedures. People in positions of responsibility should always uphold set guidelines. Otherwise non compliance can create confusion and resentment, among those expected to abide by rules and regulations.

God had anointed Abram to leadership position. Plus Abram was head of his household. God established a binding covenant with Abram. It was Abram's duty to abide by the expectations laid down by his God. But Abram probably as unconvinced that the mandated training from God was necessary. The mindset of disobedience birthed serious problems for this delinquent leader.

God had relocated Abram. God would shield him from harm and danger. But survival instincts probably clouded Abram's judgment. He likely panicked. Abram took everyone and everything, and sought refuge in Egypt. This proved to be a costly mistake. Abram made another huge blunder on his way to Egypt. He asked his wife to lie to the Pharaoh of Egypt. He instructed her tell the Pharaoh that she was his sister. He wanted their relationship kept a secret. Abram could have reasoned that a half lie was justified. Sarai was a beautiful woman. This fact induced life threatening fear in Abram. Abram became convinced he could be killed, if Pharaoh discovered that Sarai was his wife. The Egyptian king would then freely make Sarai his wife.

The Egyptians were impressed by Sarai's beauty. Pharaoh's princes also said she was beautiful. They told Pharaoh about this attractive woman. Curiosity probably excited the king. Sarai was taken into Pharaoh's house.

Abram was treated exceptionally well. This was because of Pharaoh's infatuation for Sarai. Abram was given much livestock. Pharaoh also presented to Abram an abundance of gifts. This included an assortment of maidservants and menservants.

It is irrelevant if Abram had the resolve of a saint. His wife was now in Pharaoh's custody. She probably was in his harem. She would have been with his other wives. She was on the verge of being sexually exploited.

Then there was her husband Abram. He was surrounded by a multitude of enticing temptations. It is unimportant if Abram was uncomfortable in his new surroundings. He was now intermingling with other females. The atmosphere was now ripe for anything to happen. Infidelity was now a glaring probability.

A lie had created serious complications. Abram's wife's welfare was in grave danger. Another man was about to violate her. And Abram was likely whole heartedly enjoying himself. He put his wife in harm's way by not trusting his God.

We should never flirt with the devil. This will heap live coals of destruction on our head. We should never meddle in things outside of Godly limits. We should never recklessly play with fire. It will burn holes in our soul. Those close to us could get incinerated. Selfish decisions will always cause immense devastation. Self centered actions can destroy intimate relationship.

It is very dangerous to adopt amoral behaviors. We should always cherish and protect our wife. This should be our most important earthly responsibility. This should be our first priority. We should always safeguard our spouse from harm. We invite conflicts if we behave otherwise.God knows that sometimes we will become weaklings. And He will always forgive us readily. Periodically He will protect us in advance. He saw above and beyond Abram's flawed character. God plagued Pharaoh. He disrupted the king's household, because of Abram's transgressions.

Pharaoh confronted Abram about this grave lie. This was a total miscarriage of just and upright behavior. Abram had betrayed the king. He had abused a newly formed relationship. He could have lost his life.

Abram confessed everything to the ruler of Egypt. Pharaoh returned Sarai to Abram unharmed. He then commanded his men to expel them from Egypt. Abram and his entourage departed from Egypt. (Genesis 12 verses 10 through 20.)

It is obvious that Abram had not learned from his past mistakes. He conveniently forgot about his plight in Egypt. He repeated his insane method of tricky and deception. This time it was with Abimelech, king of Gerar.

This repeat offence was maximized stupidity. The Righteous God had now changed his name from Abram to Abraham. Jehovah had also changed his wife's name from Sarai to Sarah. God also revealed more details regarding Abraham's future. But being obedient to God was a hard choice for this stubborn couple.

Abraham again told a lie. He told the king, that his wife Sarah was his sister. Sarah also joined in the cover up. She told the king that Abraham was her brother. They obviously thought that united, they could better deceive another ruler.

The king had Sarah duly escorted into his household. His intent was to take her for his wife. He was getting ready to be intimate with Sarah. He was about to consummate a relationship with another man's wife. But God intervened again.

God told king Abimelech that Sarah was a married woman. Jehovah threatened to kill the king if he violated her. As an added rebuke, God also closed the wombs of the king's women. Again God saved Sarah from humiliation and agony. Once more The Lord God came to her rescue.

Abraham was once more a coward. God had to intervene on his behalf. The King of the universe had to tell the earthly king, about Sarah's marital status. Ablimelech was understandably greatly upset. He immediately summoned Abraham into his presence. He expressed displeasure regarding Abraham's deception. He demanded an explanation.

Abraham told the whole truth. He gave his reason for lying. He feared for his life if he told the truth about being Sarah's husband. He also confessed that Sarah was indeed his half sister. The king admonished Abraham. But he permitted Abraham to reside in his country. (Full documentation recorded in Genesis 20.)

We should never start scheming to deceive. This could have a ripple effect on others. They also could suffer harsh consequences because of our dishonourable actions. We should never cloak ourselves in filthy garments. We should never hide behind evil tactics. We will eventually be exposed. Then we will be punished. Self centeredness will always produce sour rewards.

An out of control mind is dangerous. We always will embark on a one track journey. We rarely pause to reflect when we are scheming. We rarely consider the devastation we can leave behind. Selfish indulgences will always backfire on us.

It is incredible the twisted yarn we can weave just to con others. It is amazing how easily we can also deceive ourselves.

It is despicable to trick and manipulate unsuspecting folks. This is sheer lunacy. Deception can lead to death.

We should never deviate from Jehovah's guidelines. His straightforward instructions were established to ensure compliance to Godly principles. But human beings are slow learners. We are still antagonizing the all knowing God. Some are persistent with this gross ineptitude.

This is century twenty one. And many are still behaving like imbeciles. Our level of incompetence is still utterly mind boggling. Our so called superiority complex is basically no different from ancient times. Most of our sophisticated intelligence is merely recycled blunders. Twice Abraham behaved like an idiot. Twice Sarah was a co-conspirator. Twice they exposed themselves to grave danger. Not trusting God wholeheartedly caused them unspeakable grief. Minimizing the Supernatural power of the Almighty shoved them between a rock, and a hard place.

Some things have become more conservatively devious in our culture. But one thing has remained the same. This is Satan's method of conducting business. His agenda and his tactics have remained intact since the beginning.

Many reason that they can outsmart Satan on sheer will power. It is beyond stupid for anyone to behave in this fashion. Lucifer is always on call. And he stands ready to cater to the delusions of believers, and non believers. He still owns and operates the oldest evil empire on the planet. He is still hoodwinking people. He is still manipulating this earthly population. He takes great delight in tormenting and ravishing us. He is always relentlessly seducing us. Then he will mercilessly use our vulnerability against us. He will then ratchet up beyond comprehension grief.

The enemy is always eager to assist us in distorting the truth. He will show us many colorful decorative presentations. And the snake can be very convincing. But appetizing alternatives will never be acceptable. Deception is still deception. A half lie is still a lie. Distorting the truth can ruin our reputation.

Sin will always remain sin. Abraham was the mastermind. But his wife was a willing accomplice. Both could have left earth in disgrace. God will never put a stamp of approval on covert activities. But He is constantly dismantling Satan's clandestine plots. He is always looking beyond our flaws. But we will suffer the consequences for falsifying information.

God spends countless hours removing stumbling blocks from our lives. Jehovah is primarily interested in commitments from our heart. This is why we always must be totally honest with Him. And we must be wholeheartedly faithful to Him. We will be rewarded for our commitment. He will grant us peace. He will forgive and restore us.

The Lord God tested His chosen couple. He also examined their faith. They failed miserably. He knew they would stray. He also knew that they would fall back in line. And He knew that they would come crawling back. God pulled His chosen couple from the brink of disaster.God's promises will always stand firm. They will never waver. And they are never interchangeable. Abraham was a mere man. But God had made a binding decision. He wanted Abraham to build a nation. The Lord was mindful that His servant was imperfect. But God didn't grant immunity to his leader.

The Lord God gave Satan the opportunity to attack. God allowed the serpent to beguile His chosen vessel. And the devil pounced immediately and mercilessly. Satan used doubt and fear as his weapons of choice. He submerged Abraham in his emotional pressure cooker. And he turned up the heat.

He bullied God's servant. He warped Abraham's reasoning ability. Satan tricked and duped him. Lucifer encouraged God's chosen man to lie. The devil told Abraham that self preservation was a vital necessity. The enemy convinced Abraham the truth would guarantee him a death sentence.

Fright and panic set in. This created confusion in Abraham's mind. His brain was reduced to jelly. He immediately started disbelieving God's protection. He quickly formed dangerous allegiances with Lucifer and his army. He caused major embarrassment to himself.

Two leaders had welcomed Abraham and Sarah with open arms. But trickery and deception became a monumental barrier. These rulers could have decided that forgiveness was not an option. But God took control. He intervened before the situation escalated to the point of no return.

Both rulers initially had no idea they were being misled. Some could find them blameless for desiring more additions to their list of conquests. God also knew that their intentions were solely lust motivated. But He had to lock these leaders down to avert an irreversible disaster. Satan had almost demolished God's first chosen couple. Now he made another attempt to outwit God. He honed his sights on Jehovah's chosen nation. But the devil was denied the opportunity to create more disruptions. God shielded His chosen elect from danger.

God threw a huge net of protection over Abraham and Sarah. He threw Satan and his army in disarray. The Almighty kept the serpent on its belly. The enemy had to retreat in defeat. He returned to hell for a season. God's anointed couple could now breathe a sigh of relief.Abraham and Sarah made grossly irresponsible blunders. Some of their choices defied logical comprehension. Most of us could gasp for air. This was incompetence beyond incompetence. Their actions were inappropriate and dangerous, even in this culture. But these occurrences could rear its ugly head in this century.

Most would be mortified if Abraham like behavior surfaced in this era. A wife especially could be too stunned to respond. She would then unleash blind fury on the husband. Limb dismemberment would be mild compared to the pain his wife would inflict on him. Their relationship could instantly disintegrate.

She would not be through with him yet. His punishment could feel like being tarred and feathered. He then would be dragged through the divorce court. Husband stupidity would be the charge. His verdict could feel like a stake burning. She could then exile him for life.

Many friends could shun him. They could view him as an embarrassment. Other battering tongues could tear him to shreds. Society could indignantly frown on him. They could call him scum of the earth. He could suddenly feel all alone. There can be a brutal backlash when our mind manipulates our thought process.

We should candidly reflect on these examples of human fragility. And we need to be cautious. Fear is a powerful restriction. Immediate gratification can be compelling. Yielding can be even more satisfying. This will usually surface as our first compelling want.

Urgent pressure could take hold. Our flesh could start roaming out of control. Fulfilling immediate desires are human handicaps. Our values could abruptly take a vacation. Pandemonium could start ruling the moment. We could seriously harm our significant other.

Abraham was the leader. Sarah was the co leader. He should have been a role model for his wife. But he lacked discipline. He did not take his responsibilities seriously. Disaster took control. This could have destroyed a bright future for this couple. But God righteously averted this impending calamity. God sometimes will put us in unchartered waters. But He will never over expose us. And He will never allow us to drown. He will always pilot us through the choppy currents. He will catch us when we begin to sink. Sometimes He will offer His lifeline.

Chapter Sixteen
Second Generation Barriers

SARAH EFFECTIVELY ELIMINATED her competition Hagar. She could now concentrate on her most important role. This was giving miracle baby Isaac her undivided attention. She probably catered to his every need and want. But these assumptions would be pure speculation on our part. The bible gives no in depth documentation on Isaac's formative and adolescent years.

We are exposed to two incidents during his youth. One was the apparent sibling rivalry incident that Ishmael instigated. This squabble got extremely blown out of proportion. The other was when God told Abraham to kill Isaac as a sacrifice. But this was God testing Abraham's willingness to obediently follow instructions.

Sarah was in her nineties when she conceived, or actually birthed Isaac. She was one hundred and twenty seven years old when she died. Isaac was probably thirty seven years old at the time of her death. Ishmael did not attend his step mother's burial. He could have been still furious with her. Unforgiveness was probably still raging within him.

Abraham summoned his most trusted servant sometime after Sarah's death. Abraham was mindful that he was getting older. He was likely concerned that Isaac was still single. The servant was instructed to obtain a wife for Isaac. Abraham insisted that this wife be from their culture.

The servant complied with his master's directives. He acquired a wife for Isaac. She was Abraham's brother Nabob's daughter. Her name was Rebekah. (Genesis 24 verses 1-61)

We finally now get a clear glimpse at Isaac the man. We can begin to form an opinion of him. We are told he meditated in the field at eventide. (Genesis 24 verses 62-63) This is insightful information.

We can conclude that he had the ability to ponder and reflect. This revelation should not be surprising. His father steadfastly believed in his God. And most of the time he was obedient to the Almighty. It was during one of his quiet moments, that Isaac first laid eyes on his future wife. He took her into his deceased mother's tent. There he went in unto her. And she became his wife. Isaac loved Rebekah. She consoled and supported her husband, in his grief over the death of his mother. (Genesis 24 verse 67)

Father Abraham eventually gave up the ghost. He had lived a long and prosperous life. He died at a ripe old age. Both sons reunited to bury their father. Abraham was laid to rest beside his wife.

There was another famine in the land some time after Abraham's death. This was a very harsh famine for Isaac and Rebekah. God instructed them to go and reside in Gerar. This was Abimelech king of the Philistines territory. This young couple obeyed God's instructions. They relocated to Gerar. But Isaac perceived a major problem.

Wife Rebekah was an exceptionally beautiful woman. Isaac began to fear for his life as he journeyed to Gerar. He reasoned that the men of this country, would murder him to take possession of his wife. These thoughts probably petrified him. Isaac took the easy way out. He lied about his spousal relationship. He told his host country that Rebekah was his sister.

The king soon discovered Isaac's deception. He confronted Isaac. Isaac made a complete confession of the matter. The king informed his men that Rebekah was Isaac's wife.

He then issued a decree. Anyone who violated Rebekah would receive a death sentence. (Genesis 26 verses 1-11)

Isaac duplicated his parents' deceptive tactics. Father had reasoned he would be killed for divulging the truth. Now son got trapped in a similar web. But Isaac's concoction was a blatant lie. Rebekah was his first cousin. Satan had cunningly staked a claim on generation two. Trickery and deception tainted Isaac's parents. He became a repeat offender. Negative behaviours began to speedily recycle. Wife Rebekah duplicated her mother-in law's deception. She joined in a lie. Both could have been executed for lying. But once more God intervened.

Satan is still convincingly warping our thinking. He can easily overpower our mind with doubt. He will tell us that self preservation is a must at all cost. Fear and fright can easily render us ineffective. Emotional rigor mortis can paralyze our mortal being. This comatose condition will push positive thoughts to the sidelines.

Trusting God should never be complicated and confusing. Jesus is always encouraging us to pause and reflect. But we rarely rely on His ultra quiet voice during tense moments. We tend to panic when Satan begins to pile doubt in our mind. It is difficult to concentrate when Lucifer is hurling hot coals at our soul. During these frightening moments, we could begin to feel helpless and powerless.

Converting negatives to positives is never an easy task. But nothing is impossible with God on our side. A positive focused attitude will always defeat monstrous hurdles. We don't have to continue bemoaning the blunders of our foreparents. We don't need to keep on saddling ourselves with their problems. We should lay their burdens down at Calvary.

Another generation does not have to be on standby waiting to recycle misery. We should begin by concentrating on us. Ending generational dysfunctional lifestyles can start with us. Our generation can make a difference. But we will sincerely need to ask for guidance through prayer and supplication.

Prayer is the foundation on which belief, faith, and trust is built. Jesus says that we have not because we ask not. Prayer gives us hope and confidence that God will hear and answer our pleas. Prayer and meditation gives us the assurance that God can demolish all barriers from our lives. In spite of his faults and flaws, Isaac must have relied on the supernatural power of prayer.

Infertility surfaced in generation two. Rebekah had problems conceiving. Like he mother in-law Sarah, Rebekah was also barren. Her husband pleaded to God. God listened and intervened. He opened up her womb. And Rebekah conceived.

She experienced discomfort during her pregnancy. This concerned and puzzled her. She became perplexed. So she consulted the Lord. God put her mind at ease. He informed her that she carried two nations. This meant she would bring forth twins into this world.God showed her the future of her in progress babies. The older child would serve the younger child. This meant that the younger child's nation would be stronger. Both babies were born at the appointed time. These two infants entered earth one at a time.

And the first came out red, all over like an hairy garment; and they called his name Esau. (Genesis 25 verse 25.)And after that came his brother out, and his hand took hold of Esau's heel; and his name was called Jacob: and Isaac was threescore years when she bare them.(Genesis 25 verse 26.)

The children grew and matured. They developed distinctly different personalities. Esau was a skilled hunter. He naturally would be active and energetic. He likely was a very independent lad.

Jacob was a plain man who liked to stay indoors. He probably loved staying close to his mother. We could reason the Jacob was mother's pet. Rebekah loved Jacob. And Isaac loved Esau.

Being an avid hunter, Esau would understandably be exhausted when he completed his work. He would also be hungry. On one occasion, he observed his brother Jacob eating some stew when he returned home. Esau begged his brother for a portion of his meal.

Jacob refused his request. Instead he offered to sell Esau the meal. He demanded Esau forfeit his birthright as payment for the meal. Esau probably was on the verge of collapse. He likely was desperate and irrational.

He could have presumed that death was approaching. He could have reasoned that his birthright would be useless if he were dead. So he sold his birthright for a simple meal. He immediately regretted what he had done. He got extremely angry with his brother. He also despised his birthright.

Esau was older. Plus he was father's favorite. Jacob could have been envious of this fact. He could have been consumed with jealousy. He displayed an evil mindset towards his brother. But Jacob was now superior to his brother. He was one up in the pecking order status. (Genesis 25 verses 27 to 34.)

It is hard to focus when we are under duress. We can become unhinged under great stress. We will be less alert and pragmatic. Our reasoning skills can suffer severe setbacks. Normal awareness can get clouded. We could become dysfunctional. We could begin pedaling against dangerous currents.

Esau was temporarily emotionally handicapped. He was also mentally wounded. Jacob was probably was well aware that Esau was feeling weak and vulnerable. And he went for Esau's jugular. He used food as a weapon against his brother. And he succeeded.Doubt paralyzed Esau's mind. Fear entered his thought process. He became convinced him that his life was in danger. His wrong choice instincts took control. He satisfied his immediate wants. And he paid a high price. Esau probably would have reacted differently had he been alert. Jacob's proposition would have been heatedly challenged. Brothers could have become deadlocked. There likely would have been a very vicious clash. Jacob could have been badly hurt if he did not back down.

Fatigue can dull our senses. Doubt can spark irrational behaviors. We are prone to make mistakes when we become distracted. We could begin to second guess ourselves. The path of least resistance could ambush us. We could become a prime candidate for a major collapse. The after effects can be horrific.We all have our moments of weakness. Unscrupulous people can use vulnerable periods in our lives against us. Some could manipulate our condition to their advantage. They could begin to push personal agendas. We could easily buckle under pressure. We could end up regretting our decision. We could lament later.Waiting is never easy. Patience can be hard to harness. But perseverance will build character. Satan delights in attacking when our system is run down. He enjoys devouring us during seasons of despair. He enjoys pouncing on us when we are hurting.

Esau's emotional and mental condition could befall any of us. We panic easier when we feel trapped. We tend to get unnerved when we are hurting. Some could latch on to anything to ease their pain. Some could sell their soul to Satan for a loaf of bread. Some have lost virtually everything because of impulsive reasoning.

Jesus says: "And if a house be divided against itself, that house cannot stand." Mark 3 verse 25.

Mother Rebekah was closer to Jacob. He was her favorite. She gave him preferential treatment. Father Isaac apparently remained neutral. Some could even question his leadership role. Positive bonding by parents could have been lacking.

Favoritism is extremely damaging. We should steer clear of this practice. Parents should never embrace this principle. This mindset is wrong. We should never embark on this road. We should never display preference over one child. We should never exhibit partiality with one sibling.

We could end up neglecting our other children. This would be irresponsible behavior. No child is more important than the other. These actions are detrimental to the neglected child. The unimportant child can begin to feel inferior. Their value system could be compromised. They could begin to feel worthless.

The family structure should be even terrain. There should be no special privilege status. This should be null and void. We should never compare one child to the other. We should never put one child on a pedestal. The rest of the clan are not damaged goods. We should never encourage these thoughts and actions.

Our children should never have to compete for our affection. We should never indulge in separatism. We should distribute our affection and attention evenly. We should never display partiality. Our other children will feel left out. We could tarnish their confidence. This could blemish our reputation. Our offspring could view us as being unfair.

Our darlings could become resentful. We could be devalued in their minds. They could begin to distrust us. We could be setting the stage for mutiny. Unimaginable sibling rivalry could erupt. This can cause immense devastation for everyone. Parents should be truthfully aware of this fact. There could be ripple and trickle down side effects. Hostility could worm its way into our next generation.

Any child's accomplishments are important. We should never showcase bias. We should always exercise wisdom. The other children will be watching. We should never exaggerate the triumphs of a favorite child. Magnifying one child's assets can be problematic. Downplaying the importance of another child is equally bad. We should always maintain a healthy balance.

The set apart child might enjoy the attention. Our young could bask in the spotlight. These special privileges will be embraced for awhile. Eventually this child could be ostracized by the rest of the clan. This child could end up feeling alienated and lonely.

The other siblings could in time join forces. They could unleash intense fury on this labeled child. This can be a frightening experience for the set apart child. This child could start lashing out. This offspring could become bitter and resentful towards us. They could feel we had let them down.

We should always examine our motives. We should always remain impartial. We should be careful of exclusions. One child can remind us vividly of ourselves. This is not unusual. This child could be a mirrored image of us. We could gravitate to this child more readily. This understandably would be our instinctual response.

We could easily treat this child with more affection. This is never a good idea. This child is separate. We are separate. We should always remember this. But we are imperfect human beings. And we will always make mistakes.

During our lifetime we will free fall repeatedly. Sometimes we should conduct a complete inventory of our actions. There could be times when we have do repair work with our children. Level headed reasoning, hopefully should avert the need to quell a family uprising.

Chapter Seventeen
Children Need Stability

CHILDREN NEED a secure and stable environment. This is always reassuring for any child. They need to experience that special feeling of contentment. This is their security blanket. They should wake up each morning to dependable parents. This is priceless for their self worth. Nothing can be compared to unconditional love.

Parents should never function in disunity. This is extremely damaging for children. It sends them conflicting messages. This is bad for healthy growth and development. Children look to their fathers for strong leadership. They depend heavily on their mothers for nurturing. Problems will develop if children cannot rely on their parents. They will seek solace elsewhere.

A disruptive household will create major chaos. Instability will disrupt the lives of the adults and children. This will encourage major family dysfunctions. Repetitive upheavals will put any family on crisis alert. But these are age old restrictions.

Satan master minded this destructive blue print. His templates date back to our founding ancestors. His solemn vow is to dismantle the family structure. Destroying the very fabric of God's institution will forever be his primary desire. Contaminating our family is his way of antagonizing God.

Abraham's linage was plagued with serious defects. His was a murky reservoir of wrong choice decisions. Isaac inherited a lot of his father's character defects. We could learn a lot from the lives of Abraham and Isaac. We should extract what is applicable to us.

It could be reasoned that Isaac was basically a figure head. His wife was likely the domineering force. This was truly a messed up family. We could conclude that this was a two single parent family arrangement. And they resided under the same roof. Monstrous rifts could have plagued them.

Isaac focused his attention on Esau. Rebekah controlled Jacob. Parental structures probably were lacking. Guidance could have been minimal. Fights could have been frequent. Arguments could have been a way of life.

The brothers likely warred a lot. Animosity and bitterness could sometimes be severe. Sibling rivalry could have taken on dangerous undertones. Tension could have emotionally separated these biological parents.

Esau was the first born. He was first in line to receive his father's blessing. A blessing was and still is a sacred gift. It cannot be bought. It cannot be sold. A blessing was a high honor. This fact still remains intact.

Special blessings are still extremely important. They were a mandated expectation in Isaac's culture. This was a family tradition. The father normally bestowed this ritual on the oldest son. This son was anointed. He was solemnly charged to continue the family values.

He also had to preserve the family traditions. This formal ceremony was in essence the passing on of the mantle. This was the transferring of the torch to the next generation. This was ensuring uninterrupted continuance of the family linage. Some families still practice this tradition.

Father Isaac was well along in age. He was also blind. He was aware that his time on earth was coming to a close. He knew that meeting his Maker was fairly close at hand. And he knew that only he could conduct this ceremony.

He summoned his older son Esau. He gave him an assignment. He was told to hunt and kill an animal. Esau was instructed to prepare a meal for both of them. Isaac gave Esau the reason for this special meal. It was time to bestow his blessing on Esau. Isaac wanted to dine with Esau only. He likely wanted complete privacy when he blessed Esau. He could have wanted no fuss and fanfare. Complete secrecy could have been his goal. He probably wanted to avoid any uproar in his household. But the bible is silent on why Isaac behaved in this manner. This was huge a responsibility being transferred to Esau. It was also an awesome privilege. Isaac didn't invite his wife or his younger son as witnesses. He could have felt intimidated by his wife and his younger son. He could have feared reprisal from them. Esau departed from his father. He set out to execute his instructions. Esau hunted for an animal. He found one. He killed the animal. He cleaned the animal. He cooked the animal the way his father liked it. He then headed back home with the prepared meal. Excitement could have quickened his heart rate.

Mother Rebekah eavesdropped on her husband's private meeting. She listened intently to everything. And she was overwrought. She was distressed as she absorbed the implications. Esau was close to legally becoming the more influential son.

Jacob's status was now threatened. She became convinced of this. Jacob would be basically powerless. She had protected him from birth. She feared that his life would now be meaningless. She could have been terrified that she had labored in vain.

Satan used her partiality to dull her judgment. He activated her overprotective mindset. He used desperation as a weapon against her. Then the devil barged his way in. He set up shop. And he assumed residency in her soul. He impressed on her that Jacob was in danger. He insisted that she had to protect her favorite son at all cost.

She then made a decision. She took matters into her own hands. She hastily schemed up a plan to deceive her husband. Rebekah contacted Jacob. He was briefed on the meeting between Esau and Isaac. She then instructed Jacob to fetch two young goats. She was getting ready to trick her husband in a horrible way.

Jacob delivered the goats. His mother killed the goats. She then prepared a meal for her husband. Jacob was instructed to serve his father the meal. Rebekah's intention was that Jacob should pretend to be Esau. Her mind was made up. She was bent on Jacob receiving his brother's blessing.

Jacob protested his mother's unfair request. He reminded his mother that Esau had hairy skin. He had smooth skin. He worried that his father would discover the trickery. He became fearful that he would receive a curse and not a blessing.

Rebekah quickly consoled him. She would take all the burdens upon herself. She would take responsibility for all the plotting. Jacob reluctantly complied with her request. Rebekah left nothing to chance. There could be no mistakes. She took the skins of the two young goats. She affixed them to Jacob's hand. She also decorated his neck.

Her husband was blind. But his sense of smell and touch were still intact. She made sure that Jacob smelled like Esau. And that he felt like Esau. This underhanded saga was now planned to perfection. She then dispatched Jacob to his father with the meal.

Isaac became puzzled. He was surprised that Esau had returned so quickly. He was even more alarmed that the meal was already prepared. He was impressed with the speed. There was some conversation. Jacob did not even attempt to mimic Esau's voice. He answered his father in his natural voice.

Isaac became puzzled. He wanted to verify that the son before him was in fact Esau. Jacob passed the test. Isaac erroneously concluded that all was in order. He then transferred

The Barricading Yoke of Unforgiveness

his blessing on to his younger son. Jacob was now the fraudulent owner of Esau's blessings.

Esau returned to his father shortly thereafter. He presented him with this special meal. He was by now anxious to receive his blessing. He was full of anticipation. But his blessing would never become a reality. It had already been stolen by his younger brother. Esau had again been manipulated and tricked.

Isaac was understandably stunned. And he was extremely angry. His wife had beguiled him. And his younger son was a willing accomplice. But he was powerless to reverse or retract this tragedy. The transfer of his blessing was final. It was irreversible.

Reality set in on Esau. He again had been out done by his brother. Hurt and grief now consumed him. Agonizing anger and rage began to suffocate him. Hard core revenge now controlled his being. He vowed to himself to get even.

He decided to wait until after his father's death. Then he would kill his brother. An unforgiving mind had now taken shape and form. Esau's wrath petrified his mother. Her vile scheme had unraveled. Murder was now on the horizon.

This news grieved Rebekah to the core of her being. She passed this frightening information on to Jacob. The bible doesn't say how Jacob reacted to this devastating news. But this sudden turn of events would have created grave concerns for him.

Rebekah had masterminded a coup. She had deliberately deceived her husband. She had also betrayed her older son. Her actions had now backfired on her. The fate of Jacob was now uncertain. She likely panicked at the thought of losing her smothered son. Her life would be meaningless if Jacob were murdered.

Rebekah likely gave a full report of her devious actions to her husband. He would have understood the gravity of the situation. Jacob was now the blessed heir apparent. Jacob's murder would be devastating. Isaac's linage would grind to a halt. The family's reputation would be tarnished. Isaac had to protect Jacob at all cost.

God's set aside couple was in knee deep trouble. They had blundered badly again. They had strayed dangerously off course. They had exhibited poor child management skills. They had functioned independently. This was their downfall.

They banded together when calamity struck. They united on one accord. They now began to communicate. They dialogued. And they reasoned intelligently. They focused on this urgent matter. Then they made plans for conflict resolution.

Esau was out of control. This was a major concern. The brothers needed space. Separation should be a temporary solution. It was imperative that Jacob leave home. Isaac hoped that Esau's temper would soon subside.

Isaac then called Jacob. Again he blessed him. He charged him no to stray from his culture. He then warned him not to take any Canaanite wives. He was then sent to reside with Rebekah's brother Laban. And an impending murder was averted. (Genesis 27, and Genesis 28 verses 1 to 10)

Murder will always be devastating for any family. This can be likened to a monstrous tornado. The aftermath will always be horrific. It will shock everyone to the core of their foundation. This violent upheaval can disintegrate the family structure to shreds.

It is always heart rending when a tragedy occurs within a family. But sometimes a crisis will be the only time that some families will unite. Most back stabbings will be put aside for this season. Grief and togetherness will usually overshadow everything else.

Esau could have murdered Jacob on the spot. This would have been extremely debilitating for his parents. They would have had to live with the shame within their community. The stigma and scorn could have ruined them. Esau would have become an outcast and a vagabond.

The plight of Isaac and Rebekah is not past tense. Their struggles could torment any of us. We will always run afoul when we fast track God's timing. We put everything in disarray when we meddle with His schedule. We should never get impatient. Patience will always silence impatience.

Rebekah obviously discounted her conversation with God, concerning the disturbances in her womb. She conveniently forgot that God had already pre-destined the future of her sons. God expected mother to nurture and guide the twins in an upright God fearing way. Her duty was to leave the details to God. But she became impatient.

She was determined to do things her way. She deviated from God's plan. She took matters onto herself. Rebekah played the role of the meddler. This resulted in her messing things up. Her disobedience to God severely damaged Esau.

Any of us could be forced to deal with similar circumstances as Esau. We will become angry when we have to confront betrayal. We will get hostile when we are blatantly tricked. We will hurt deeply. And our suffering is never minimal. The residual effects can roam freely for a long time.

We will be highly offended when our friends backstab us. We could respond in a cold hearted manner. Eventually many of us will shrug off this needless load. Many will deliberately avoid contact in the future.

But it is hard to forgive when our flesh and blood turn against us. This is definitely the vilest act of transgression. It is not an issue that we can easily reconcile. We could easily seek revenge for family treason.

It will hurt even more when our parents dupe us. We expect them to be always there for us. We are supposed to look to them for guidance and protection. Then they callously let us down. There is never any justification when they gang up on us. This grave injustice can leave permanent scars.

It literally can drive some of us to the grave. Only death and hell can be worse than our parents trampling on us. Nothing can be compared to the agony of a deeply wounded soul. It can be likened to rapidly hemorrhaging to death. Repeated cruelty can ruin us.

Chapter Eighteen
Choices

JACOB SUFFERED from a severe personality disorder. Jacob was a deviously bad fellow. He was unethical and unscrupulous. He took wrong choices to new levels. Jacob wantonly ignored Godly principles. He initially was a cold and cruel individual.

Jacob was cunning and conniving. He was greedy. He was a selfish person. Jacob was a thief. He was beyond evil habitually. Young Jacob basically mutilated his character. His diabolical actions put enormous stress and tension on his family and himself. For a season Jacob was Satan's disciple. Many of us could fit Jacob's mold. Many of Jacob's deficiencies could be incubating in some of us. A lot of us could be duplicating his lifestyle on a daily basis. Many self proclaimed believers are also guilty. Sin has entombed many like an embalmed corpse.

Some could turn against family and brethren. They could resort to back stabbing in the blink of an eye. Some will think nothing of robbing others of their joy and assets. Some of us have become heartless and ruthless. Many will stoop to any level to achieve an objective.

Some end up belittling themselves. We berate ourselves by cheating others. We lose our dignity when we resort to trickery. We will be cursed when we rob from another. We should never envy things that are not ours. We should never crave our brethren's possessions. Malicious intent could eventually turn to torment.

Practicing immoral activities is dead wrong. We will never be justified. We will suffer severely when we are the instigator. It is a deadly sin to be a silent partner. We should always give peace a chance. We should never contemplate strife. God will punish us when we indulge in evil.

The fast track of life has two fundamental mottos: Destabilize and destroy all opponents. And enforce an agenda by any selfish and unscrupulous method available. Many of us still gloat in this feeling of dominance. After eliminating all perceived threats, some could have difficulty sleeping.

It is relatively easy to join forces with unethical behaviors. Controlling evil intentions can be difficult. Honesty and level headedness should be our guiding light. We risk losing everything when we behave dishonestly. But many still refuse to listen and think.

They continue to profit from the misfortunes of others. There is no greater curse than the bitter tears of the downtrodden. Wickedness could trap some in that horrible dungeon of despair. Some could experience that bottomless pit of terror. Many could implode with a loud noise.

Jealousy and greed will breed discontentment. They sometimes work together. There can be an insatiable crave to "have like". To be like "so and so," is a damaging mindset. A "must have" mentality can rapidly snowball into an obsession and an addiction.

Impatience has become a way of life for too many people. A lot of us can become dissatisfied with blessings God has bestowed on us. So we begrudge others for their blessings. Some of us relentlessly murmur about our current lot and portion in life. Some complain to God that He is unjust and unfair. Many vehemently showcase their displeasure and dissatisfaction.Many have turned to the world to fulfill their unrealistic goals. Covetousness is the speed dial approach to living above our means. Some could aggressively attempt to be on par with the presumed more affluent. Many could drown themselves in debt just to compete. But like Jacob, these are serious symptoms of a personality defect.

Jesus says:"They that be whole need not a physician, but they that are sick." Matthew 9 verse 12

Unless there are major physical, emotional, or mental health related issues, many will not seek professional help. We discussed in chapter one, that we should always prioritize immediate action, concerning any health related issue. But the majority will reason that they can medicate themselves. Many have ended up on the bed of affliction, because of this warped sense of reasoning.

The most difficult task for any human being is that of honest self evaluation. A lot of us are pathetic in truthfully dealing with ourselves. This is because the majority of us are horrible role models for ourselves. It is never easy uprooting deeply embedded demons within us. Some will only submit to help after a literal collapse.

The first step to wholesome healing is recognizing that we have a problem. The next phase is wholeheartedly surrendering to an appropriate treatment plan. But making that initial move can be frightening and intimidating. Fear of the unknown could make some of us extremely uncomfortable. But our anxiety level should be minimized, once we are in the presence of an attending physician.

A doctor will routinely ask some pertinent questions. General enquiry relating our current condition is always probed. A thorough examination is usually conducted. Personal data is always recorded. Sometimes more in depth questions will be asked. This could include our background and family history.

These questionnaires could be considered very invasive. But there is a reason for this at times embarrassing intrusion. A detailed overview of our condition is imperative. There could be some underlying family disorders. Some family irregularities could be hereditary. We could be affected now, or at a later date. This could potentially be detrimental to us.

The topic of emotional and mental health issues could also be discussed. These investigative procedures are oftentimes appropriate. The background of our ancestors could be queried in depth. Some of us could get highly offended. But these enquires are necessary and vital. The professionals always need to get a comprehensive understanding of our condition.

A psychological or a psychiatric assessment could be suggested. The results could determine if a treatment plan would be necessary. This request could make us even more uncomfortable. Some could even panic. Confronting complex issues tend to be very scary. But we always need to get a comprehensive understanding of all relevant issues.

We could have to sort through generations of family irregularities. This could be a monumental task to undertake. This could be a hard choice. But our focus should be on wholesome healing. And we should be committed to change. Our physical and our mental health depend on each other.

We should investigate all level of disturbances. We then should absorb all information. We should understand what we are focusing on. It can be dangerous to begin to guess. An ailment could be wrongly diagnosed. This could result in wrong assessments of a problem. This could lead to a misinterpretation of the findings. Harmful medications could be prescribed.

We overburden our emotions when we misinterpret. Misinterpretation is the leading cause of mistakes. We lead ourselves astray by not establishing all the facts. These problematic conditions affect trained professionals and laymen alike.

We have just theorized what a detailed medical examination should entail. Secular and spiritual guidelines follow the same basic pattern. But there are profound differences. A comprehensive evaluation is done by trained human professionals. Spirit and soul treatment is administered solely by the Spirit of the Living God.

We must be physically present for the earthly doctor to administer treatment. The Holy Spirit will make a house call when we earnestly request His help. The earthly doctor might prescribe pills or other medicines. Doctor Jesus will prescribe for us prayer and fasting. He will closely monitor our commitment and dedication to follow instructions.

Our obedience to God must supersede all our humanistic inclinations. The Holy Spirit is the only person capable of pulling us out of our emotional dungeons. But we should first recognize the urgent necessity for spiritual and emotional restructuring. Then we should be willing to embark on an honest soul searching pilgrimage.

God made us with one spirit, one soul, and one body. But He designed us with multiple emotions. God freely dispenses choices to us. It is our responsibility to differentiate between appropriate and inappropriate behaviours. There is no greater joy than a spiritual awakening. Our spirit will begin to unite in harmony with our emotions.

Doctor God is the wisest physician in the universe. He supervises all earthly doctors. Some may mutiny and rebel against him. But all are accountable to Him. God's examination requirement is more through than any human professional is capable of. His diagnosis is never wrong. Neither is it ever incomplete. And we can never lie to Him.

Only Jesus is capable of completely healing our broken heart. He can instantly fill that lifeless void within us. God can miraculously mend the woes in our lives. This includes all the burdensome loads we have been saddled with from previous generations. Our God will put peace and joy within us in the twinkling of an eye. Only the Holy Spirit can give us a divine makeover.

God will replace envy and jealousy with satisfaction an understanding. He will remove from us the urge and the desire to covet. No longer will we steal joy and possessions from others. He will teach us how patiently wait on Him. It is only God who can destroy the demons within us.

God will assist us in sorting out hereditary family irregularities. He will gently guide us through our unmanageable issues. He will teach us how not to arbitrary target any one. He will reveal to us that most parents are not bad people. But stubborn and ignorant individuals are in abundance. Many will stray when they put God on the sidelines. They will pay a steep price for disobedience.

Parents should never get entangled in inappropriate behaviors. They can severely damage their offspring. Jacob was an all around rascal. He was ruthlessly evil to his brother. Then he conspired with his mother to destroy Esau. He suffered harsh consequences because of his mother's deviousness.

Esau could have immediately murdered Jacob. Rebekah's damaging indiscretions would have created this tragedy. She would also be guilty of murder. No offspring should be saddled with carrying lifelong burdens, because of an evil minded parent.

Chapter Nineteen
Unresolved Issues Relocate with Us

Young exiled Jacob eventually arrived at his uncle Laban's residence. Laban welcomed his nephew passionately. Laban invited Jacob to reside in his household. But there was a major downside to this arrangement from the onset. Both men were crooks.

Laban was a cunningly seasoned crook. Jacob was an inexperienced crook in training. Both men had constructed their internal infra structure on a dishonest foundation. Trickery, manipulation, and deception had tarnished their reputation. Mistrust eventually birthed tension between these men.

Laban was blessed with two daughters. The older was named them Leah. The younger was named Rachael. Jacob immediately fell in love with Rachael. He asked for her hand in marriage. But there was a situation that had to be addressed. Jacob had no assets to present to Laban as a dowry. He requested working seven years free for Laban. Laban agreed to this request.

Jacob laboured willingly for seven years. He then formally asked permission to marry Rachael. Laban agreed. Laban celebrated his daughter's matrimony with a wedding feast. During the course of the evening, Laban presented to Jacob a daughter. Jacob presumed this was Rachael. Jacob went in unto her. And she became his wife.

Shock and bewilderment greeted Jacob the next morning. He discovered that he had been tricked. Leah was now his wife. This was a blatant violation of trust. He confronted his Laban. Laban then imparted to Jacob, valuable information that he had deliberately withheld.

He now told Jacob the custom of the land. Leah was the older daughter. She was therefore in line to be married first. So he had fulfilled his part of the agreement. He told Jacob that he could also marry Rachael. But he would have to work another seven years for free. Jacob agreed.

Jacob toiled for the allotted time. Rachael became his wife fourteen years later. Jacob was now the husband for both sisters. This was an acceptable practice in Jacob's era. A man could take unto himself multiple wives. Some cultures still practice this way of life.

Rachael was beautiful and vivacious. She was more loved and highly favored by her husband. Leah was a simple woman with tender eyes. God blessed Leah's womb. She was always conceiving. She kept on adding new life to this world.

Like her in-laws before her, Rachael was barren. She envied her sister. She craved for her sister's fertility. She badly wanted things that Leah probably took for granted. Rachael's inability to conceive obviously made her resentful. At times she was bitter towards her sister.

Jacob probably spent many sleepless nights reflecting on his life. But he was responsible for creating this huge mess. He was likely now regretting all the havoc he had caused. At home he was basically the bully. He was also the pampered one. Before his current misfortunes, Jacob probably had not worked an honest day in his life. Jacob could have now felt like a victim and a pawn.

Working fourteen years without pay is tough. This is no joking matter. Jacob's selfish and self centered lifestyle carried an expensive price tag. His rotten habits resurfaced to haunt him. But his problems were self inflicted. Dishonesty will always return to haunt and taunt.

Jacob had little time for a pity party. He now had a large family to tend to. There were frequent wars between his wives. He likely had to settle intense heated issues with sisters. Rachael probably created most disturbances. Her inability to conceive was likely the cause of many disruptions. Jacob had problems galore. He constantly was on the lookout for trickery from Laban. Oftentimes his wives were locked in a bickering marathon. His kids were probably driving him crazy. He was literally jammed to the hilt. Jacob basically had no wiggle room. He was sinking fast without a life jacket.

Jacob's problems just would not give him a break. He was isolated from a meaningful support system. His wives were too busy tending to their own conflicts. He badly needed some guidance. He urgently needed to hear from his God. But God remained silent.

Genesis 28 verses 10 to 22, is very insightful. Jacob communed intimately with his God en-route to his uncle Laban. But he still had to seek repentance for his evil deeds. The consequences of his sins had to be dealt with. God was not about to exempt him from his corrupt lifestyle. Jacob and his mother had teamed up against Esau. He had also grieved and disappointed his father. He was now living in torment. These issues had to be reconciled. Jacob had made numerous wrong choice decisions. He was now receiving more than a double portion of punishment.

Leah delivered six sons and a daughter into this world. God had mercy on Rachael in due season. He opened up her womb. And she conceived. She brought forth a son. She named him Joseph. Jacob now had his love child.

But this new earthling was at risk. His father's devious lifestyle was still very much active. Son could easily be contaminated. Mother Rebekah had overprotected Jacob. But he had invented many deviant plans on his own.

Jacob had demonstrated the ability to put his underhanded schemes into action. He had also learned more cunning trickery from his mother. He was close to the pulse of most of her dirty bag of tricks. Joseph was a prime candidate to be eventually tarnished. We cannot sugar coat Jacob's delinquent actions. We cannot cover up his deplorable way of life. Jacob was now a fully seasoned crook. He had arrived as an unrefined crook in training. The experienced crook was Laban. But Jacob eventually calculatedly turned things in his favor.

Jacob was responsible for tending to Laban's livestock. The men had an agreement. Jacob would keep the blemished livestock as payment for his work. Jacob masterminded an exceptionally covert plan. He discovered a way to cunningly trick his employer.

He installed a rod in the animal's drinking troughs. This startled the pregnant animals when they came to drink. The frightened livestock produced spotted offspring. Jacob then claimed the ringed flock.

He fed them better. They flourished better. They were healthier. His stock increased more than Laban's. He was now wealthier than his boss. Jacob had engineered a coup. And he succeeded. He emerged as the more cunning and underhanded crook.

The bible says: "For the Lord seeth not as man (or woman) seeth; for man (or woman) looketh on the outward appearance, but the Lord looketh on the heart." 1 Samuel 16 verse 7 part B.

Jacob was robed with multiple filthy garments. But he always rose above his infirmities. He unwaveringly trusted his God. He had a steadfast belief in God. He was committed to serve God. God judged Jacob by the sincerity of his heart. And his God protected him during his perils. Jacob had outright tricked his father-in-law. He was now more powerful than Laban. Their relationship took a nose dive. Laban became angry. Laban's sons began to grumble. Tension was now thicker than molasses. Deep and bitter wedges escalated to breaking point. Meaningful communication was perhaps lacking. Productive dialogue likely became obscure. Hostility most likely reined unchecked. Jacob was now at a dangerous impasse with Laban. This was a major stumbling block. And it loomed large and menacing.

Jacob had to make a swift decision. He had to sever ties with Laban and his sons. Jacob's wives had donated their two maid servants to their husband. Jacob sired four sons with his two additional wives. He now had four wives. His clan consisted of eleven sons and one daughter. Jacob once more found himself in a precarious condition. He was no longer welcomed on Laban's soil. He now had a large family. The livestock he had swindled from Laban had multiplied abundantly. He had to move on. But his options were limited. One wrong move could spell trouble.

The Spirit of God intervened. He paid Jacob a surprise visit. God instructed Jacob to leave Laban's domain. The Lord told him to return to his father's country. The die was now cast. Jacob had to obey God's directive. He immediately started making plans. He had to make a hasty retreat.

Jacob's entire entourage had to leave Laban's grasp. He consulted with wives Leah and Rachael. He gave them a detailed breakdown. They also were angry with their father. He had swindled them out of their inheritance. They made a unanimous decision. It was time for a change. They had to move on. But they needed to execute their flight plan carefully.

Hasty decisions can induce worry and doubt. Panic can impair clear judgment. The fear of the unknown can generate peak anxiety levels. Jacob and family began to frantically make plans. They hastily assembled their personal belongings. Jacob readied his huge caravan. They then activated their flight plan. They departed from Laban's domain like thieves in the night. Jacob also faced a much more grim reality. This was a monstrous obstacle. It loomed larger than life in Jacob's mind. This was a predicament that he could bi-pass no longer. He could not ignore or downplay this crisis any longer. He could not evade this menacing threat indefinitely.

This problem truly frightened him. But he had to accept the rendered verdict. His past had finally caught up with him. This terrified him. This glaring truth haunted him. He now was at his lowest ebb. He feared for his life.

Jacob could not return home without crossing paths with his brother Esau. Laban was still fiercely angry with Jacob. And he was aggressively pursuing his son-in-law. But Jacob had to press on towards home. And he couldn't take a short cut home. Jacob had jumped out of the proverbial frying pan into the raging fire.

He had to be reflecting on all his bad choices. He was basically now out of Laban's grasp. But his major fear would be facing his older brother. Jacob was dreadfully afraid of his brother. But he was obeying God's command. He kept on moving. His goal was to make it home.

Jacob knew he would eventually come face to face with Esau. He was clueless how Esau would greet him. He didn't know if he would emerge dead or alive when they met. Brothers had been separated for a very long time. But Esau was probably still bent on revenge.

Jacob made a preemptive move. He dispatched a scout party to meet and greet his brother. He furnished his men with gifts for his brother. This could be likened to an insurance policy. Their role was to announce Jacob's impending visit. This was a long overdue reunion.

Gifts were usually presented to the visited by the visitor. This was a display of respect and honor. It was the custom in Jacob's culture. This was a good will gesture. Gift giving is also a part of our current culture.

Jacob had a bad reputation. He was a cunning manipulator. And he was a crafty shyster. Now he was desperate. So his true motivation could be deemed questionable. Jacob could have been attempting to bribe his brother. He could have reasoned that a peace offering would minimize potential hostilities.

This gesture however, could have been a sincere show of remorse. Esau probably was still bitter. This could have been an "olive branch" attempt, to minimize hostilities. It could also have been a show of repentance on Jacob's part. But Jacob was in for a surprise. Esau returned all of his brother's gifts. Jacob was told that Esau was on his way to meet him. Esau was also armed with four hundred men.

This news petrified Jacob even more. He now could have smelled the sting of death. Jacob began to pray earnestly to his God for deliverance. He reasoned that Esau's wrath was about to overpower him. He would be a dead man without God's intervention.

Jacob hastily divided his camp. He concluded that an attack from his brother was imminent. Jacob issued instructions to his servants. He instructed them how to act when Esau arrived at their camp. He then rested with them for a while. (Genesis 32 verses 1 to 21.)

The bible says that during the night Jacob arose. He took his four wives with him. He took his eleven sons with him. They all passed over the Ford Jabok. He sent his family over the brook. He stayed behind to commune with his God. It was during this period, that Jacob experienced an event that forever changed his life.

Jacob became involved in a wrestling match with a man. The bible does not document why Jacob was wrestling with this man. The holy book is silent on who started this fight. The bible reveals only that these two men were involved in close combat.

They jostled all night. They fought until daybreak. At the break of dawn this stranger told Jacob to release him. But Jacob refused to let him. Jacob was determined to win this wrestling match. Jacob must have realized that this person was no ordinary man. Jacob demanded a blessing from this stranger. The stranger complied. He blessed Jacob. He then changed Jacob's name to Israel.

A perceived imminent attack from Esau was looming. Jacob did not request that his life be spared. He did not request super human strength to confront his brother. He did not petition a battle ready army. He did not ask for the necessary expertise to fight Esau. He made no mention of skills to defeat his brother in battle.

Jacob remained focused. He wanted one thing from this apparent heavenly representative. He wanted a blessing. He asked for a blessing. Matter of fact he demanded a blessing. And he received his blessing. He emerged from this encounter with a permanent limp. But he was a forever changed man. (Genesis 32 verses 24 to 32).

The bible says: "For thy name's sake, O Lord, pardon mine iniquity; for it is great." Psalms 25 verse 11

We may have orchestrated countless problems. Our lives could be completely covered by numerous mudslides. We could have been despicably evil minded. We may have become below human level disgusting. But everything will change when we experience an encounter with God. Our sins and our iniquities He will remember no more.

Sometimes everything will come crashing down on us. But we should never react in despair. We should never succumb to desperation. We should hold fast to the helm of His garment. Our healing will begin when we reach out in faith. The Spirit of God will purge us of all infirmities. Jesus will bathe us in His precious blood. He will wash and purify us. This is His promise to us.

Peace should flow through us like a river. We should rejoice nonstop. We should be totally convinced that there is a God. Our soul should become thirsty because of this reality. We should humbly petition Him for a blessing. We should wait in quiet complete submission. And we will receive our blessing. In humble reverence, we should give Him thanks.

The bible says: "Let the wicked forsake his (or her) way, and the unrighteous man (or woman) his (or her) thoughts; and let him (or her) return unto the Lord, and He will have mercy upon him; (or her) and to our God, for He will abundantly pardon." Isaiah 55 verse 7.

We will feel terrible pain from self inflicted wounds. At times we could stumble like a drunken sailor. Sometimes we could blunder to below zero degrees. Our mistakes could stretch to infinity.

Remorse could ignite our insides. This could feel like a roaring fire. We could be likened to charred rubble. Wrong choice decisions can incinerate us. Worldly insane indulgencies could hold us captive. The elements of this world take pride in brainwashing us.

We could start behaving in oneness with evil. Our carnal nature's job is to be deviant. Our abnormalities could seem right. We could feel justified. Then we could suddenly wake up. The bull horn could be blaring. But we could feel powerless to stop. We could be staring at the gushing waters. And we had never learned to swim.

Remorse could begin to drown us. We could become confused and disoriented. Darkness could begin to blanket us. This is when Satan will pull us into his torpedo boat next to him. This would the last place we would want to be. The devil would put the boat on auto pilot and abandon us.

That deadly precipice would be glaring at us. The bottomless pit would be anxiously waiting. Then sanity could suddenly pay us a visit. Spiritual intervention would begin to soothe our pain. We should then cry out: "Thank you God. Please forgive me Lord. And please help me Lord."

The "me" formula is like a dragnet. We could start ignoring upright principles. We could neglect our parental responsibilities. We could become deviously inventive. Conflicts with our spouse could be hard to resist. We could shove our family in a darkened corner. Everyone would begin to suffer. "Please teach me how to change Lord." This is the prayer we will need. Change can be a huge and frightening decision. It rarely happens overnight. This usually evolves over time. But the effort is well worth the rewards. We should discover that love is a gentle soothing experience. God designed it to be free flowing. He decreed it everlasting. Strife and bitterness are opposites.

Love will always smooth over a multitude of ills. Our emotions should become more manageable. Life should become clearer and brighter. The present and the future should begin working in unity. God's Spirit is our greatest teacher. But we should absorb what we learn. And we should put them in practice. The Lord God will guide and sustain us all the time.

Chapter Twenty
Greed

COVETOUSNESS AND ENVY birthed greed in the Garden of Eden. The serpent convinced Eve that God was treating her unfairly. Dissatisfaction prompted her to begin craving to acquire what was off limits to her. She then made the decision to indulge in immoral activities. And she followed through by charting for herself a disastrous course.

Jacob inherited his conniving and unscrupulous way of life from first generation Eve. These hereditary dysfunctions likely had been dormant for centuries. Jacob reactivated this devious mindset. This demonic compulsion propelled him to covet his brother's status, within the family structure.

There are several probabilities why Jacob chose to strong arm Esau out of his birthright. The most plausible could have been that he just wanted to be superior to his brother. And this self centered mentality, has saturated every culture and nationality throughout the world. This must have mindset has infiltrated virtually every corner of the globe.

Greed has transformed itself into hard core compulsive lifestyle. Greed is an aggressive pursuit to accumulate unnecessary excesses, for the purpose of displaying an air of superiority. Greed is maximized selfishness. It is aggressive self centeredness. Greed is extremely addictive. Greed is the cornerstone that can transform evil thoughts into malicious actions.

Oftentimes we misdiagnose and narrowly define greed. We tend to view this imbalance solely as excessive hoarding. But greed can quickly mushroom into a beyond destructive force. The tentacles of greed go deeper than abnormal stockpiling. Greed is more profound than merely acquiring material possessions.

It is the relentless pursuit of amassing personal acquisitions, by any underhanded method that is available. There is generally no remorse after a targeted objective has been achieved. Greedy people are always on the prowl to conquer and devour. An unsuspecting population are easy targets. Many can be left feeling broken and bitter.

The ruthless mentality of greedy individuals will plunder far and wide. They have no respect for moral and ethical principles. They will resort to any unscrupulous method to grab and hold. They love to demonstrate an air of superiority. Many are consumed with a spirit of dominance.

Greed addicted people have some basic similarities: Many are egotistic and pompous. They love to showcase an aura of greatness. Presenting a flawless sense of accomplishment is important to them. Many build their own pedestal. They mire themselves in self exaltation. They are usually power hungry. They love to boast about their personal achievements. Most believe that success can purchase dignity.

Greed addiction has some definitive character deficiencies: Many are grossly dishonest. They also love to invent their own spotlight. Involvement in anything should to revolve around them. They delight in tackling issues that gives them an audience. They will eagerly get submerged in multiple projects. But their goal is always to derive exceptional benefits. They are obsessed with abnormal levels of mistrust and paranoia. They can become very delusional. They frequently verbalize that society is always conspiring to destroy them. They behave as if everyone is on the prowl extract their wealth. Many are consistently overburdened with anxiety.

Most greedy individuals are basically cowards. They hide behind an ill fitting mask. Some are constantly at war with themselves. Many lack self confidence. Good versus evil issues oftentimes will plague them. This would be like looking in the mirror. Their consciences could convict them.

Greedy people always push to be number one. Instant recognition boosts their ego. They are usually jealous of other people's success. Envy is second nature to many of them. Many resent other evil competitors. They could end up sabotaging their perceived opponent.

Greed driven individuals hate to have their wants delayed. They love to obtain things in a hurry. But their desires could be put on hold. This could propel them to angry outbursts. Their sights could be fixated on something. Not everything is for sale. This could further infuriate them. They oftentimes behave like spoiled brats.

The Owner of the universe puts things in proper perspective. Our needs are always urgent priorities. God will promptly attend to them. He will routinely put a question mark to our wants. This is plain and simple language. It should be easily understood. God owns all the wealth in this world. He will tend to our wants after He has supplied our needs. So what is the problem?

God's assurances are straightforward and uncomplicated. And He will always manifest His promises into reality. But a lot of us disbelieve. We instead will heed the call of the world. It is easier to live what we can see. Hoarding can be more practical. Empire building will keep us in abundance.Binge consumption is an unhealthy habit. But many are obsessed with overstuffing themselves. They are consistently overstocking their barn. Some will stockpile to accumulate. These indulgences are very important to them. Enough is never enough for many.

Many people love to display their righteous garments. They profess to be rock sold believers. They are quick to condemn the so called ungodly world. They constantly breathe fire and brimstone on the general population. They demonize the "on the way to hell" materialistic world. But their personal lives tell an unworthy story.

Their hearts are freezer cold. They are evil and corrupt. They also hoard and stockpile. They also plunder. They are equally selfish and greedy. They will rob the poor and needy. They will break the backs of the less fortunate just to accumulate.

They should take a snap shot of themselves. And they should put it on the wall of disgrace. They should be condemning themselves. Fire and brimstone should consume them. They behave no better than the society that they enjoy pushing under the bus.

Then there are some seasoned religious dignitaries. Their greed can surpass worldly boundaries. Many are makeshift pious. They display surface level humility. But they indiscriminately plunder their flock. They will consistently take more than they put in. They are always backstabbing others of like mind.

The Son of God has instructed us how to approach our Father. We first must give honor and praise to God. This is our first expectation. He then instructed us to request our daily bread. Taking by force is never mentioned.

Jesus said that our Father will supply all our needs. He made no mention of our sometimes unreasonable wants. God said we should trust Him under all conditions. He didn't say we should envy our neighbor. We must be confident that He will satisfy all our needs. God will decide when to distribute our wants. Our steadfast belief in God should be our reinforced foundation. And we should exercise our faith when we pray. Our unwavering trust in the Almighty is the best stress blocker. A steadfast reliance on God will pull us through all adversities. We wouldn't need God in our lives if we could fix all our issues. We need the practical necessities of life to live. Necessity and excess is as far apart as north and south. We eat to satisfy our hunger. This maintains and sustains our body.

This is a need and a necessity. We over indulge when we over eat. We are being greedy. We should never take more than we need. These are definitely not necessities.

We should never adopt the conqueror take all mentality. We hurt others when we take by force. They will legitimately become angry. They could retaliate violently against us. They could find it hard to forgive when we trample on them.

We should never enter that emotional highway named greed. It will only take us into that city called covetousness. Major problems will be awaiting us in the capitol. We should steer clear of unhealthy trails. We could get pricked by briars and thorns. They could get lodged in our veins. Infections could poison our system. Some infections can kill us.We should never grab all just to add more. The evil elites are notorious for this. They reason that the world owes them favors. Some will extract their "favors" by force. They live a universal motto: Giving is weakness. Taking is strength. They are convinced that these are the fringe benefits of comfort.We should never copy cat evil doers. We should always focus on fairness. The disadvantaged are always struggling. They need help. We should never exploit the poor. This will destroy the needy. They all need an advocate.

The world has taught us how to be dishonorably dishonest. We are often instructed that this should be our goal. We are encouraged to strive to achieve it. Electronic crookedness has become very wide spread. A lot of us have embraced this evil. A multitude has accepted this demonic trend. Some are comfortable with it.

 Some of our fellow citizens will adamantly glorify greed. Many are proud of their accomplishments. They truly believe that this a new era. Some will even brag that they redefined the rules. But envy and greed has been around longer than modern crooks. Dishonesty is older than all our current crooks combined.

Greedy people are excessively competitive and compulsive. They are very combative. They are never satisfied with their measure of blessings. They are never contented with what God bestows on them. Greed put Eve and Adam at odds with God.

Cain became angry with God for accepting his brother's gift. He was overcome with envy because of this fact. He wanted everything for himself. He became ruthless. He turned against his brother. Greed laid the foundation for murder. His greedy appetite backfired. He harvested sorrow instead.

Greed incubates on emotional and mental levels. This is dangerous for our mind. Greed is a fearless adversary. Anyone could be overpowered by this evil. The instinct to grab and hold can be tempting. A sneaky coup is considered good for business. Greedy people rarely negotiate. They just take. God abhors greedy people. Jacob preyed on Esau's the weakened state of mind. Greed caused him to swindle his hungry brother's birthright. He wasn't satisfied with his own birthright. Raw greed also motivated him to steal his brother's blessing.

The whole world needs to be reminded about some simple truths. These are uncomplicated facts about the Spirit of the living God: The Spirit of God is always abounding in abundant love. The Spirit of God is all the time full of compassion. The Spirit of God will righteously impute wisdom. The Spirit of God is patience and long suffering to us who believe in Him.

The Spirit of God is forgiveness and cleanliness. The Spirit of God will always righteously administer grace and mercy. The Spirit of God will supply all our needs. He will fulfill our heart's desires in due time. The Spirit of God is sinless. He detests evil. Manipulative and greedy people He detests.

Wrong choice decisions can be expensive. There will always be related consequences. We will suffer for our wrong choice mindset. We could be damaged by wrong choice actions. Greed ranks very high on the list of wrong choices.

Those who follow in the footsteps of our greedy ancestors should take heed. Otherwise their self centered gluttonous way of life will become their downfall. Their thievery will be posted on numerous billboards. The public harshly scorn and ridicule them. They will be put on trial. Universal guilty verdicts will put them behind bars. Jesus will query why they shamed His cross.

Jesus has cautioned us: "For what is a man (or a woman) profited, if he (or she) shall gain the whole world, and loose his (or her) own soul? Or what shall a man (or a woman) give in exchange for his (or her) soul? Matthew 16 verse 26.

Society has endorsed a motto that says only the fittest and the strongest should survive. Many have embraced this self fulfilling doctrine. But nothing or nobody will last forever. This includes the strong and the feeble. It also incorporates the affluent and the vulnerable.

God issued to all humankind temporary citizenship. He will eventually revoke our passports. Others will inherit our assets and liabilities. They will control our sometimes wealthy empire. Eternity does not have an offshore account. The bank of heaven will not accept earthly deposits.

Everyone will eventually make a peaceful, or a painful planet exit. Then the rich and the poor will come face to face with God. The condition of our soul will determine whether God is pleased or displeased with us. He will either accept us or reject us. This is our most important legacy that we will leave behind.

We all at some point must say goodbye to all our earthly possessions. We will leave everything behind. But we could have ruined countless lives when we had breath. We will not see that expensive casket we will be buried in. We are immediate dust if we are cremated. The earth will then reclaim us empty handed.

Everyone will have to answer in person to that final roll call. All names will be tabulated. Some will be marked present. Some will be marked absent. Those with an absent slip will be denied entry into heaven. Many will have conquered and gained the whole world. But they will have lost their soul. Only Satan will rejoice.

Chapter Twenty-One
God Always Gives Second Chances

MANY WRONG CHOICE DECISIONS hounded Jacob. He flaunted his selfishness. He demolished his relationship with his brother. He outsmarted himself. His greed turned against him. He ran from his home like a common thief. Misery and torment became his personal diet. His problems multiplied and flourished.

God never gave up on Jacob. He allowed Jacob to mess up his life. The Lord watched as Jacob tumbled. But His Spirit was always just a prayer away. God was satisfied that Jacob's heart was pure. He blessed Jacob abundantly. This was in spite of all his terrible deeds.

Jacob still had unresolved issues. He had to make things right with his brother. This was a major stumbling block. This was a huge distraction for Jacob. He had to confront these barricades. He had to deal with his spiritual and emotional crimes. This restricted Jacob's overall progress.

God put Jacob on a corrective path. This was a pre-destined collision course. Now he had to make right all of his wrongs. God offered him this unique opportunity. His only requirement was to comply. Only then could Jacob come in full alignment with God.

God will sometimes institute a binding mandate. And we dare not disobey Him. This would be a fate likened to death.

His will and His wisdom will always prevail. His irreversible directives are always a must. They will supersede our idiotic melodramas.

Jacob's years on the run came to an end. He finally came face to face with his younger brother. He could easily have yielded to Satan's manipulative antics. He could have made a wrong decision. Jacob could have resorted to his old methods of trickery.

His habitual deceptive lifestyle could have been activated. His cowardly selfish ways could have rushed to his defense. But he resisted these temptations. This was a potential life and death meeting. He didn't attempt to worm his way out of his predicament.

Instead he kneeled before his brother. He was completely subdued. He displayed sincere remorse and true surrender. He had wronged Esau. He had transgressed against Esau. He had been needlessly cruel. He had recklessly inflicted grave harm on Esau.

The bible says Jacob bowed seven times before his brother. Jacob was finally now contrite. He was completely chastened. He was a broken man. He was extremely humble. This was an act of complete repentance.

Jacob was a horrible person. But he repented of all the wickedness. All he wanted now was forgiveness from his brother. It had been a long hard road for Jacob. God was pleased. And Esau was happy. Jacob's honesty made a huge difference between life and death.

Very little has changed since Esau's and Jacob's era. Most things have gotten progressively worse. Many Jacobs still walk and talk with us. Evil is still rampant in the land. Many human hearts have gotten colder and more frigid. Humanity has fine tuned trickery. Deception has been remodeled. Most of society is in on the take.

This world is at a new and dangerous level. The strong are on steroids. They refuse to bear the infirmities of the weak. The poor and the needy have become the outcasts in society.

The crooks and the thieves have taken over the world. This is the prevailing reality. And it is raging out of control.

Many no longer love their neighbors as themselves. This has been put in the archives. Robbing and mutilating our neighbor is now part of the new world order. Some people will literally kill for one dollar. The world appears to be on a collision course to extinction.

Giving is hard to find. Our wants have pushed our needs on the backburner. "Flawless" people now rule. Most people won't even admit to mistakes. Hurting others appears to be the new positive. Forgiveness has now become antiquated. Getting even is also part of this new world order.

There is a frenzy to hoard. This can be likened to the gold rush of old. Few refer to the past to balance the present. Many say the teachings of old have become irrelevant. Some view them as primitive. Honesty is now a concept of the past. Sophisticated thievery leaves no trace.

The bible says: "For the wages of sin is death; but the gift of God is eternal life through Jesus Christ our Lord." Romans 6 verse 23.

The bible says: "If we confess our sins, He is faithful and just to forgive us our sins, and to cleanse us from all unrighteousness." 1 John 1 verse 9

This planet is full of blemished people. We are all defected merchandise. Some are damaged goods. Some have open sores. We all come to God as filthy rags. He will never send us to the back of the line. He will accept us as is. He will always incorporate us into His fold. But we must be willing to change our decaying ways. Otherwise we will mourn when it is too late.God always rejects an impure heart. But He knows that our minds are battlefields. Confession will mature us. It will cleanse our soul. These measures will purify us. The saying "confession is good for the soul," is a time tested truth. A hardened heart will guarantee us a seat at Satan's head table.

Spiritual death is a dreadful thing. It separates us from God. It is a terrible price to pay for   indulging in evil mindedness. A devious lifestyle is an insurance policy to hell. Stubbornness is not good for us. Eventually it can ruin us.

Strife will always cause us anguish. An "always ready to rumble" attitude has no place in Jehovah's kingdom. Today we are alive. Tomorrow we could be dead. We are a called and chosen generation. Our lives are pre-ordained. Everything about us is pre-destined. We should never forget these facts.

It will hurt when we are unfairly treated. We could feel dismembered. We could easily take the retaliatory road. We could perceive this as our only option. Our wounds can become more painful, when our persecutors laugh at us. We will be incensed by their insensitivity.

We could become livid when they enjoy carefree moments. We could view this as an insult to us. We could suddenly feel like assassinating them. But some could reason that this method of punishment would be too tame. They had caused us too much grief. They should deserve a harsher penalty. Mutilation would be appropriate.

Some people are beyond comprehension evil. Only God knows why some turn into vindictive monsters. We will be offended when strangers invade our personal domain. It can be utterly devastating when family and friends turn against us. Those close to us should be watching our backs. Our wounds will bleed longer when they deliberately backstab us. Forgiveness could be tough to negotiate.

The trials of life are always brutal. We can feel like live coals burning wildly within us. Hell's fiery showers are mercilessly relentless. Our sanity could become questionable during these moments. We could question why we were being treated so unfairly. Oftentimes our questions will go unanswered. It can be frightening when our mind turns against us. But God will grant us clarity in due time.

We will see no end in sight when we are hurting. But we should never feel defeated. God sees our injustice. He feels our pain. He will repay. These are the moments when we should meditate on Romans 12 verse 19: "Dearly beloved, avenge not yourselves, but rather give place unto wrath: for it is written, Vengeance is mine, I will repay, saith the Lord."Sometimes we will endure endless nightmares reliving painful periods. Life is full of sneaky curve balls. Missiles will always be constantly hurled at us. Helplessness could overwhelm us. We could literally fall asleep at the helm. We could begin steering in the wrong direction. We could put ourselves in grave danger.

At time we could fantasize about just lying down. We could picture not waking up. Death suddenly could appear appealing and real. This would be a relief. Nothing could be worse than living in petrifying hell holes. But this would be a mistake. Hell is not a pretty place.

Chapter Twenty-Two
Family Responsibilities

OUR FOUNDATIONAL PROFILE is cemented at a tender age. Professionals contend this occurs between age three and age five. We should pay close attention to these findings. There is a multitude of wisdom in them. We should absorb much of these researches.

We should also pay keen attention to our tiny people. We could learn a lot from them. We would be better equipped to curtail their first act of defiance. Their rebellious nature begins very early. Their first word is always "NO." They will yell this first word. It is clear and precise. They will enforce their "NO" with actions if necessary.

Their limited vocabulary is now crystal clear. Our little angel is growing and maturing. Our offspring has moved to another level. They now possess measured doses of independence and understanding. With this limited knowledge, comes the period of throwing temper tantrums.

We could be well seasoned veterans. We could be trained professionals. We could be experts in child psychology. We could be well adjusted parents. Our success history could be widely documented. They could even be offered as teaching manuals.

Then a new occupant is added to the land. Our eloquent credentials suddenly will be of little value. Our multi level experience could become questionable. When a new arrival glides to earth, everything will change in a hurry.

It is an awesome experience holding an infant for the first time. Our emotions will routinely dictate our reactions. This is because our feelings are now in control. These precious moments are usually filled with anxiety and nervousness.

All text book researches could evaporate like a vapour. Our previous knowledgeable insights could become antiquated. Enhanced diligent child caring techniques could suddenly be redundant. Every child is distinctly unique. Their individual needs are different. There are no universal treatment plans.

"One method fits all" philosophy will not work. We are one of a kind. They are one of a kind. We need to understand this fact. We should internalize this reality. Each occupant should be recognized as being different. They should be dealt with accordingly.

Every new little citizen sets their own guidelines. They come with new sets of challenges. We will now have new obligations. We will encounter fresh mandates. And there will additional responsibilities. Parenting is a "hands on" learning experience. It is an on the job training adventure.

Parents tend to ignore early signs of defiance. Our bundle of joy is too cute to do any wrong. We oftentimes downplay our concerns. Most of us will silence warning bells. Many will turn a blind eye instead. We could frequently make excuses for their inappropriate behaviors.

We usually disregard their small acts of disobedience. We could instead try to rationalize these mini acts of rebellion. We tend to label them as normal trials. We could mistakenly put them in the "mini terrible" department.

We sometimes laugh at these disruptive behaviors. We oftentimes term them silly. We tend to cater to their inappropriate wants. Sometimes we pacify their temper tantrum rants. But they are testing us. And they are determined to win.

Boisterous behaviour is a normal part of any infant's life. This sometimes stressful phase is understood to some degree. It is basically an accepted norm within any culture. This is a process that every child will go through. But this is a manipulative tactic. They just want to see if we will fall victim to their dramatic antics.

Their rebellious rumbles will be temporary. Eventually they will get tired from their kicking. Their screaming episodes will eventually put them to sleep. They will quickly learn our expectations. And they will fall back in line with our guidance. But seldom do we just watch from a safe distance.

We should never ignore the onset of our child's disruptive behaviour. We should never label our children as little terrors in training. Acting out behaviours should never be condoned. They should never be deemed acceptable. Unfortunately oftentimes they are tolerated as growing up pains.

It can be a nerve wracking experience for parents and care givers, when infants and toddlers begin to intermingle with their environment. Most little people are naturally active and rambunctious. They will meddle with everything that they can get their hands and mouths on. They will break anything that is not firmly nailed down.

Too often we over compensate our disorderly young. We often term them the "bad little baby" syndrome. Oftentimes we end up under reacting to them. We could make fun about our "bad little baby's" antics. We will have missed the mark. We should have disciplined our "bad little baby's" bad behavior.

Society will accept most infant's disruptive behaviors. This melodrama is understood. It is the child vying for attention. Oftentimes we will act and react mostly with humor. We routinely watch infants flaring around on the floor. Many will ignore their screaming and hollering.

There are times when we could get annoyed and frustrated, dealing with our pesky little meddlers. But we should never respond by becoming heavy handed or punitive. They can only learn by experimenting. We should lovingly but firmly monitor their activities.

The inappropriate behaviour of a two year old is sometimes tolerated. Small delinquent actions of age three to five are oftentimes minimized or overlooked. Deviant behaviours in older children should follow stricter disciplinary guidelines. We should never sweep inappropriate behaviours under the rug. We should always promptly address them.

Children begin vying for independence at a very tender age. Their tiny mind will instruct their developing brain to start investigating their surroundings. It is usually during these early periods, that our angels begin to forcefully express their opinions and displeasure. This is when they will begin to interfere with things that are not appropriate or safe.

It is at this stage when the word "don't," can become a permanent part of a parent's vocabulary. But children always need a safe and stable environment. This will give them the security to explore and learn. A disruptive household will encourage instability and negativity in their lives. We should be mindful that children learn by mimicking the actions of parents, adults, or older siblings.

Society will respond differently to our "should know better" child. Lashing out would not be condoned. Smashing items would not be tolerated. This child would be treated in a whole different way. Immediate action would be taken to correct this inappropriate occurrence.

A zero tolerance policy could be imposed. Responses could be harsh. Our out of control child would be held accountable. Their punishment could be severe. It could be off to jail and imprisonment. This most likely would be an appropriate related consequence. Our delinquent child could suffer gravely for their wrong choice decision.

A volatile family climate will inevitably impair healthy growth and development in children. Parents who are prone to angry outbursts will produce offspring, who are also predisposed to fits of rage. Sometimes children are mystified that they are held accountable, for inappropriate behaviours that had become entrenched in their system. Countless children oftentimes suffer because of their parents' unruly behaviours.

Monitoring our children and setting appropriate standards; should begin during their formative years. We should effectively deal with unhealthy behaviors at this tender age. This will be positive nurturing. Negative behavior resurfacing should be minimized. Rebellion should not be a point of contention at older ages. This should avoid heartaches for our children and for our self.

Accurately understanding infants can be very complex. Deciphering mixed messages can be confusing. We will struggle with trials and errors. We will fumble. And we will stumble. Eventually we will understand these intense challenges. In due time, we should recognize wrong choices easier. We should be able to plan the right path. But we should always rely on God for guidance.

Our job description to care for, and nurture our children was written by God Himself. No earthly title that can be compared to the serious responsibilities of being a parent. The dedication and diligence required to be an effective care giver, can be overwhelming at times. Multi tasking is not an expectation. It is a way of life.

Some parents put their lives on hold, and focus exclusively on child rearing. Scripture tells us to train up our children in the right and proper way. Nowhere is it suggested or implied that we should deny ourselves the necessities of life. We cannot adequately care for our children if we neglect to care for ourselves. Whatever we do, should be done in moderation.

The Spirit of God should always be the guiding beacon in our lives. We should concentrate on His Living Word as our focal point. God should be the correcting force behind everything that we undertake. His assurances should be the center piece of our sincere commune with Him. He will teach us how to persevere amidst adversities. God will encourage us how to maintain a balanced lifestyle.

These are binding assurances that we have from our most High God. Our only requirement is to concentrate on our most important lifelong responsibility. This is to guide and nurture a new generation in the right and proper way. Unfortunately, many parents get sidetracked and pressured by influences outside of Spiritual guidelines.

Being blessed with the responsibility of diligently molding a new life; is an awesome honour and privilege. Carefully structuring positive influences in a child has to begin from infancy. If major internal imbalances surface during latent years, the parents will have erred in judgment at some point.

Sometimes the guidelines for living can become blurred, complicated and confusing. Circumstances and situations can pressure us into making survival decisions. Oftentimes these conditions do not meet our ideal criteria. But at times we have to settle for second best.

Parents have to make a living like everyone else. The workforce will rarely give special allowances, to those who also have to tend to the needs of their family. Employees are expected to perform to the maximum requirement. Otherwise a termination letter will send us to the back of the unemployment line.

The economy is rebounding from a very painful recession. But many employers still behave as if a collapse is still impending. Some will use this as an excuse to saddle their employees with additional gruesome tasks. It is not unusual for a worker to be burdened with responsibilities designed for multiple assignments.

A heavier workload will mean more hours spent on the job. Many parents exhaust a lot of time toiling to complete a day's work. This will obviously drastically shorten the quality time we have for our children. These are the realities for many working parents.

Stress and strain will eventually take a toll on our body. Being overtired will cause our system to start shutting down. We obviously will be dead tired when we get home. But oftentimes our children will be anxiously waiting for our return.

They gladly greet us at the door. They immediately express their love for us. Their body language tells us that they are starved for our affection and embrace. But all we want to do is unwind, and plan for tomorrow. We could become aggravated and irritated. We could respond to them in an impolite manner because of emotional fatigue.

Our dialogue could sound like incoherent grunts and groans. We could unintentionally become hostile towards them. This would make them feel alienated and rejected. They could retreat from us highly offended. They could begin to feel unimportant.

We eventually will fall asleep, sometimes burdened with mixed feelings. Our children will go to bed feeling distraught and lonely. We tended to our needs today. Our children tended to themselves today. No parent tended to the needs of their children today.

There is a monstrous hurdle challenging all human beings. This is the relentless manipulation to conform to the dictates of the world. Society exalts productivity and glorifies success. This entrenched rule basically covers all aspects of the public and private sector. Many parents can feel compelled to push themselves to exhaustion to conform to the standards and expectations of others. We will become a casualty by listening to the dictates of society. The blame will lay exclusively with us, when we permit worldly influences to control us. It is impossible to be faithful to God, and prioritize materialism all at the same time. We will be setting ourselves up for unnecessary heartaches.

We should never swap our family responsibilities for financial gains. But oftentimes the demands of our job could conflict with the needs of our family. We always need to focus on which is more important. We could hate our job and love our family. We could love our job and tolerate our family. We could end up losing both family and job.

Maintaining healthy balances can become complex and confusing. We have to work to afford food and shelter. Juggling work and parenting is never easy. It is presumed that issues are tougher when we are single parents. Single parents and couples face similar battles and challenges.

Child rearing is always hectic. Family life can be taxing. The stresses on full time employed couples can be tremendous. Single parents encounter similar hurdles. Our children can fall through the cracks when our choices are limited. They will lack consistent positive input. This could put them at risk to be damaged by negative influences.

We will make money as long as we live. We will lose money as long as we breathe. Our children are always observing and growing. They will mature with or without our positive input. We are afforded one clear window of opportunity. This is to instill positive values in them.

We could create untold grief for everyone if we sidestepped our obligations. Our offspring could run afoul with the law. They could become casualties of society. We could exert a lot of energy on damage control. We could desperately try to keep them from jail time. Lawyers are expensive.

Our savings could be depleted. We could lose everything. We could spend numerous years reflecting on what might have been. We can always regain lost revenue. But money cannot compensate for a ruined young life.

Money cures all ills. This is a lie. The world sold us this rubbish. A lot of us have bought this fiction. Money is never the answer to everything. Our love for our family should be more important than money.

We have been indoctrinated that we should stock pile for our offspring. We are told that they will understand. This also is hog wash. Our children learn by observing us make healthy balances. This will prepare them for the future.

We need to make a living. But we need to give them their fair share. They need our affection and attention. They will be happy with us. They will appreciate our values. They will understand that they are more important than us acuminating wealth.

This world is grossly unfair. There are no quick fix answers. There are no miracle remedies to the disparities in society. But this is the universal truth: It is impossible for our children to properly train up themselves. The world will bludgeon their survival instincts.

Our offspring will always fail relying solely on themselves. They need our love. They need our protection. And they need our positive dedicated influences. They are always observing and learning from us. They will mature as balanced or unbalanced members of society.

Every offspring has certain mandated responsibilities, and obligations to their parents. They are the first persons that children bond with from infancy. We the children begin life by adoring and clinging to our parents for comfort. Unfortunately some parent and child relationships get estranged, as youngsters grow and mature.

The scriptures give specific instructions to children: "Children, obey your parents in the Lord: for this is right." Ephesians 6 verse1

Some children can get very defensive when their parents quote scripture to them. Many behave as though their parents are brainwashing and manipulating them. But every child should always listen to, and obey their parents. Obedience is virtually impossible when defiance and disobedience becomes a major stumbling block.

Friction and tension will be minimized within the household when we abide by our parents' expectations, and follow their guidelines. Our parents are not our enemies. But sometimes they will need to firmly admonish us when we get involved in inappropriate behaviours. They have been around longer than us. They can visualize potential dangers. Their duty is to protect us from the demons of life.

Ephesians 6 verse also instructs all youngsters: "Honour thy father and mother; which is the first commandment with promise;"

We honour our parents when we learn to appreciate their roles as our guardians and protectors. We will hold them in high esteem when we understand the decent values they are trying to instil in us. We will gladly absorb their priceless words of wisdom as we grow older. We will be blessed with a happy and fruitful life. Our descendants will be recipients of a rich inheritance.

Every parent also has certain mandated obligations and responsibilities to their children. It is the duty of every parent to be nurturing, kind, and compassionate to their offspring. We should always be willing to listen to our young. Our most important role is to lovingly guide these little people, by instilling in them Godly standards. Teaching them positive values, will be priceless preparation for adulthood.

Many children tend to get obnoxious and stubborn as they get older. Some could become belligerent and defiant. But deep down, they are yearning for our guidance and support. Parents need to demonstrate empathy and patience. Our child is struggling to cope. We also passed through this phase.

Parents should never respond to their children in a hostile manner. Some parents vent their anger and frustration by hurling insults at their young. Some will resort to using the most demeaning and vilest vulgar language, to verbally chastise their young. They end up shaming themselves. They are now parents in bad standing.

No parent should ever provoke their child to anger and wrath. They should never embarrass their offspring by berating them. They should never degrade them by belittling them. Some youngsters could take extreme measures to retaliate.

Parents are expected to be positive role models. They should behave in like manner.

Parents should never attempt to control children through fear and intimidation. Brute force will compel them to comply. But they could end up resenting and hating us. Sadly some parents are bent on being dictators. Their behaviour can make them oblivious, of the long term damage that their dictatorial attitudes can cause.

Our conscience is our spiritual guidance system. This internal probe will eventually convict young and old. But it is more pronounced in older folks. Some parents will be overcome with guilt after they have behaved dishonourably. Some will try to redeem themselves by showering their children with multiple gifts. But oftentimes the damage will have already been done.

Most children are happy to receive gifts, especially from their parents. But presents will not ease their pain when they are experiencing emotional distress. They could begin to internalize that their parents hated them. Deep distrust could erode parent and child relationship.

Trust is not a shelf commodity that can be bought or sold. It has to be earned. It is extremely difficult to regain our children's trust, after some parents have physically or verbally abused them. One violent episode by parents or caregivers can permanently scar a child's self esteem and self worth. There are many grieving adults meander though life because of pent up bitterness.

Family obligations and responsibilities should be joint expectations. Children are required to abide by the appropriate behavioural standards set by their parents. Parents should set above reproach standards for themselves. They should positively lead by example. Children will from time to time rebel. But a healthy environment will stabilise the stormy periods of living.

Chapter Twenty-Three
Always Remain Focused.

WE SHOULD ALWAYS BE MOVING progressively forward in life. We should always maintain a positive outlook. We should consistently be motivated. We should be focused and disciplined. We should be dedicated and determined in pursuit of our goals. And we should always demonstrate and eagerness and willingness to learn. This will enable us to succeed.

It is our right to strive for greatness. This should be our earnest desire each and every day. We should be excelling as long as we live. This should be our noble ambition. It is our duty to be the best we can. We should always concentrate on our abilities. We should always maximize our God given talents.

We may be actively and aggressively exploring methods to improve ourselves. We may be pursuing our life's dream. We may perceive this to be our most important desire. This should be our ultimate goal. This should afford us a yearned for affluent lifestyle.

We had commenced our journey as a numbered employee. Our career had started in the mail room. Then God's Spirit breathed on us. Our commitment dedication and planning brought positive results. Our dream is now a reality. We now own the company. We are the president of this ultra powerful conglomerate.

We should be overwhelmed with joy. This experience should be truly heartwarming. We should be justifiably contented. We should begin to live our dream. We had fought long and hard. We have finally arrived at this well deserving moment. No one is going dampen our happiness. We have rightfully earned this quality of life status.

It is our right to feel proud of our accomplishments. We should immediately thank God. We should claim this reality. We should embrace this feeling. We should cherish this moment. We should then begin to live this new era. Moving ahead in life is our responsibility. We should always embrace success. None of us should ever forget this fact.Finally arriving at this point will be an amazing feat. It will be the first hurdle completed. It is imperative that we remain level headed. Humility should be our focus when we reach to important bench mark. We should also keep images alive of how we got here. This will demonstrate our resolve and our commitment. Our continued success will depend on these factors.

We should be keenly mindful of the anchoring system behind our success. Any other route could be inviting disaster. It is never an easy task climbing to the top. But we can easily slip at the top. One mistake could result in us tumbling to the bottom. This would be a free fall. And it would be painful. We should never forget these facts.

We should never get caught up in egotistic attitudes. We should never deliberately showcase ourselves. We should not dwarf or discount our support system. Otherwise we could lose our sense of balance. We will lose focus when our balance is impaired. We could begin to bump into walls.

We should always put God in the equation. It was Divine help that got us thus far. An irresponsible attitude would be a recipe for failure. We should never get swell headed. We should not take our success for granted. Stupidity can be our downfall if we embrace this mindset.

Arrogance can cause us to sidestep our moral and ethical duties. We are now expected to be role models. But we could become insensitive in our interactions. We could become self centered and egotistic. Our peers will begin to be disgusted with us.

We should always make arrangements for quality family involvement. But we could lose perspective. We could put our family on hold. This would be a huge mistake. Our loved ones will be watching us. Our most important duty is to our family. We should never minimize our responsibilities. We will become seriously maladjusted if we ignore our family.

Self exaltation will put us on the negative watch list. We should never substitute our intimate relationship for financial gains. Our spouse could become resentful. Strife and bitterness could impede honest dialogue. This could put a huge strain on the family unit.

We could start drifting apart. Our relationship could fall on hard times. Unfaithfulness could rear its ugly head. Our spouse could eventually leave us. Our "for better or for worse" commitment could be ruined. Anger and loneliness could be a brutal reminder of our mistakes.

Our children could turn against us. They could blame us for the breakup of their family. They could resent being around us. They could begin to hate us for ruining the family. Strife could take control of our fragmented family. Our children could become unmanageable. Their bitterness would be aimed at us.

They could eventually begin to feel abandoned. This would disturb us greatly. We could spend many sleepless nights reflecting. Bemoaning our wrong choices could put us in a depressed condition. Forgiveness from our spouse and our offspring could be a steep mountain for us to climb.

Devastation within an intimate family circle is never an easy bridge to repair. Nothing should ever supersede the needs of our family. We should never repeatedly say "yes" to the world, and "no" to our family. But materialistic enticements can easily corrupt us. We could be saddled with hectic work schedules. But we ought to be careful not to neglect our family. Sometimes we will have to strategize a plan B work sheet. Sometimes it is necessary to designate a trusted experienced adult. Their role should be tending to the needs of our family in our absence. This arrangement should be appropriate under these conditions. But we will need to remain clearly focused. The demands of our job should never conflict with the needs of our family.

Professionals of the highest caliber could care for our children. But we are the parents. We should never function as absentee caretakers. We would be setting ourselves up for untold calamities. Our children deserve our positive involvement in all areas of their lives.

We should be available to them on a consistent basis. This means under all conditions. They will learn by watching us. Our positive examples are their greatest teachers. They always should see us fulfilling our duties and responsibilities. They will also observe how their parents relate to each other.

They need to see us interacting positively with each other. We need unconditional love and affection from each other. We need to show each other commitment and respect under all conditions. We should always treat each other with understanding and dignity. Our children will feel secure.

Our family duties are crucial. Our responsibilities are not part time jobs. Casual labor is not part of our job description. Fulfilling our obligations is not an absentee vocation. Neither is it a silent partner inactive commitment. We are required to be active and visibly committed.

God expects us to provide a loving and caring atmosphere for our family. We should always be available to tend to their needs. Our Maker knows that we will never be perfect. We will always be part of His training program. But we must always cultivate an eager to learn attitude.

We could learn a lot from other life forms in the wild. We might consider them primitive. But their parenting skills are superb. They take their responsibilities seriously. The parents are always committed to consistently meet all the needs of their young.

They exhibit excellent nurturing and grooming skills. They take meticulous care in selecting the proper foods for their infants. All nutrients are screened before being fed to the offspring. A wrong diet would be disastrous. Preserving their species is very important. These fragile babies will eventually become their parents' replacement in the wild kingdom.

God gave us dominion over all species on earth. He designed us superior to them. But most species take better care of their offspring than many human beings. Like the creatures the wild, God expects us to diligently care for our young. We ought to be feeding them physical and spiritual contamination free foods. But we must be willing to do the necessary preparation.

It is our duty to prepare fertile soil for our children. Our children need and deserve the best. We should always be planting healthy seeds for them. But we first must irrigate and prepare the ground. We are the ground. God expects us to be contamination free. It will become problematic if we are badly polluted.

We should separate the wheat and the tare in our lives. We should burn the tare. We should plant the wheat only. Our wheat should be disease free. They should grow and flourish. This is called responsible parenting.

We should harvest the pure wheat. Everyone should reap healthy grains. Our spouse should be satisfied. Our children should eat in abundance. They all should ingest healthy nutrients. They should be now be feasting off the fat of the land. Their lives should be enriched. They should feel satisfied and secure.

Sadly; we could encounter a huge problem. We could end up planting wrong seeds. We could even forget where and when we had planted. We could plant the wheat and the tare together. It would be a disaster come harvest time.

Feeding time could pose a problem. We would be unsure what we had reaped. We would not know what we were feeding our family. Things could become even more chaotic. We could end up serving contaminated substance. This would be a disaster.

We will damage our family when we feed them unhealthy foods. We should always scrutinize the types of seeds we implant. We should be extremely selective. We should be vigilant. Wrong seeds for us will mean wrong seeds for our family.

Fertile soil and healthy seeds will produce a good crop. Inferior soil and decaying seeds will produce a bad crop. Harvest time will come and go. Tabulating the plusses against the minuses will determine if we had a good or bad season.

Many of us are ambling aimlessly through life. Some picked up multiple bad habits. They eventually could become part of our makeup. Over time we could distribute them to others. Our family could become the unwilling recipients of negative influences. They could become casualties.

A lot of us are quick to tabulate the flaws of our spouse. Yet some of us will refuse to retire issues that accompanied us into our relationship. Many of us find it difficult to admit that we too are flawed. Some conveniently forget that they too had baggage when they joined hands.

Before our children there was us. Everything started with us as a couple. There are times when some of us lose sight of this fact. Some of us develop amnesia. But the whole process was put in place by us two. We eventually made the decision to tackle life in unity and honesty.

We all enter into relationships carrying separate assorted luggage. Eventually we will have to open our mixed merchandise bags. An honest relationship demands that we patently sort out all our baggage. We should tag the usable and reusable bags. We should put them aside. These we will sort through for current and future meaningful usage.

We then should gather the damaged goods. These burdensome excesses should be deposited in another pile. We should put them all together. Then we should burn this garbage. We should watch together as they become ashes.

We all enter relationships with our preferences and our biases. This is normal. This is a part of us. We are our present and our past. We will need to discuss our likes and dislikes. Then we will need to come to an understanding. There should be no hidden agendas when we tabulate our assets and liabilities.Some of us emerge from a large family. An outgoing personality could be second nature to us. Some are from an only child family. We could be less energetic to freely mingle and socialize. These issues should be discussed at an early stage. We should honestly acknowledge each other's strengths and weaknesses. Then we should come to an understanding and agreement.

Some parents enjoy molding their children in accordance with their customs. Those from large families tend to embrace this tradition. Some parents could be uncomfortable with this practice. It could be a drastic departure from their accustomed lifestyle. They could feel more comfortable focusing solely on their immediate family.

This obstacle could pose serious conflicts. It is imperative that we sort these issues out. Then we should arrive at a compromise. Potential conflicts should be sorted out before we introduce children to our union. Our focus should be on what is best for us and our offspring.

It is essential that together we work through our differences. Only then can we proclaim that we are truly one. Stability should always govern our relationship. It will be easier for our offspring to conform to our values and our structures.

Some cultures practice the extended family setting. This is their norm. There is presumably less pressure on one couple in these environments. Reliable adults are readily available to offer support and guidance. Many are also excellent mentors.

The boundaries are normally well defined within the confines of this culture. The extended family structure is usually tight knit. Our offspring is always included. They are embraced in this community. They are also an intricate member of a much larger extension. A positive support system is routinely always on call.

Children tend to be evenly developmentally balanced within this environment. Tending positively to their needs is rarely a complex issue. Neither is it a burdensome task. It is a shared responsibility. These youngsters tend to intermingle easily. They have more spiritual and emotional resource tools available. This support system is readily accessible to them.

The functions of the extended family should be a safe haven. Everyone should be above reproach. But it behooves parents to exercise wisdom. We should prudently and vigilantly exercise discretion and caution. We still should monitor our children.

We should always thoroughly investigate their daily exposures. Godly influences could be ever so present. Exceptionally good intentions could be overflowing. But there also can be devastatingly evil and demonic disasters lurking. We should never forget that we are primarily responsible for the protection of our children.

Some cultures practice the nuclear family structure. A nuclear family could consist of a single parent and offspring. It could also be a couple and offspring. Sometimes this is the norm versus the exception.

The borders of the nuclear family can be somewhat confining. Distance oftentimes could separate them from family and friends. Nuclear families tend to rely heavily on each other for support. They sometimes function with limited resources. This can put strain on the family.

The nuclear family is supposed to be close knit. But things could get hectic if tempers flared. A neutral referee could be hard to find. The family could become isolated. This could put excessive strain on the family unit. Daily healthy living could become challenging. Prioritizing effectively could be an uphill battle. They could implode at times. This could construct a major barrier.

Families can experience hardships by not having a viable support system. A spiritual and emotional vacuum could develop. They could feel like they were walking a tight rope without a balancing pole. Severe damage could occur if someone fell off the rope. The family could suffer hard to repair casualties.

There is nothing wrong with the nuclear setting. This could be a chosen way of life. This could be an inherited lifestyle. But togetherness should be the key to success. Most of us have done exceedingly well within this community. A multitude of us have emerged exceptionally well balanced. Some have graduated with exceptional excellence.

Some are success stories of the extended family environment. Some are success stories of the nuclear family community. But our major success will be the positive values our offspring inherited from us. This will be our ultimate important achievement. We will be remembered for these assets.

God designed the blue print for family planning. He cemented the foundation. He supplied the building blocks to house our family. We are responsible for firmly cementing our family structure. Our children are recipients of a healthy lifestyle because of us.

Chapter Twenty-Four
Casualties

SOME COULD REASON that Jacob's parents chose a nuclear family lifestyle. Some could conclude that Isaac and Rebekah kept to themselves. This could have put tremendous strain on their relationship. Problem solving could have been problematic. The Holy Book is silent on why parents adopted this living arrangement. But their chosen way of life almost destroyed their family.

Jacob had endured numerous painful experiences. He had encountered severe hardships. He had lived through hell on earth hard times. These were self inflicted burdens. They were related consequences because of his evil mindedness.

God granted Jacob the opportunity to clean up his act. He successfully mended fences with his brother Esau. But disturbances continued to plague Jacob's family. Problems resulting in severe casualties became permanent fixtures in Jacob's life.Some issues were more serious than those of his grandmother Sarah. They were worse than Esau's birthright that he had claimed ownership to. It was more damaging than when he formed a devious alliance with his mother, and stole Esau's blessing.

Dianah was Jacob's only daughter. She became the first casualty when she relocated to her new community. She apparently ventured out alone to visit with her peers. This proved to be disastrous for her. She was raped by the prince's son of that country. He developed affection for her after she was molested. He then asked his father's permission to take Dianah as his wife. (Genesis 34 verses 1-4)

Jacob heard about this horrible deed. But he remained silent until his sons returned from the field. Her brothers became angry when their father relayed the incident to them. The prince pleaded with Jacob to permit his son to marry Dianah. But there was a major problem. The men of the country were uncircumcised.

The prince met with his men. He suggested that all males be circumcised. This would enable his son to marry Jacob's daughter. There was some negotiation. An understanding was reached. All the men agreed. And all were circumcised. But sons Simeon and Levi were not satisfied with this arrangement.

They were still furious. So they had a change of mind. They violently attacked and plundered the city on day three. This was while the men were still sore from circumcision. They slew all the males including the prince and his son. They then took their sister back home. (Genesis 34 verses 5-26)

Jacob was greatly distressed by the actions of his sons. He feared reprisal from the surrounding cities. He made the decision to immediately relocate. God gave Jacob and his entourage safe exit. The Lord terrorized the surrounding cities. Jacob and his family journeyed safely to Bethel.

God again appeared to Jacob. The Almighty told Israel (Jacob) to relocate to the land that He had given Abraham and Isaac. Most loved wife Rachael gave birth to another son en route to their new destination. She died shortly after childbirth. Before her death she named the baby Benoni. Meaning: "Son of my sorrow." His father renamed him Benjamin. Meaning: "son of my right hand."

Israel continued on his journey. He pitched tent beyond the tower of Edar. It was here that first born Reuben transgressed against God and his father. This was a vile and despicable act. He became intimate with his father's concubine Bilhah. (Genesis 35 verse 22)

This was an act of open disgrace. It was also the lowest form of disrespect. Rueben had shamed his father. He had defiled his father's bed. Jacob heard about this hideous act. It must have grieved him to the depths of his soul. But the bible is silent on how father initially reacted, to this deplorable incident.Jacob eventually was reunited with father Isaac. The Bible is silent as to how this reunion went. Isaac died at age one hundred and fourscore years. Esau and Jacob buried their father.

God had bestowed much favor on Jacob. He was still alive by the grace of God. He should by now have gotten tired of his former rotten lifestyle. He should have rid himself of them. He should have learned from his mistakes. Jacob should by now have learned healthy habits. He should have turned his life around.

Jacob should now be a better role model for his children. He should have been teaching them how to avoid repeating his unhealthy lifestyle. They could have been spared the harsh consequences of duplicating his turbulent lifestyle. But he obviously wasn't listening to his God. He just refused to let go of most of his old self.

Jacob carried his burdensome past with him. He began to reactivate harmful blunders. His first mistake was to enshrine Joseph in over protectiveness. This was a repeat of his mother's mistakes. Jacob now created an environment for Joseph to become a casualty.

Father granted extra privilege status to this young lad. This created instability in the household. A disruptive atmosphere now threatened the stability of the family. Sibling revolt began to fester. Joseph was now at risk to be hurt. Excessive smothering was about to seriously damage Joseph.

Joseph was second to last in the family pecking order. But he received more attention than his older brothers. The other children undoubtedly felt alienated. This created a climate of resentment. Jacob's actions birthed major imbalances within the family structure.Jacob added fire to his sons' fury. He built a coat of many colors for Joseph. This further fanned the flames of animosity. This fueled hotter rage. The older brothers would have felt totally discarded. They probably concluded that Joseph was the showcase of the family. A showdown was now in the making.

Joseph also created problems for himself. He should have known that his brothers envied him. He should have been well aware that they were jealous of his special status. This glaring fact obviously did not disturb him. He could have been living in fantasy land.

Joseph displayed a lofty attitude toward his brothers. Plus he was always having dreams. These dreams portrayed him as being superior to them. He relayed these dreams to brothers. This was very bad for Joseph. They hated him more. Sibling wrath erupted against Joseph. (Genesis 37 verses 3 to 11.)

Joseph's brothers were out working in the field. They were tending to their father's flock. Jacob commissioned Joseph to spy on his brothers. His brothers saw him coming from afar. They began to mock his dreaming abilities. Their pent up rage reached boiling point. Ten brothers eventually ganged up against Joseph.

Joseph was likely labeled an arrogant fool. And brothers' negative perceptions kept on gathering steam. They could have been plotting revenge for a very long time. Their pent up hostilities finally reached boiling temperatures. Their pressure cookers exploded with a violent bang.

Their emotions collided head on. Hostility towards Joseph increased. Things quickly turned ugly. They all developed a one accord evil mind. Wrath now took complete control. His brothers became insanely furious. They suddenly decided to murder Joseph.

Oldest brother Reuben quelled this mutiny. They instead threw Joseph in a pit. They likely intended to leave him there. They then noticed a group of approaching Ishmeelites. Their caravan was headed for Egypt. Brothers sold Joseph to these Ishmeelites for twenty pieces of silver.

Joseph was now a slave. His new masters were Ishmeelites. Were not the Ishmeelites from the tribe of Ishmael? Ishmael was Isaac's half brother. Would it be safe to conclude that Joseph was sold to his flesh and blood?

Ten brothers completed their transaction with the Ishmeelites. They then slaughtered a young goat. They smeared the blood on Joseph's coat. They presented Joseph's blooded coat to their father. They then gave a lying report.

They told their father that Joseph had been killed by an evil beast. Jacob would have been obviously stunned. He was exceedingly upset. He could have suffered a fatal heart attack. He mourned the loss of his favorite son for a very long time.

Abraham's third generation recycled evil indulgences. His great grandson Joseph became the newest casualty. God's chosen generation had once more drastically deviated from His covenant. These are some of the tragic results that human reasoning can produce.

It is never easy reversing generations of entrenched negativity. Sometimes it is easier to remain and keep suffering. Many can get complacent with accustomed unhealthy environments. But we could get stuck indefinitely in a comfort zone of irregularity.There are no instant fixes to life's problems. But everything in life comes with a price tag. Some are expensive. Most are not. Good deeds come with an affordable price. Sometimes we are afforded an installment program. But negative behaviours have no resale value.

Joseph's mother had died while he was still young. Jacob probably reasoned that Joseph was helpless and defenceless. He could have concluded that he needed to shield his love child from danger. Father likely didn't trust his older sons. Jacob could have been consistently intervening on Joseph's behalf.

We could explore countless probabilities. These theories would crumble under minute scrutiny. Jacob was the problem. He alienated the rest of his sons. He embraced an above reproach treatment for Joseph. This was bound to mushroom into emotional upheavals. Jacob inadvertently set Joseph up for an agonizing fall.

Joseph could be classified as a spoiled brat. His father instilled in him a false sense of self importance. Joseph obviously loved and adored his father. He could have felt justified with his special treatment status. But he was also to be blamed.

He refused to activate his right versus wrong inbred instincts. He suppressed his God infused right choices. He silenced his conscience. Instead he remained in his well fortified cocoon. He embraced a life of wall to wall protection. He displayed selfishness and an air of aloofness.We all need an earthly teacher. Learning is difficult without guidance. But not everyone is a good instructor. Jacob was a bad tutor. And Joseph misguidedly embraced his toxic environment. He could have perceived this to be a less problematic path. Facing growing up challenges could conveniently be put on hold.

It is our duty to instill Godly values in our children's lives. We should begin grooming them during their infant years. Our instruction manual gives us clear guidelines regarding this. This will glue together a rich resource bank. This will enable them to utilize a firm foundation as they get older.

The bible gives specific instructions pertaining to youth. It speaks candidly about the benefits of getting older and wiser. But the bible is basically silent on the years between being young, and getting older. We could label this period as our in between years. We all fall into this category. No one can escape this cycle.

Our rebellious nature wakes up when we begin to explore life. Unhealthy behaviors could intensify as we get older. We could start ignoring our foundation structures. We could develop a "know it all" mindset. We could start believing this. We could begin acting accordingly. We could easily fall by the wayside.

We could become pig headed. We could become strong willed. We could become puffed up. We could turn our back on wisdom. We could give understanding a bad makeover. We could begin to dialogue in self righteous terms. We could easily confuse our left and right turns.

Our in between years are always problem prone. We could stray miserably off course during these periods. Unhealthy indulgences will always escalate. We will blunder repeatedly. We will create needless heartaches for ourselves. We will drift aimlessly without knowledge. Sometimes we will collide. We could suffer immensely. We could easily fall victim to the dictates of our flesh. Our abnormalities could stretch to the entrance of hell's gate. We could exhaust countless years chasing the pleasures of this world. Some of us will trample on our moral and ethical responsibilities. This would be insane. We will be hit by that word called stupidity. Stubbornness will rub our nose in the mud. The bible is assuredly the wisest book ever written. There has to be a reason why it is silent on our between years. God gives us a lot of latitude. But we are expected to make healthy choices. This includes our in between years.

Most of our devious nature is magnified during our in between years. We could be considered a risky investment during these years. Our parents will consistently warn us about life's pitfalls. This could have little impact on most of us. Some will refuse to listen to words of wisdom.

Many will keep on plowing ahead aimlessly. Some of us could treat our parents as antiques. We could start believing that our generation has all the answers to life. We will finally have a show down with the world. Our brutal collision could make headlines. But this one thing is sure. We will over time get older. Hopefully we will be wiser.

Eventually we could have to make some difficult decisions. Right choice reasoning will never change. This will pull us from the brink of disaster. We will be happy to return to solid ground. We will gratefully thank God for praying people.

Many of us will suffer severely during our in between years. Then some of us will eventually limp back to our roots. Hopefully we should have learned from our mistakes. We should now be back on the banks of sanity. Most of us will apologize to our parents. We will thank them for not giving up on us. They will embrace us. Then they will point us back to God.

We will now acknowledge a forgotten truth. Our situations were not unique. Our parents had also taken a flight from life. They also had blundered miserably during their in between years. They also had not listened to Godly advice. They also had refuted wisdom principles from their parents.

They also had endured countless harsh winters. They had lived through scorching summers. We are now where they had been. Our fore parents also messed up during their in between years. Their siblings also suffered severe mishaps during their in between years. Most repetitive un-Godly acts occur during our in between years.

Many parents are responsible for coordinating dysfunctional living environments. Some of us could inherit unhealthy lifestyles. We could be involved in family cover-ups. We could be the keeper of dirty little secrets.

Some secrets could begin with us. Our demons can sometimes behead us. This would be horrible for our in between years. The burden of guilt could cripple our ability to function positively. Misery could keep us confined.

Some of our fore parents' siblings brutalized their consciences. They joined forces with evil during their in between years. They held on to harmful secrets. Jacob's sons orchestrated a massive cover up. They concealed the truth about their younger brother. They deliberately lied to their father. They had to live with this lie.

They were saddled with a horrendous burden. Guilt would have plagued them. Daily they had to feel the weight of their diabolical actions. They had to function with this misery. Shame and embarrassment must have tormented them.

This could have felt like a fate worse than death. Sin will never just evaporate. Brothers had badly tarnished their characters. Positive interaction among them could have been extremely strenuous. Straight forward honest communication could have been sporadic. This could have been truly agonizing for them.

Their consciences would have pronounced hard labour prison sentences on them. Daily they watched their father grieve. Honest dialogue with him would have been virtually impossible. This was a below low blow to their father. But they could not turn back the hands of time.

Their anger towards their father was legitimate. He did not evenly distribute positive interactions with his other sons. He had treated them grossly unfairly. Favoritism will always divide and devour. Seething rage knows no boundaries. Any conspiracy is bound to produce stress. It is never easy living under the curse of a lie. Jacob had focused misguided affections on Joseph. He was in effect cloning Joseph. His other sons revolted against him. Selfishness became Jacob's downfall. Losing Joseph gravely wounded him. This hurt more than all his other escapades combined. Jacob was now a broken man.

Repetitious dysfunctions will always recycle and flourish. Destructive disruptions will reproduce and replenish. Amoral lifestyles will quickly gather steam. It will continue to climb the abnormal generational ladder. It can become a deadly virus. It can catapult itself into terror zones. Disproportioned anger always has a catastrophic conclusion.

Raw rage can have a snowball effect. We could be damaged. Those around us could suffer. Our out of control temper will eventually subside. Our heart could convict us. We could become dissatisfied after executing our displaced objectives. Remorse will set in. Regret usually is the aftermath of hard core vengeful vendettas. Our emotions could hold us hostage for many seasons.

The Barricading Yoke of Unforgiveness

Chapter Twenty-Five
Never Give Up

THE BIBLE STATES: "And Joseph was brought down to Egypt: and Potiphar, an officer of Pharaoh, captain of the guard, an Egyptian, bought him of the hands of the Ishmeelites, which had brought him down thither. Genesis 39 verse 1

Joseph's life had taken a rapid downhill spiral. The founder of the tribe of Israel's favorite son was now a slave. And his father was not around to help. Joseph could have thought being thrown in the pit was a prank. But he would have been shocked being sold as a slave.

Now he was alone. And he was defenceless in a strange land. Volumes of thoughts could have circulated though Joseph's brain. And they wouldn't be amicable thoughts toward his brothers. This lad was having a tough time coping with his in between years.

Joseph had every right to be bitter. He could have secretly plotted to one day seek revenge. But he came from a long line of praying families. In spite of their flaws, they never stopped communing with God. This was a good habit Joseph learned from them. He must have cried out to his God during these bewildering moments.

The bible continues: "And the Lord was with Joseph, and he was a prosperous man, and he was in the house of his master the Egyptian." Genesis 39 verse 2

The bible also says: "And his master saw that the Lord was with him, and that the Lord made all that he did to prosper in his hand." Genesis 39 verse3

The Lord God granted Joseph divine status. He bestowed extra special favors on this lad. Joseph's master was pleased with him. His master's household was also pleased with this young fellow. Joseph was quickly promoted. His title was to oversee all the affairs of his employer's household.

Satan was gravely displeased with Joseph's treatment. Joseph had gained trust and respect. This high level of honor and prestige enraged the devil. He had a conversation with Joseph's master's wife. He convinced her mind to join forces with him.

His master's wife aggressively tried to seduce Joseph. She pursued him relentlessly. Joseph declined her sexual advances. Joseph was very straightforward with his employer's wife. This would be an abomination before God. It would also be gross disrespect to his master.

This explanation did not deter her aggressive tactics. She continued to harass Joseph. Compromising in her favor was her goal. She was relentless. Eventually Joseph found himself alone with her. She again offered herself to him. Again he rebuffed her. Then she took her aggression to the next level. She grabbed his garment. He yanked himself free and fled the house.

His employer's wife realized she was holding his garment. She used this piece of evidence against Joseph. She immediately called out to the men in her house. She reported to them that Joseph had attempted to seduce her. And she had his garment to prove her point. She also relayed this false information to her husband. He was understandably exceedingly angry and disappointed with Joseph.

He had his slave thrown the king's prison. This accusation could have gotten Joseph executed. But the Spirit of the Living God intervened. Joseph's sentence was commuted to a temporary prison term. The Lord remained with Joseph. And

He blessed him. God granted him special treatment with the prison guards.

Joseph had rejected Potiphar's wife's sexual advances. His actions were based on Godly moral and ethical principles. For this he was framed. He was accused of attempted rape. This was a death sentence crime. And he had no way of proving his innocence.

Joseph was rewarded with evil for doing what was right. The bible makes no mention of Joseph's state of mind surrounding these accusations. But we know that his heart was always in harmony with his Lord. And God was right by his side throughout this ordeal.

Joseph's era has long passed. This is here and now. This is this culture. This is this century. Any of us could get framed for attempted rape. This is not speculation. This is real. And this could happen.

Our employer's wife could develop a mindset like Potiphar's wife. She could make a sexual pass at us. Moral principles would mean nothing to her. She would be furious if we declined her offer. She could end up framing us. We would be powerless to defend ourselves.

We would be terminated from our job. We could even be criminally charged. We could be ruined. Our reputation could suffer severely. Our character could be tarnished indefinitely. Current or future relationships could be jeopardized.

Jesus says: "But I say unto you, that whosoever looketh on a woman (or man) to lust after her (or after him) hath committed adultery with her (or him) already in his (or her) heart." Matthew 5 verse 28

The bible says: "But every man (or woman) is tempted, when he (or she) is drawn away of his (or her) lust, and enticed." James 1 verse 14

Our roving eyes can get us into trouble. Lustful thoughts can give us immense satisfaction. Flattery will tickle our fancy. Sexual temptation is usually hard to resist. Our flesh always loves to take control. We could easily yield to clandestine propositions.

Immoral and unethical behaviors love to mingle and spread bad tidings. Our carnal past never goes to sleep quietly. Secret sins will always walk out of our closet. Everything done in secrecy will always be revealed. Then we will be truly humiliated.

We could blindly drift into a compromising position. It is easy to accept an enticing invitation. Resisting sexual temptations take courage and integrity. The urges of our flesh are always unruly and unpredictable. We could thoughtlessly comply. Our selfish acts could incur irreparable consequences.

We could broaden these real life examples. The scope is large and very wide. Our imagination could gallop wildly. The oversized list of lust is literally endless. Nothing is impossible when our flesh begins to prowl. No one is immune to the power of persuasion.

We could include casual peer relationship flings. It could be an on the job encounter. It could be an off the job arrangement. We could include infidelity to our wife or husband. We could target a tryst with the partner of a close confidant. We could mix in a sexual involvement with our next door neighbor.

God's Tabernacle should be solicitation free. God's home should be protected property. His sanctuary should be neutral ground. It is designed as our safe haven. His temple should be a zero tolerance zone. But infidelity is running rampant in His places of worship. Clandestine perverseness among believers has taken a turn for the worse. Cover up has become galore.

Infidelity among believers is real. And it is dangerous. Scruples will rapidly diminish when our flesh is charged to go. But we will be creating a serious breach in God's kingdom. There will be a brutal backlash. God will always see us. And He knows our names. We eventually will be exposed. The Lord will render unto us appropriate verdicts. Compromising requests will always tickle our fancy. Implementing carnality has no boundaries. The rigorous push to participate is always very powerful. But our egos can ruin us. Lustful seduction is always temporary. Our indiscretions can easily slaughter us. Shame and humiliation would be our just reward.

    Covert indulgencies are never prejudicial. Neither are they gender biased. Sexual propositions could confront any female. They could be hounded relentlessly. They could feel pressured. This could prove extremely stressful. Resisting could be subject to retaliation. But yielding to illicit temptations will always bring disaster. A lie can literally speed up our demise. It can permanently send us to reside on the other side. This could be heaven. Or it could be hell. The school of public opinion is a very battle hardened one. This institution rarely verifies the facts. It can be a nightmare when we are unjustly accused.

    Enduring vile and cruel treatment will always be a humiliating experience. We will feel defiled. We can be forced to live in misery because of a lie. This will be harsh and demeaning. A lie is not an easy distress to reconcile. This is very frightening. It can be life threatening. Forgiveness could be hard to contemplate during these horrible moments.

    Jesus says: "Blessed are they that are persecuted for righteousness sake: for theirs is the kingdom of heaven." Matthew 5 verse 10

    A tantalizing invitation oftentimes is hard to resist. Lust is a powerful emotion. It is never easy to put the gravitational pull of our flesh on hold. It is easy to be slain by desire when the atmosphere of intimacy is appeasing and appetizing. But we should steer clear of anything that would cast ill repute to our character. Our values should be unwavering among our fellow human beings.

    Saying "yes" can be relatively easy. Participating in "yes" can be even easier. But it is easier to turn a "no" to a "yes", than vice versa. We could be ridiculed for taking the moral and ethical high road. We can suffer persecution for our core beliefs and practices. Jesus paved the way before us. He set all the examples that we should follow.Jesus is God in the flesh. We are mere human in dirty clothes. Forgiveness is not an overnight flippant trial and error. It is hard to forgive when we are in the heat of battle. But the need to forgive should always be a compelling choice. We all need peace in our lives. Only God can turn evil into good. Like Joseph, we should always let go of vile accusations.

Handing over our revenge reins might prove difficult. But we always need to surrender that trigger labeled "getting even" to God. We also need to relinquish that gun tagged "revenge." This will give us time to reflect. Jesus is better equipped to handle anger management. He is that Power that is greater than us. Being falsely accused is definitely heartrending. We have little control over bogus claims. Clearing our name can be tedious. But holding on to injustices will only prolong our pain. Living with intense fury can damage our health. Functioning with rage can cripple us.

Our accuser could be stubbornly bent on pursuing false accusations. Legal proceedings could be brought against us. An earthly judge and jury could be convened to decide our fate. Our faith will now be put to the test. But when we trust God, we will always be vindicated. We will groan in gratitude. We will actually feel pity and sadness for our accuser.

This is a glimpse of the perils of being falsely accused. Many have had to endure this brutal injustice. Lives have been ruined. Boiling point indignation would be completely understandable. But we will always need to forgive those who have wronged us. This will lead to God's enduring closure. There is no other recourse that has been offered to us.

Mother Rebekah had shielded and overprotected Jacob. Joseph was a clone in progress. Then he was sold as a slave in Egypt. But he gained instant privilege with his new master. This made him important. It would also have made him influential. Joseph was probably enjoying the same levels of comfort that he was accustomed to at home.

Then Satan visited his master's wife. And everything changed suddenly. He was thrown in prison as a common criminal. Joseph was now essentially as a non entity. He was stripped of everything that had made him special. He was now in a dungeon. His world looked collapsed.

There is no record of Joseph being angry with his God. He never complained. He never sulked. He never murmured. And he was not bitter. He accepted his current predicament. He never ceased to reach out to his God. God was obviously pleased with Joseph. Even in the dungeon Joseph gained favour.Jehovah should be our God when we are prominent. And He should be our God when things get rough. We should trust Him when we are on our mountain tops. And we should hold on to Him when we are in our murky valleys. We should rely on Him when we are being pampered. And we should depend on Him when everyone forsakes us. God will never turn His back on us.

We should thank on Him through good times. We should exercise faith in Him in bad times. God expects us to be reliable and loyal to Him. He will strengthen weaklings. But He will not work through stubborn weaklings. Stripping us is sometimes part of His process. Then He will restore us to higher glory. This is His promise.

The prison guards admired Joseph. They gave him a promotion. Two of Pharaoh's employees, were Joseph's cellmates in the dungeon. One was the king's chief butler. The other was the king's chief baker. Joseph was assigned to supervise his two fellow inmates.

They both had vivid dreams while incarcerated. They were perplexed by their dreams. God had previously blessed Joseph with a special gift. He was able to predict future occurrences via dreams. Now The Lord promoted Joseph. God added the gift of dream interpretation.

Both cell mates relayed their dreams to Joseph. Joseph easily interpreted their dreams. He told the king's chief butler that he would be reinstated in his job. The chief baker's dream meant that he would be executed. Joseph's interpretations proved accurate.

Joseph asked the chief butler to petition to the king for his release. But the chief butler forgot about Joseph's request for clemency. He apparently was too happy to be reinstated in his old job. He didn't deliver Joseph's message to the king.

Joseph languished in jail for being innocent. This was bound to torment him. Joseph wanted his freedom back. God decided that Joseph should remain in prison. We also sometimes will try to wiggle out of God's grasp. But He will keep us confined until He is good and ready.

God would have known Joseph's thoughts. Joseph's mind could have kept on drifting in negative directions. His heart could have gotten polluted. His whole being could have needed purging. God would have deemed it necessary to keep him confined.

This would give Joseph time to focus. He would be able to reflect on his circumstances. He would be able to pray without being distracted. He could peacefully meditate. He would have the opportunity to re-connect with his God. Being confined by God was good for Joseph.

He would be cleansed of unrighteous thoughts. God would purify his messenger's spirit. His soul would be restored to God's grace. He would be re-fashioned. He would become a clean vessel. And God could begin to work through him. Joseph would then be ready to effectively represent the King of kings.Joseph had a coat of many colors. His life was full of many colors. He had more dark shades then bright stripes. All this changed when God took permanent control. Jehovah clothed Joseph in a sparkling robe of righteousness. Joseph was now ready to reflect the true image and likeness of his Maker.

It is vitally important to exercise diligence. We should always wait for God's answer. Being lied on is never an easy cross to carry. We tend to feel abandoned during these trying moments. Loneliness and uncertainty are frightening roads to travel.

We could start relying on ourselves. We could begin to take matters into our hands. But internal burdens can literally destroy us. We should never forget that Jesus is our permanent companion and reliable defender. Joseph was eventually vindicated. He defeated Satan by having faith in his God.

We need to follow Joseph's examples all the time. Our lives could literally depend on the depth of our faith. God will always come to our rescue. He will also rejuvenate us. He will heal our land. He will command our adversaries to be at peace with us.

God will make our enemies our footstool. But we should never resist Him. We should never doubt Him. We should never argue with Him. He will always work with us. He knows us better than we will ever know ourselves. He will always grant to us what is best for us.

He will fix our wronged yesterdays and today. He will brighten our tomorrows. He will transform us to reflect us His dignity and integrity. He will bestow on us highly favored status. He will promote us to positions of honor beyond our wildest dreams.

The bible says: "When my father and my mother forsake me, the Lord will take me up." Psalms 27 verse 10

Joseph's parents did not deliberately forsake him. But they were not around to guide and comfort him during this perilous period in his life. Rachael's death could have left Joseph with feelings of abandonment. The unanswerable "why did this have to happen me," thoughts could have haunted him.

"Why did she have to die so soon" questions could never be answered. More unanswerable questions likely tormented him while he worked for Potiphar. He probably constantly reflected on his family. He must have pondered if his father knew that he was now a slave in Egypt.

These silent questions could have gathered steam during his incarceration. This could have induced roaming feelings of despair. Jacob had been Joseph's backbone. Now he was severed from this vital link. He could have concluded that he was now an orphan. But the Spirit of God was now his mother and his father.

We can easily feel and understand Joseph's pain. Most of us can readily empathize with his plight. We could sympathize with his dilemma. Joseph's woes were horrific. They could have pushed him to insanity and beyond. But Joseph was chosen by God before his birth. He was commissioned by his Maker for a specific task. This was executing the Almighty's agenda throughout Egypt and beyond.

God can choose any of us for an assignment. He will set us apart. He will fix everything in us that needs fixing. He will cleanse and purify us. He will then anoint us. He will consecrate us. He will sanctify us. Then He will bless us. We will now be ready to comply solely with His directives and His objectives.

God knows our spiritual and secular limits. He distributes to us no more than we can handle. God permitted the dire hardships in Joseph's life. He lived with and endured adversity. He probably viewed his life as an uncontrollable uncertain mess. But God never abandoned Joseph. God was grooming and fine tuning his servant. This was a training process that Joseph had to endure.

God is still searching for new recruits. He is still purging. He is still grooming. And He is still fine tuning some of us. He is still looking for pliable people. He will demonstrate His abundant and supernatural manifestations through those whom He chooses. Our 21st century pride is irrelevant to God.

The bible says: "Be strong and of a good courage, fear not, nor be afraid of them: for the Lord thy God, he it is that doth go with thee; he will not fail thee, nor forsake thee." Deuteronomy 31 verse 6.

The bible also says: "And the Lord, he it is that doth go before thee, he will be with thee, he will not fail thee, neither forsake thee: fear not, neither be dismayed." Deuteronomy 31 verse 8

At times we can be bombarded from every conceivable angle with evil. But we should never doubt. And we should never permit fear and fright to conquer us. We should never waver or falter in our faith. God is always well able deliver us from all perils.

We could suffer harsh and unusual restrictions at times. But we should always stand our ground. God is literally a breath away. Our centuries old reckless lifestyles have always caused Him great grief. Our technological advanced age means nothing to God. The Lord still sits on His Righteous Throne.

Jesus still holds us accountable for our wrong choice decisions. He is still sifting through our junk impacted minds. He knows when we are dishonest before Him. And He knows when we are whole hearted commitment to Him.Nobody ever deliberately welcomes problems in their lives. Trials and tribulations can suddenly stop by unannounced. And they could begin to terrorize us anytime. We should never falter during these moments. And we should not get submerged in a pity party. We should be thankful that God has confidence in us.

We will at times experience and endure hurt. Sometimes we will be severely challenged by disappointments. All these measures are appropriate and necessary. God ordained these tests. We should always bury our anchor deep. We should never be intimated by humankind. We should never feel threatened by their vile actions.

Warriors should never run and hide. We should be aligned with the will of God. Humility should be our strength. We should remain clearly focused. God will hide us in His miracle crevice. He will always protect us from lightening storms.

We should refrain from evil indulgences. We should be hush. And we should remain still. We should cling to His promises to protect us. He is always replacing our re-start buttons. He is our rock of ages. He will never leave us in the rain. His blankets will keep us dry.

God will instill within us supernatural courage. His strength will be our might. His wisdom will guide us. He will bestow upon us His power. But we must first ask for forgiveness of our sins. And we must believe that His pardon is everlasting. At His discretion He will install within us insight.

His discipline will be our light by day. His wisdom will be our comfort by night. He will teach us methods to keep Satan at bay. He will infuse within us understanding. God will show us how to put an end to wretchedness. We will meekly say: "Hallelujah to the Lamb of God"

Our biblical ancestors should have shown more restraint when confronted by evil. They should have been more resilient. They should have exhausted more Godly efforts. This would have reversed their negative repetitive pathway. Many innocent lives were badly scarred and mangled. This could have been avoided.

Secular understanding will never unravel God's mysteries. Humankind oftentimes will ask God too many "whys." We just need to reflect on misfortunes and shake our heads. We then need to ask God for clarification. His Spirit will reveal some of His mysteries in due season.

God says: "I form the light, and create darkness: I make peace, and create evil: I the Lord do all these things." Isaiah 45 verse 7

God does nothing by chance. He is never a bad or good luck God. He grants blessings. Or He withholds blessings. He will not bless a dirty mind. He will not sanctify a hardened heart. He oversees all things. He institutes all things. But He has given us the capability to reason. He gave us the ability to make choices.

God knows everything that Satan does. A lot of us blame every disturbance in our lives as being evil. Not every surface level disruption is a problem. God will sometimes place a perceived crisis in our lives. This is necessary to test our obedience to Him.

God put Job through a rigorous re-training program. God told Abraham to kill his son Isaac. He exiled Joseph to Egypt to purify him. He will always put us on the examination table.

God will give Satan the liberty to test our faith. God is harder on His lead shepherds in training. The devil will interpret this as killing time. Satan will inflict double portions of torture. He would love to kill us. But that decision will never be his.

God alone sits at the judgment desk. We should be keenly mindful of this fact. Not every presumed problematic distraction is a dooms day attack. Not every eye level bad situation is necessarily rooted and grounded in evil. Humankind is obsessed with drawing negative conclusions.

Sometimes we needlessly exert our energies running in the wrong direction. We routinely quickly blame every unexplainable disruption on the devil. We love to yell foul. Then we sternly rebuke the enemy. This is not always the case. Sometimes our Higher Power is taking charge. Jehovah will at times employ unusual methods to get our undivided attention.

He will destroy our earthly security blankets. Then He will systematically strip some of us of all our materialistic props. He will dislodge us of all worldly assets. He will wedge us between a rock and a hard place. He will then bring us low. We will now be completely at His mercy. Only then will He begin to work on us.

Most of us have become experts in sweeping issues under the rug. Dirt will not automatically cleanse itself. Our room will get smelly. Eventually we will need to sweep or vacuum clean. It is impossible to permanently hide our problems. The storms of life will not disappear by blocking them out. We can never take a flight from life. But some are gluttons for punishment.

Nobody likes to be exposed to too much heat. But God's purifying vat is extremely hot. It can get messy being on His potter's wheel. But His intense chastisement is always good for us. God is not interested in our moans and groans. Total dependence on Him is His ultimate expectation.

Some stubbornly refuse to swallow God's cleansing medicine. Sometimes our Maker will apply more pressure. Many will resort to game playing. Some will try to jump off His potter's wheel. But God will push us back into His purifying vat. Eventually we will get exhausted.

It is insane to recklessly resist God. His microscope is always probing. We will never be able to sway the mind of God. All we should to do is open our hearts to Him. God chooses those who are pleasing to Him. He will never settle for second best. And we can never out run God.

Chapter Twenty-Six
Triumphing Over Adversatives

The Spirit of God visited the powerful Pharaoh via two visions. They were not pleasant. This king of Egypt was gravely disturbed by these dreams. He probably reflected on them for a while. Then he made a decision.

He summoned all his magicians. He also assembled the wise men of Egypt. He told them all about his dreams. He requested an interpretation. But none could interpret the king's dreams. Then the king's chief butler remembered Joseph. He now relayed Joseph's delayed message to his ruler.

He gave a full report to the king. A Hebrew man had been his cell mate. The chief butler had a disturbing dream in prison. His had relayed his dream to this Hebrew. And his dream was accurately interpreted. This young man was still incarcerated. He was a servant to the captain of the guards.

Pharaoh demanded a meeting with Joseph. They hastily brought him from the dungeon. Joseph shaved and changed his raiment. He was then brought before the king. God's completely refurbished servant now stood before Pharaoh. He was now ready to represent the King of kings.

Joseph was no ordinary prisoner. He was God's anointed. And he was ready for duty. Divine radiance would have covered Joseph from his head to his feet. Pharaoh was likely stunned by Joseph's appearance. The king would have been immediately impressed. Joseph would have gained instant respect and admiration.

The king chit chatted with the prisoner. He had heard about Joseph. He was told that Joseph could interpret dreams. Joseph took no credit for these statements. He told the ruler that it was God who would interpret his dreams. The Egyptian king then repeated his visions to Joseph.

The first dream was about seven fat cattle and seven malnourished cattle. The malnourished cattle came out of the river. They ate the well fed cattle. The second dream was about seven ears of corn on one stalk. And they were healthy. Then seven thin weather beaten ears of corn sprung up. The seven thin ears devoured the seven healthy ears. (Genesis 41 verses 1 to 7)

Joseph wasted no time. Pharaoh's dreams were quickly interpreted. Both dreams were actually one dream. Egypt would enjoy seven prosperous years. Then there would be seven years of famine after this prosperity. This information gravely distressed the king. This was a frightening problem. This was a potential national disaster. But God had a solution to this dire situation.

He used Joseph to show Pharaoh an alternative. Egypt should sow and reap corn in abundance. All the food should be gathered for the seven prosperous years. They should be stored at various locations in cities. There was great urgency to move forward. Preparations should begin immediately. The famine was established by God. And God would bring it to pass shortly.

Capable people would be needed to oversee this massive operation. He advised the king to appoint discreet wise men. The king quizzed his servants. He needed the most qualified person. Pharaoh insisted that this selected individual be spirit filled.

But this was a problem. None of Pharaoh's inner circle was spirit filled. Magicians are never God sanctioned. Earthly wisdom will always remain just that.

Pharaoh's search ended before it started. The most qualified man was standing before him. The decision was easy to make. God's ambassador had put the king's magicians and wise men to shame. Joseph spoke with Godly wisdom. The king appointed Joseph to coordinate all operations. Pharaoh promoted Joseph to rule over all Egypt. Joseph was now second in command. The only person more powerful was the king himself. Pharaoh adorned Joseph in expensive clothing. He placed his ring on Joseph's finger. He put a gold chain around his neck. And Joseph rode in the king's second chariot.

The king also selected a wife for Joseph. Joseph was now fully in charge of all activities in the land of Egypt. And he executed the planning and preparation with Godly precision.

God can promote us as He did Joseph. But we must first meet His standards. And we should let God have His way. We might endure mourning for many nights. But our joy filled days will delete our fretful nights. He will elevate us to sit with kings and queens. We will lead nations in His name. Our prosperity will be a wonder to behold.

The famine came. And the famine spread. The famine quickly covered the land. Hardships for everyone got progressively worse. Many people were now on the verge of starvation. Egypt was the only food source for all the people both near and far.

Other vicinities were also gravely affected. They had to travel to Egypt to purchase grain. Everyone had to be screened by Joseph. His crew was very busy. They were tirelessly processing and selling grain.

One day Joseph got the shock of his life. Ten men showed up to purchase grain. They were his brothers who had sold him into slavery. Joseph immediately recognized them. But his brothers did not recognize him. So Joseph kept his mouth shut.

Many years had passed since his brothers had exiled him. Joseph was thirty years old when Pharaoh made him ruler over Egypt. For seven years prosperity was in abundance under his leadership. Then the devastating famine came. Joseph was by now in his late thirties. And his brothers suddenly reappeared in his life.

God's divine anointing would have been on Joseph. This would have altered his physical appearance. God could have also veiled his brothers' eyes. This would have made it impossible to recognize Joseph. This likely was a bitter and sweet reunion for Joseph.

There could also be other speculations why Joseph was now unrecognizable. But this was the reality: They were here to purchase food. They stood before the second most powerful man in Egypt. He was their literal life support system.

Only he had the authority to authorize their purchase. He alone could grant them this privilege. But he had the absolute power to deny them everything. Denying them food would be a death sentence by starvation. This would spell disaster for Israel. His entire family would not survive this famine.

His brothers were fortunate not to have recognized their younger brother. Recognition would have been dangerous for their health. Fear and fright could have paralyzed them. They could have dropped dead of multiple heart attacks. Trying to flee Egypt would have been futile. Joseph could have gotten them immediately executed.

Joseph used their lack of remembrance to his advantage. He did not communicate with his brothers in their native language. He used an interpreter to converse with them. He began jabbing daggers into the hearts of his brothers. Then he went for their jugulars. He wasted no time going on the offensive. He became extremely hostile to his ten evil brothers.He did his best to belittle them. He viewed them with disdain. He glared at them with hard core suspicion. He barraged them with insults. He hurled wild accusations at them. He angrily questioned their real motivation for wanting to purchase grain. He bluntly accused them of being spies. They now literally feared for their lives.

His brothers volunteered additional information to prove their innocence. They informed Joseph that there were twelve sons from one father. Their father was still alive. One brother was no longer around. The youngest brother still lived at home. But Joseph continued to treat his brothers as spies. Eventually he relented on his accusatory line of questioning.

Joseph demanded the youngest brother be brought to him. This was the only way they could prove their innocence. He imprisoned them for three days. He then released them. His condition was that they bring Benjamin to him. They all agreed.

Then they remembered what they had done to Joseph. They began to lament about the evil way they had treated him. Reuben reminded them that they wouldn't listen. He told them that Joseph's blood was still on their hands.

Joseph overheard their squabbling. He went aside and wept. He regained his composure and rejoined them. He kept Simeon behind. He bound him before their eyes. He then instructed that all their sacks be filled with grain. He also had all their payments returned to their sacks. Then he ordered them from his presence.

His brothers returned home. Bad brothers were more distressed and afraid when they opened their sacks. All their monies were still in their bags. They had received a grain shipment for free. They even now blamed God for their plight. Jacob also became frightened regarding this unexplainable occurrence.

Sons then had a meeting with their father. They briefed him on what had transpired in Egypt. He became extremely angry. He chastised them for divulging too much information. He had lost Joseph. Now he feared losing Benjamin also.

For a long time Jacob wrestled with sending Benjamin to Egypt. Then their food supply began to dwindle. He finally relented. He sent Benjamin to Egypt. Jacob also instructed his sons to take a double portion of money with them. He also sent gifts as a good will gesture.

Nine brothers escorted Benjamin to Egypt. They again all stood before Joseph. Joseph saw his youngest brother. But he remained silent. Instead he left instructions to bring them all to his home. They left with Joseph's steward.

The brothers told the steward about the monies left in their sacks. He calmly lied to them. He told them that their God had given them a treasure for their sacks. He told them that he had taken their money. Simeon was released back to them.

Joseph again greeted brothers when he got home. They presented their gifts to him. Pleasantries were exchanged. He looked at Benjamin again. He then ran to his chambers and wept bitterly. He finally regained his composure and rejoined the group.

They ate. And they drank. Everyone was merry. But Joseph remained mute about who he really was. Instead he instructed that their sacks be filled again with grain. Joseph set his brothers up a second time. But this time he did so with a twist. He commanded that his special silver cup be put in Benjamin's sack. Then he bade them farewell.

He then called his steward. He told him to overtake and apprehend his brothers. His steward was instructed to retrieve the cup from Benjamin. This was done. Everyone was then brought again to stand before Joseph. (Genesis 44 verses 1 to 13)

Joseph pretended to be full of fury. He accused them of violating his trust. His brothers were now devastated. They immediately knelt before him. There was a lot of weeping and wailing. There was a lot of begging and pleading. They felt trapped. A terrible shame had befallen them.

They were utterly dumbfounded. Explanations became questions. They tried to negotiate for their lives. They offered to become Joseph's slaves. His brothers were now completely humiliated. They were beyond measure remorseful. Their evil deeds had brutally resurfaced. And this tormented them like brimstones from hell.

Joseph could contain himself no longer. He sent all his employees away. Then he wept uncontrollably. He finally revealed his true identity to all his brothers. There would have been an eerie silence in this room. A pin drop would have sounded like an atomic blast.

They were suddenly speechlessly bewildered. Weeping would have turned to hollering. Shock would have turned to cold sweat. They should have thanked God for granting them favor. This startling revelation could have put them in multiple graves.

This was definitely a beyond imagination reunion. Joseph then told them to come closer. They were now more fearful for their lives. But they reluctantly complied. He tried to console them. Then he reasoned with them.

God had reversed their evil intentions. Being sold into slavery was actually a good deed. God turned a horrible experience into a life saving adventure. He asked them to stop grieving for what they did. He told them to stop being angry at themselves. He then forgave them.

God used Joseph to preserve life. God placed him in a strategic location. He was God's instrument. He became the forerunner for his family. God used him to save his family from starvation. He invited his family to live with him. He instructed them to bring their father to Egypt. (Genesis 45)

The Barricading Yoke of Unforgiveness

Chapter Twenty-Seven
Revenge Is Never Sweet

JOSEPH HAD MEMORIZED three generations of trickery. He then took covertness to another level. He put new meaning to the word "clandestine." He declared war on all ten brothers. Joseph skillfully and cunningly manipulated his brothers to their knees. He then terrorized them nonstop. This confrontation had been years in the making.

Most of us could agree with Joseph. Some might view his actions in a positive light. All ten had received their just reward. The consequences imposed were appropriately rendered. Some may even be congratulating Joseph. He had organized and executed a brilliant master piece deception.

The gang of ten had imposed degrading measures upon Joseph. Now he had sneakily turned their evil against them. His brothers finally experienced raw fear. They now got a taste of their own bitter medicine. This must have made their bellies churn in agony.

Some of us might reason that Joseph's actions were appropriate. His brothers had been exceptionally cruel to him. Many could view Joseph's actions thoroughly justified. Some could legalize and legitimize his methods. Some could conclude that revenge would have been appropriate punishment.

Generational deception had produced severe damage. Treachery had plagued his ancestors and his immediate family. But his brothers took wickedness to an all time low. Contemplating murder was bad enough. Selling younger brother as a slave could be considered a fate worse than death.

No measure of reasoning could justify the agony they imposed on their father. They reduced him to live constantly with tormenting grief. Sorrow could have easily put him in the grave. A multitude of us could verbalize that they should have suffered more.

Our assumptions and hasty conclusions would be grossly inaccurate. Joseph did not set out to seek revenge. He did not let his temper control him. He was very level headed. Calm prevailed from his first meeting with his brothers. Deplorable behaviors and underhanded trickery were the golden rules of Joseph's linage. But Joseph's mindset was goal oriented focused.

Joseph's communication with his brothers was at times double edged. His dialogue was harsh. But they were fair. His intentions were never to hurt. He did not harm his family. His behavior was always on a dignified level. And he succeeded on a positive note.

Joseph had been a show off kid. He was considered a pest and a nuisance. But God transformed this spoiled brat into a wise and prudent ruler. Joseph's right heart attitude kept him on track. God used Joseph to protect His chosen nation.

Joseph's strategy cemented his family together.   God used him to put them in a new land. His family received a fresh start in life. They now had a clean re-beginning in a new environment. We could conclude that Jacob's God had mercy on him. God provided him another chance to clean up his act.

Some of us have lived through hell on earth predicaments. Sometimes our hurricanes will continue to batter us. Oftentimes our accustomed habitat will continue to simmer. Our familiar environment could be ripe for repeat offences. Our bloodied hatchets could refuse to stay permanently buried. The grave could have difficulty containing them. Our signed good will peace treaty could be flushed in the sewer. Our gesture toward genuine forgiveness could be trampled on. Revenge seeking occurrences could keep tracking us down.

Our God will know that we could easily drift back. Our filthy environments could be lurking to ambush. But the Spirit of God will always present to us alternatives. Our Father will always make tangible solutions available to us. He will remove us in due time from still toxic conditions.

Oftentimes He will present to us the opportunity to relocate. But fear and stubbornness could be a barrier. Sometimes God will have to assume direct control. He will force us to make that change. Humankind will always need multiple second chances.

We should always determinedly confront problematic conditions. We should always learn from the hardships of life. This is the only way to grow and mature. Life can present itself as a dangerously confusing war zone. But if we never went to war, we will never enjoy the joy of winning. And we will never experience the pain of losing.

Human beings love to win. We can recklessly trample on others when we are on top. We tend to sulk and mope when we lose. Some of us can get mean and nasty. We will not win every battle. But we can emerge intact. The cycle of life affirms this fact.

We may never win the war. We may never take the spoils home with us. But this is factual: The battle is never ours. It never will be ours. It will forever be the Lord's. He will always bring us out alive. All that we need to do is petition Him for help. And He will do the rest.

There are times when we could lose our vision. We could overshoot our runway. We can become disoriented and confused. We will sometimes need a compass to turn us around. Having a reliable compass is always a wise idea.

We all need a guidance system. It can be a life saver if we got lost. But we will need to properly utilize it. A compass is designed to point us in the right direction. Our secular and our spiritual compass operate under similar guidelines.

We should always concentrate on where are coming from. Otherwise we will be pointing our compass inaccurately. We should get our bearing accurately programmed. Today we are here. But we had to come from somewhere yesterday. We need yesterday and today. Then we move on to tomorrow.

This is now. We are the now. We are here. We can make a difference. But we must make the effort. We can make a huge impact in the lives of others. Steadfast determination will enhance our faith. God should always be our compass.

The bible declares in Ecclesiastes 1 verse 9: "The thing that hath been, it is that which shall be; and that which is done is that which shall be done: and there is no new thing under the sun."

Life and history can be likened to a large wheel. Life and living moves from the beginning around to the beginning. We recycle occurrences that have transpired before. There is little that we do that has not been done before our time.

Jacob's fourth son was named Judah. Generations of bad examples also rubbed off on him. He too charted a path of trickery and deception. He yielded to selfishness. This caused him major embarrassment.

Judah took unto himself a Canaanite wife. He sired three sons in this union. Their first born was named Er. Judah procured a wife for son Er. The maiden Tamar became Er's wife. The bible states that Er was a wicked man in the sight of God. Er died because he was evil. Tamar had not yet conceived.

There was a custom within that era and culture. There was a protocol when a widow was childless. The next in line brother had to marry his brother's widow. The first born within this union would be in the deceased memory. The child would be reared as the dead brother's offspring. This would guarantee continuance of the dead brother's linage.

Judah's second son Onan took his older brother's wife. Tamar was now Onan's wife. God was also displeased with Onan. He also proved to be an evil husband. His brother Er lost his life because he was all around wicked.

Onan was wicked on a different level. He conspired with himself to indulge in a wrong choice decision. He ignored God's mandated obligation. He disrespected God. He decided to do his own thing. He disobeyed his reproducing and his replenishing responsibilities.

He refused to honor his dead brother's memory. Tamar was unable to conceive because he was selfish. The Lord was displeased with Onan. A very angry God pronounced judgment against Onan. He lost his life because of his wrong choice reasoning.

Judah had a third son. This lad was young. He was not yet of marrying age. Judah told Tamar to return to her parents. She should remain a widow. Youngest son would be her husband at the appointed time. But Judah had other plans.

Judah probably blamed Tamar for the deaths of his two sons. Time for marriage to son number three came and went. Judah did not produce his son. He retracted on his obligation. He refused to release his son to Tamar. He fabricated excuses.

Tamar then concocted a plot. It was get even time with her father-in-law. Judah was now a widower. Tamar donned the clothing of a prostitute. She successfully seduced Judah. Tamar took no currency as payment for her services. She kept his signet ring, his bracelets, and his staff as collateral. Then she went her way still in disguise.

Judah received a message three months later. His daughter in law was pregnant. Judah thought that Tamar had strayed. His youngest son was still in hiding. She could not have been pregnant for his son. Tamar had violated her matrimonial vows. She had brought disgrace to his family.

Judah decided that Tamar be punished for this shameful act. She had to be put to death. Judah summoned Tamar into his presence. He demanded accountability for this unpardonable offence. But Tamar had an insurance policy. These were Judah's signet ring, his bracelets, and his staff.

Tamar then confronted Judah. She still had the items in her possession. She showed him his merchandise. Judah realized that he had been tricked. He was responsible for Tamar's pregnancy. Twins were earthbound. And he was their father.

Generational abuse of moral principles had once more reared its ugly head. Abnormal behavioral patterns once more recycled. These deficiencies now claimed Judah's generation as its newest victim. He was now caught in the same old dishonorable and undisciplined trap.

There was different twist to this debacle. His daughter in law turned his cunning and manipulative tactics against him. She successfully tricked him. She deviously outsmarted him. This caused him major embarrassment. Jacob was a more cunning crook than Laban. Tamar turned out to be a more sophisticated crook than Judah.

Revenge is oftentimes considered as being sweet. But the aftermath can be as bitter as gall. Tamar cleverly conned Judah. She seductively manipulated him. She produced more leverage than he had bargained for. She won the battle of deceit. But this was a wrong choice decision on her part.

Two new male lives were added to the population. Tamar was now a single mother. She was saddled with huge responsibilities. She had to care for two innocent infants all alone. There would have been stigma attached in her era. (Genesis 38)

Chapter Twenty-Eight
Cleansing

THE UNPREDICTABLE AVALANCHES of life can be relentlessly merciless. Exposure to harsh spiritual winters can take a devastating toll on us. We could suffer severe psychological frostbites. We could endure prolonged mental arthritis. Our soul could be tormented by excruciatingly bitter painful nights and days.

Countless scorching emotional summers can have a debilitating effect on us. We could become overexposed to the severe elements of drought. Unquenchable thirst can leave us parched and dry. Dehydration can literally kill us.

The Word of God should be our insulation. His Spirit is available to us during all our seasons. No one should have to suffer needlessly. The agony of loneliness and hopelessness can be brutal. Helplessness is an extremely painful condition to endure. Internal collapse is always a gut wrenching experience. But this is the grueling reality of a life without God.

No one is an island. Self reliance will only take us thus far. Life is never without alternatives. But we should first look around us. Then we should diligently seek guidance. We will find solace when we ask for help. God did not design living to be complex. We are the culprits who have complicated the simple principles of life.

God is our well of Living Waters. His fountain is never frozen. And it will never run dry. His river is never polluted.

We can always drink freely. Thirst will become an issue of the past. But God had set high standards to sip from His cup. Our hearts must be pure. Our minds must be free of corruptible thoughts. And our hands must be clean.

Cleanliness of heart is next to Godliness. God has to prepare us before we can touch His righteous cup. He will put us through a rigorous cleansing program. Dangerous toxins in our mind can leave contaminated deposits in our heart. There are times when the Holy Spirit will have to put us under His supernatural shower.

God will immediately turn on His spiritual taps. He will saturate our insides from head to toe. Sometimes He will use His holy scrubbing brush on our minds. There are times when God has to use heavenly chemicals to clean deeper.

God has to scrape the filth from our souls. Only then can God sweep us clean. He will vacuum the harmful residues from our heart to Godly perfection. We will stand before Him as a clean vessel. God will shred our dirty unrighteous garments. He will adorn us in brand new robes.

God will then invite us to dine with Him. He will engrave love and forgiveness in our hearts. He will hold His holy cup for us to drink from. We will begin to savor the honey dew drops from heaven. We will drink until we thirst no more. But evil will be lurking even as we drink. The snake will squeeze in beside us at God's supper table.

The devil is still furious, that he was expelled along with his rebellious angels from heaven. He will forever hold a grudge against God. And he is always relentlessly trying to get even with his Creator. But God is still Satan's Boss. The Greatest Designer designed Lucifer. The product will never be superior to the producer. Demon Satan is that product with a fast approaching expiration date. Satan will be livid when God begins to reverse entrenched layers unforgiveness from within us. He will begin waging ruthless guerilla warfare to re-capture our mind. The devil specializes in pre-emptive strikes. He is a murderous strategist. Satan can never outsmart God. But he can easily outwit us.

Satan will attempt to snatch us from the presence of God. Then he could brutally terrorize our mind into submission. He will cunningly negotiate an alternate form of forgiveness. We could accept lip service forgiving as an appropriate compromise.

Forgiveness can be compared to deliverance from substance abuse. Our disease will remain in remission proving we obey our treatment plan. But a relapse is one slip away. We cannot re-experiment on a lesser scale. This would be like playing Russian roulette. Our demon will progressively become more aggressively destructive. We will end up in a worse condition than before.

This brief analogy represents the dangers we face when our mind begins to subvert our heart. Surface level forgiveness is a dangerous manipulative mindset. We will rapidly relapse. Unforgiveness will now become our tormentor.

We are constantly being bombarded with encouragements to forgive. But the truth of the matter is that eloquent words are vastly different from reality. Being told to "let go and let God," sometimes is not as easy as it sounds. Some could tune out these wise words.

There are times when adverse conditions will severely impede healing. Some situations could be beyond grave and complicated. Lingering horrible memories could seriously restrict our healing process. Fear of more damage could create wider divides. But this is the naked truth: Unforgiveness will remain a stumbling block when conflict resolution is absent.

Restoration on all levels should be our goal. But we should first re-visit all the gory issues. Then we should honestly flush them to the surface. Healing can never begin until sincere reconciliation is in progress. There are times when it is easier to mend fences with others. Rebuilding our tattered bridges can prove more challenging.

Forgiveness for us comes directly from the heart of God. Forgiveness for others has to originate from our heart. God will not accept forgiveness from our mind. Many continue to live in misery because of this delusion. This is because our mind will routinely rebel against this vital element of closure.

Cleansing begins with genuine forgiveness. A vast percentage of our population has been grossly misled. Many wrongly conceptualize this very important method of closure. Forgiving in not a pardon issued to someone else. Forgiveness is not granting someone a fake conditional release.

Forgiveness is not an act of charity. It is not a reprieve to a person on spiritual and emotional death row. We cannot put forgiveness on the bartering block. Forgiveness cannot be auctioned off to the highest bidder. Forgiveness can never be bought. Neither can it be sold. Forgiveness should be unconditional.

Forgiveness is freedom from bondage. But some treat forgiving as a good will gesture. This life changing experience is never to showcase our superego. Some still view forgiveness as strings attached contribution to society. Forgiveness is dismantling the fortified walls of strife and anger.

We cannot put forgiveness on an installment plan. Forgiveness should not be put on some vague "to do" list. It should never be shelved for future consideration. We should never reason that we have the right to grant, or withhold forgiveness. Forgiving should always be the here and now. Forgiveness and opinions are not compatible. We all know how this mindset will end.

Forgiving is the most important step towards healthy growth and development. Forgiveness is the foundational infra structure to experience harmony. It should rekindle our spirit. It should rejuvenate our soul. It should revitalize and heal our body.

Jesus cautions us: "Judge not, and ye shall not be judged: condemn not, and ye shall not be condemned: forgive, and ye shall be forgiven." Luke 6 verse37

Many of us behave no differently than the unjust judge. Some will become judgmental and condemn without thoroughly investigating the facts. Some will render swift verdicts with extreme prejudice. But our rush to judgment mindset could backfire on us. We could be the one standing before the unjust judge. We could be that person begging for clemency and mercy.

When we become judgmental, we should be mindful that judgment could also be pronounced on us. Condemning anyone will put us the forefront to also be condemned. It behoves us never to recklessly judge and condemn anyone. Conclusions based solely on opinions are oftentimes wrong. Prejudicial bias can cause us to misjudge.

No one should ever arbitrarily judge and condemn another human being. Unforgiveness is on the horizon when we begin to embrace this misguided mindset. But it is virtually impossible to extend forgiveness and compassion, when our inflated ego is out of control. Many could remain deadlocked in a mindset of strife, to punish perceived offenders. Some will leave earth tightly clutching unforgiveness.

We should always vividly remind ourselves why Jesus visited earth. His unbiased examples should serve as a template for all humanity. There were times when He had to sternly admonish the population. But he was never closed minded or judgmental. He frequently rebuked the people for their anti God lifestyle. But Jesus never arbitrarily condemned anyone.

Jesus endured the vilest form of torture, by those who wrongfully accused Him. But the Son of God held no grudge against those who condemned and sentenced Him to death. Jesus freely forgave all who judged and convicted Him, as He slowly suffocated to death on that cross. We should focus on Jesus' actions on that cross, whenever we decide to judge and condemn anyone.

Jesus reminds us: "For if ye forgive men (or women) their trespasses, your heavenly Father will also forgive you." Matthew 6 verse 14.

Most entertain preconceived notions regarding God's expectation to forgive. Jesus will freely forgive our sins seventy times seven. Yet many will insert conditional clauses before God regarding others. Some of our stipulations are beyond preposterous and dumb. They could make God shake His head in bewilderment.Most of us come to God in a bankrupt condition. Many will only yield to Him after all humanistic agendas have been depleted. Some will finally surrender when the sharks of life begin to devour our flesh. Many of us wasted countless years battering the harsh elements of life.

Most will crawl to God totally exhausted. We are in desperate need of some relief. All we want to do is ask Him to forgive us of our wrong doings. Many of us reason that this will be acceptable to God. Most could conclude that forgiving others can come at a later date.

Then Jesus cautions us: "But if ye do not forgive, neither will your Father which is in heaven forgive your trespasses." Mark 11 verse 26.

God will always have compassion on a broken heart. He will grant grace and mercy to even the vilest offender. But His directives are very specific. We must forgive others if we expect Him to forgive us. Some of us could bluntly refuse to obey Father God. Stubbornness could cause some to retreat in defeat.

Some will grant forgiveness through long range binoculars. We could rationalize that we had met God's criteria. We could fantasize that we had fulfilled our obligation. We could delude ourselves that God will be satisfied. We could begin to concentrate exclusively on our recovery program.

Then Jesus shatters our lopsided thinking: "Therefore if thou bring thy gift to the altar, and there rememberest that thy brother (or sister) hath ought against thee; Matthew 5 verse 23

And He becomes more specific: "Leave thy gift before the altar, and go thy way; first be reconciled to thy brother,(or sister) and then come and offer thy gift." Matthew5 verse 24

Jesus' blunt instructions could shock a multitude of us. These words could slice and dice us to the core of our being. Adherence to Jesus' directives could be tougher we had bargained for. But we can never challenge God's authority. This would be like handing Satan a loaded gun. And he will shoot to kill.God's wisdom is infinite. Our wisdom is limited. His love knows no boundaries. Our love is oftentimes conditional. His grace is sufficient under all conditions. We cannot dispense grace. Jesus sacrificed His life at Calvary for us. How many do we know who would sacrifice their life for us? Many could feel intimidated absorbing Jesus' expectation. Doubt and fear could paralyze a host of us. We could respond with anxiety and apprehension. But writing our instruction manual eroded our infra structure. Obeying our guidelines put us in this predicament.

Some of us could still be shaking reflecting on horrible previous injustices. We had fled the tormenting war zone. We had dragged ourselves to safety. We barely made it. We arrived with a multitude of displaced parts. We are now in a safe and secure place. Our rescue is now a reality. We reasoned that we were a safe distance from our attackers.

We decided to be an absentee forgiver. Our adversaries were out of sight. And so were we. This should pacify them and us. We would tend to our wounds from afar. We reasoned this to be logical thinking. Anger and bitterness could still rear its ugly head. But no one would be around to vent it on. We concluded that forgiveness from afar was safe.

Conjured up forgiveness is not genuine forgiveness. Some could honestly believe this to be the correct approach. But our decision would be based solely on our limited intelligence. The impact of Jesus' words, could feel like an armor piercing bullet. Leaving His sacred altar and returning to the past will not be an easy task.

Even more complicated, Jesus says we must do this in person. We could be saddled with a terrible burden. The sharp jagged fangs of bitterness could begin to inflict more damage to our heart and soul. Our brain could begin to implode from the emotional shrapnel.

We could suddenly feel like running from His presence. This would be a bad idea. Pain and gain are oftentimes intertwined. We should always stay the course. And we should diligently follow God's instructions. There are no other alternatives to move forward.

Embarking on any emotional pilgrimage is never an easy experience. Making amends can be even more nerve wracking. Some of us made hasty exits because of betrayal. Abuse still made some of us quiver. The list of negatives could stretch to infinity. Our pain eventually subsided. But brewing hostility accompanied us everywhere.

Now Jesus expects us to return and confront our past. This could be like returning to countless devastating crimes scenes. Some could be overcome with nasty migraine headaches. Others could tell God that He was being unfair. But the Spirit of God will remind us this is not a multiple choice request. He will also tell us that the clock is ticking.

We could now discover some buried facts. We were not always totally blameless. Sometimes we had skillfully crafted a hostile environment. There were occasions when we were the instigator. There were times when we were the passive aggressor. We had sneakily taken flight. Then we screamed foul.

Forgiveness should now be a joint venture effort. Confronting our past is never easy. Exhuming emotional graves is even worse. Honest self examination can be a very terrifying experience. But Jesus' directives will be crystal clear: "Repair our internal house before we return to His altar bearing gifts." There is no other route for spirit and soul cleansing.

This expectation could be the toughest task ever undertaken by many. Most could have to immediately commence shredding current priority hit lists. Many of us could have to start a journal. The long lists could encourage some to generate files in alphabetical order. A multitude could now have to earnestly fast and pray.

We had endured excruciating pain for too many years. Most of our grief was deeply buried in our subconscious. Unearthing and dealing with these horrendous issues will be extremely difficult. But we are expected converse and dialogue, with those who had imposed raw evil on us. Just thinking about this task made our stomach churn in disgust.

Infidelity will forever be a touchy topic. Reliving painful memories can be just awful. It is a major reason why some become callous and uncaring. This is a monumental problem in society. We hear about it. And we read about it. But it becomes dangerously personal when we live it.

Coming face with a cheating spouse is always tough. They had desecrated their sacred vows. Coping with this serious breach of trust issue had taken a toll on us. We had cursed the day we met them. We had pronounced multiple death sentences on them. This horrible person was still on our short hit list.

Granting forgiveness could induce shock and bewilderment in them. They could react as if we had pierced them with a lightening rod. Shame and remorse could overwhelm them. Multiple emotions could bring them to tears. But it is important that we remain focused.

We could eventually have to pray for them. Then we should close that painful chapter in our life. The heavy burden of hate should now finally be lifted. We should begin enjoying freedom from bondage. We should be overjoyed that we had listened to Jesus.

Everything will change when our goal is peace versus war. Supernatural transformation can sometimes be instantaneous. Honest communication should never be one sided. Meaningful dialogue should always encourage self examination. Truthful exchanges can work miracles.

Focus should always be on conflict resolution. This will lay the foundation for mutual understanding. We can never undo yesterday's mistakes. But we can make the choice to change today. A positive attitude will assuredly make a difference. We will show compassion versus embracing hostility.

Most of us put our heart and soul in a relationship. Some of us make unwise choices. Sometimes we enter in relationships to escape our deplorable living conditions. We eventually could envision our mate as our god. Embark on this approach is neglecting to examine our own imbalances.

Both spouses could have emerged from similar dysfunctional backgrounds. They could set unrealistic expectations on each other. But arguments will never resolve anything. We should always deal with our individual issues. Otherwise we will be setting ourselves for failure. Even after embracing Jesus, some have difficulty with self examination.

We always should recognize our assets and liabilities. This should be our first approach to cleansing. Not dwelling on the past should help us to heal. This should pave the way to forgiveness. And we should find peace for ourselves. Flash backs could resurrect themselves periodically. But making amends should be permanent.

Displeasure will become apparent when we are denied freedom of expression. We could easily get frustrated and angry. Pent up emotions can carry serious side effects. It is very unfortunate when unresolved issues linger untouched. Not being able to interact on any level will always encourage stress.

There are times when people who damaged us literally disappeared. Initially we felt a sense of relief. But over time we began to track them down. Not to forgive, but to punish for violating us. Sometimes we reasoned that we had conquered these horrible nightmares. But they always returned to torment us.

Death is that final curtain call. This is usually a tough period for the living. Some will mourn the dead. But some could become very angry. We could feel cheated. We could rationalize that the finality of death had robbed us. It had erased all our yearning for healthy recovery. We could feel like killing the dead all over again.

We were denied access to confront them when they were alive. Honest dialogue probably could have encouraged a clearer understanding of them and us. All hopes of getting answers to our numerous "why" questions, died with them. We could feel defeated and powerless during these moments.

Mortality will always cause us to pause and reflect. Prayer and meditation will always flush truth to the surface. We could discover that we too had hindered our path to cleansing. We had kept silent when we should have expressed our hurt. Our efforts may or may not have produced positive results. But we would have verbalized our pent up anger.

Many of us will eventually visit the tombstones of our parents. Some will rant in rage to the dead. Oftentimes we will verbalize our pain and suffering in graphic details. It is less threatening to have a conversation with the deceased. We could experience relief venting in this manner. Forgiving them should be easier than we had envisioned.

Sometimes we would visit the graves of other horrible family members. They were beyond evil caregivers. We would curse them until we broke down in tears. We used vocabulary that cannot be put in print. We finally forgave them for all the pain they had inflicted on us. Oftentimes we would depart feeling less burdened.

We could also visit the headstone of our wicked employer. They had intimidated and abused us. Then we were discarded like a dirty disposable rag. Belittlement turned to humiliation and rage. They were totally unapproachable during their lifetime.

We assumed we had closed that chapter in our life. But we are here glaring at that cold stone. And our nightmares resurfaced. They had hurt us badly. They had defamed us. We express our outrage in crystal clear words. But there was compassion in our commune.

We also were at fault. We should have legitimately fought back. But we remained silent and passive. We gave them permission to bully us. We were also to be blamed. We finally tell them that we forgave them. We also asked the dead to forgive us.

God is everlasting to everlasting. We have a beginning. We have an end. It is appointed unto us once to die. Then our judgment comes. God knows about us when we are alive. He knows about us when we are dead. God sees us even beyond the grave.

The road to healing is never easy. Wholesome recovery is always challenging. Genuine forgiveness will always be daunting. Assessing and reassessing ourselves will never be an obstacle free highway. Some could get stuck in a rut for a very long time. Many still struggle with multiple issues.

We should never surrender to a life of despair. We should always explore ways to ease our pain. It is our right to express outrage regarding unfair treatment. Harmful issues should always be addressed. We should always defend ourselves against injustice.

No one has the right to arbitrarily trample on us. We should never believe otherwise. We should never consider ourselves weaklings. Forgiveness is not a weakened state of mind. It takes a lot of character and courage to say: "I forgive you." But many still continue to listen to the advices of "Joe Public."

Forgiveness is that calm and quiet pathway. It should lead to heart cleansing wholeness. God is always encouraging humans to forgive each other. This is His divine offer to us. But we should be willing to dismantle conflict prone environments.

Forgiving should result in lasting peace. We should exhale a huge sigh of relief. Warmth should surpass limited human understanding. Earthly comprehension will not fathom our joy. We should be able to lay our emotional daggers down. We should then permanently bury them.

Forgiving is and intimate contract between God and us. It is important on all levels. Forgiveness is that final act of sincere surrender. But we should be committed to change. Only then will we be granted permission to mend fences and repair bridges. Forgiving should be considered mandatory. The need to forgive is a crucial lifeline. God offered this helpline to all humanity. This is also a mandate from heaven. Our Heavenly Father decreed this expectation. Purity of heart and mind are prerequisites to cleansing.

We should never perpetually live in the misery of victimization. We do not have the luxury of this escape route. Embracing negativity will smother our growth. We all need freedom from bondage. We cannot claim victory in hiding.

It is imperative that we return to Jesus' alter. And we should be prepared to give a detailed report. Sometimes we will still be dragging some unresolved issues. But we should always return knowing that we had done our best.

There are times when our burdens will be too heavy to pull back. Jesus will meet us half way. He will grant us permission to vent our anger and frustration to Him. Jesus will fix situations that we are literally unable to address. He will introduce to a new sustainable lifestyle. God will guide us to find peace and closure. He will tell us: "Well done thou good and faithful servant."

The Barricading Yoke of Unforgiveness

Chapter Twenty-Nine
New Beginnings

It is our responsibility, to probe every process that will lead to conflict resolution. Genuine forgiveness will never become a reality, until we reconcile all levels of disturbances. Only then will we begin to experience the joys, of complete spirit and soul cleansing. For many, this should usher in an era of spirit filled new beginnings.

Sadly, even our most diligent efforts to settle disputes, could encounter major challenges. Those embroiled in controversy with us, could stubbornly refuse to discuss reconciliation. This could be a heart rending setback for us who are determined to settle conflicts. Some of us could lament that our treatment program was incomplete.

Unforgiveness is an extremely tough barrier to dismantle. This burdensome yoke will never voluntarily set us free. It takes concentrated efforts, and steadfast commitment, to pry ourselves loose from this demonic restriction. But not everyone is mature enough to understand the necessity, to undertake sincere grievance resolution. For some, this could be a gruesome and tedious struggle.

Jesus gives us straightforward guidelines, regarding dealing with tough situations such as these: "Moreover if the brother (or sister) shall trespass against thee, go tell him (or her) his (or her) fault between thee and him (or her) alone: if he (or she) shall hear thee, thou hast gained thy brother (or sister).

"But if he (or she) will not hear thee, then take thee one or more, that in the mouth of two or three witnesses every word may be established."

"And if he (or she) shall neglect to hear them, tell it unto the church: but if he (or she) neglect to hear the church, let him (or her) be unto thee as a heathen man (or woman) and a publican". Matthew 18 verses 15-17.

Jesus' wise instructions should be considered mandatory for all aspects of problem solving. Jesus' guidelines apply to church goers and non church goers alike. Not everyone is involved in the formal act of worship. But all human beings should have a spiritual connection with their Higher Power.

We cannot suddenly wish forgiveness into existence. We will need a starting point. The ideal setting should be to have a one on one discussion to repair a damaged relationship. But embarking on the path to genuine conflict resolution, could make some nervous and jittery. Sometimes we will need a neutral referee to act as a trusted mediator. Genuine forgiveness sometimes can appear to be an uphill battle. Reconciliation could remain a work in progress for a very long time. Sometimes constructively venting our anger will reduce tension. This is healthy and appropriate. But our goal should be clarity and understanding.

Forgiveness is virtually impossible when we are hurting profusely. It is difficult to rational when we are surrounded by evil. This is because problems are always searching consistently for ways, to keep hate alive. Sometimes we might have to take a leave of absence from volatile mine fields. But we should never put too much distance between our conflicts and us. This could hinder progress.

We should not wait indefinitely to return. The longer we wait, the more reluctant we could become to return and focus on problem solving. There could be several attempts made to find a common ground. Some could still have emotional bayonets drawn. The atmosphere could still be dangerously tense. One wrong word could spell disaster.

Not everyone has easy access to elders of a church. Sometimes we might have to solicit the help of more wise unbiased individuals. Their role would be assisting in bridging the gap between war and peace. Impartial input should make discussing hurtful issues easier. Tension should be minimized when experienced councillors are present to monitor proceedings.

Nobody ever wins when tempers begin to flare. We can only do our part to encourage change. It takes at least two to make change a reality. Peace is only possible when we focus on the positive. But some people live in ice boxes. Some act as though they will roam earth forever. They conduct their affairs as if they will never die.

Some could have wrong us. We could have offended them. We could attempt to repair breaches. But many could remain aloof and uncaring. They could burn our peace treaty olive branches. They could stubbornly refuse to even listen to us. But avoiding verbal interaction will retard healthy growth.- Some could refuse to seek peace because of fear. They could feel intimidated that they too would have to examine themselves. This would sabotage progress. We could feel that they were holding our emotions hostage. But we should never give up on peace.

We should explore every path that could lead to an amicable solution. We should put forth our best efforts to broker unity. This is extremely important. But some could refuse to ratify a peace treaty. We would now be at a potential volatile junction. Bystanders could get hurt.

We should still proceed to ask for their forgiveness. And we should forgive them for not forgiving us. This would be like heaping coals of fire on their heads. But we will have done our part before God and humanity. We will have exercised our right choice decision.

Sometimes will have walk away from toxic situations. We could have to remove ourselves from potential harm. There are times when we will have to watch explosions from afar. But we will be satisfied that we had done our best. Our consciences will be at peace.

Jesus reminds us: "Blessed are the pure in heart: for they shall see God". Matthew 5 verse 8.

God's Spirit is a candle illuminating within us. He constantly searches the innermost parts of our belly. Only His Spirit can convict our hearts. God is the only person capable of reconstructing our minds. It is Jesus who will convince us of the necessity to forgive.

God monitors our thoughts and actions. Jesus will comfort and chastise us as long as we live and breathe. He affords us countless choices and opportunities while we are alive. He liberally gives us new beginnings to do repair work. Our choices and chances are revoked when we stop breathing.

We cannot be faithful to two masters. We must be completely committed to God. Otherwise we will cheat with the devil. But God will never abandon us because of our stupidity. Only His Spirit can melt our hearts and turn us around. Forgiveness is top priority to God.

Human beings are habitually destruction prone. We are always tripping and hurting ourselves. Band aid treatment is usually ineffective on a gaping wound. We always need to quell the bleeding. Then we will need to examine the condition of the wound. There is no greater pain than emotional distress.

Forgiving should mean reconciling our excruciating past. We should now have the freedom to embrace a new beginning. Everyone needs to experience happiness. A forgiving spirit should be the first step that should make closure a reality. This life changing experience is paramount to wholesome recovery. The storms of life will subside when we begin to live forgiveness.

Sometimes surgeon Jesus will have to operate. Only Jesus will know how to effectively treat our injury. He will be by our side to comfort and support us. The Holy Spirit will closely monitor our healing process. Our healing is called forgiveness.Our mind will protest until it is silenced. But eventually our heart and mind will unite in oneness. Actions should now speak louder than words. There are abundant rewards for making right choice decisions. We should enjoy calm and joy beyond our wildest imagination.

A mind free from corrupt viruses is essential. We should now be able to maintain a balanced and stable life. A Forgiving heart should bring relief to our soul. It should be a joyful occasion when we are finally free, from the barricading yokes of unforgiveness. Peace and tranquility should begin to radiate within us. Forgiving should reinstall new meaning and purpose in our lives.

Our contentment should defy mere human understanding. We should now confidently continue to pursue our God given destiny. This renewed energy should fell like a divine miracle. Forgiving should be that special reenergised interconnectedness.

Heaven will rejoice when we reconnect with our Father. We should enjoy a happy reunion with our loved ones. We should bond meaningfully with our neighbors. And we should understand the importance of loving ourselves.

We should now have the courage to embrace the present. We should sing and dance. We should smile and laugh. We should shake loose sulking and depression. We should embrace the enrichment of harmony and unity.

Managing stress should become a reality. We should begin fulfilling dreams we had perceived were impossible. We should now joyfully worship God in truth and righteousness. We should feel like the lost sheep that was rescued. In humility we should say: "It is well with my soul."

The Barricading Yoke of Unforgiveness

Chapter Thirty
Sin Will Mutilate Great Rulers

KING DAVID was God's chosen and anointed vessel. He was a mighty ruler and warrior. David loved God wholeheartedly. God said that David was a man after His own heart. The Word of God declares this in Acts 13 verse 22 part B.

David was the greatest king who ever ruled Israel. The Lord God bestowed abundant honor and favor on David. He had immense earthly power. Godly guidance was his beacon. But David was not immune from succulent pitfalls. This is a powder keg cocktail. It can reduce the greatest warrior to his knees.

David's relationship with God infuriated Satan. He paid the king a surprise visit. The snake persuaded the mighty king to detour from Godly principles. He used the lust of David's flesh against him. David yielded to mind and body turbulent temptations. Satan then sliced and diced God's servant mercilessly.

David took regular strolls on his palace roof. This probably gave him a good vantage point of his city. This could have been a time of relaxation for the king. He undoubtedly could meditate while he walked. This would also give him alone time with God.

David had a peculiar sighting on one of his strolls. He observed a very beautiful woman. She was washing herself out in the open. And she was completely naked. David's curiosity was aroused. He sent and enquired concerning the identity of this damsel.

He received an answer. This ravishing beauty was a married woman. She was married to one of the king's soldiers. Her husband's name was Uriah. This information should have squashed this king's lustful curiosity. Warning bells should begin to ring in his mind. But evidently he just ignored this loud noise.

He instead dispatched his messengers. They visited the woman's home. They brought this vivacious woman to him. Her name was Bath-sheba. She was indeed the wife of his soldier Uriah. Her husband was in the battle field. He was fighting the king's enemies.

Bath-sheba washing herself was for a reason. Her purification period was complete. She had been cleansing herself. The king had no business on his roof top. He should have been in battle with his men. But he chose to remain behind. Disobedience is bad for our soul.

The king and his solder's wife probably chit chatted. They could have exchanged pleasantries. But conversation and dialogue would have sounded shallow and superficial. The yearnings of the flesh would be the dominant force. Fulfilling lustful desires would have been urgently compelling.

King David deliberately disregarded moral and ethical boundaries. His mind was made up. Greed got activated deep within his bowels. He surrendered to the enticing appetite of his loins. He wantonly entered forbidden territory. He began intimately entertaining another man's wife. He then took ownership to someone who was not rightfully his.

Immediate gratification proved too difficult to resist. They crossed the taboo line. The king and this married woman consummated their relationship. This was an abominable act in the eyes of God. It was also illegal within the laws of the land. They laid the foundation for heartbreaking consequences.

Temporary pleasurable irresponsible indulgencies created complications for them. This moment of illicit passion resulted in a pregnancy. An innocent child was now earth bound. Their momentarily lapse of judgment suddenly became a complex issue. This lustful encounter began to tilt at a dangerous angle.

A monstrous problem was now in progress. Bath-sheba sent word to the king. Her message confirmed her pregnancy. The king sent word to her husband Uriah. Soldier was told he was needed at the palace. Uriah arrived at the palace.

David masterminded a devious cover up. He spoke with Uriah. They broke bread. He then ordered Uriah to spend some time with his wife. This appeared to be a genuinely sincere gesture from the king. But the king was laying a trap for his soldier.

This was a well thought out covert plot. Uriah was supposed to engage intimately with his wife. She would then announce her pregnancy. Everyone would be happy for this couple. Uriah would be called a proud father. But this is not the way events unfolded. The king's plans backfired.

Uriah did not spend the night with his wife. He slept at the palace doorsteps instead. David was informed of what Uriah had done. Uriah was once more summoned before the king. The king again told husband to return home. He was even given extra time off. But Uriah still did not visit with his wife. He remained in the palace.

David's attempts to trap Uriah had failed again. A very angry king dispatched soldier back to the battle field. King David then issued a decree via a letter. His instructions were very specific. His directive was blunt. Uriah should be positioned in the hottest part of battle. Uriah must also be killed in battle. And Uriah was the bearer of his death sentence letter.

The king's orders were activated and duly executed. Uriah was killed on the battle field. The king was an adulterer. Now he was a murderer. The greatest king had stooped to the lowest crime. He had murdered an innocent man. (2 Samuel 11 verses 1 through 17)

Temptation completely devoured David's judgment. He took that which was off limits to him. He acquired illicit pleasures from another man's wife. She was not his to have and to hold. Uriah knew nothing of the king's dubious intents. He was a naive bystander. He admired and loved his king.

Some people will smile and be surface level nice to us. But their mind could be full of corruptible thoughts. They could cunningly attempt to trick and entrap us. They could get frustrated when their devious maneuver failed.

Anger could overpower them. They could become deeply incensed. They could begin plotting against us. They could harbor unforgiveness against us for not complying with their demands. Covetousness has gotten many innocent persons killed.

Our consciences will convict us when we participate in wrongful activities. There is no greater remorse than the burden of guilt. The consequences can have far reaching repercussion. But some will stoop to underhandedness to deflect self examination.

Some could begin to "hen peck" to ease their shame. Others could instigate arguments hoping for a showdown. Many could become hostile if their strange behaviors were questioned. Many could get furious if their clandestine objectives failed.

Some could resent us because they were consumed with guilt. They could strategise ways to convert guilt to hate. They could exhaust sleepless nights plotting against us. They could begin to malice us. A malicious mind can become extremely vindictive. We could be mortally wounded, because someone close couldn't deal with the after effects of guilt.

David became enraged because he could not manipulate Uriah. Fear perhaps motivated him to plot Uriah's murder. Desperation could also have played a role in his decision. He resorted to hate Uriah without just cause. David's unforgiving mindset was totally one sided.

The king laid eyes on Bath-sheba. He desired her. She was off limits. But he took possession of her without thought of consequences. His actions were dangerously dead wrong. But he was recklessly bent on flesh fulfillment. David's runaway emotions conquered him.

Instant gratification can spark unpredictable chain of events. This can ignite long lasting destruction. Our curious mind can place us in some precarious situations. Lust could visit anyone at any moment. It could present itself as a hard to resist proposal. Uncontrolled desires can crucify us.

Temptations will confront us as long as we live. This is a reality in our daily pilgrimage. We don't have to be on the prowl looking for trouble. Trouble can blindside us anytime. The route that can cause us to stray is irrelevant. The problem is with the consequences. Deviant behaviors run deep and wide. King David was an experienced warrior. He was always engaging in wars. He was always capturing lands. He always controlled populations. All Israel knew that their king was mighty. He was their lord and master. Bath-sheba knew this too.

King David's strolling routines were probably consistent. The people would have been aware of this. Bath-sheba would have known about her king's strolling patterns. She would be aware that her ruler could observe multiple activities from his vantage point.

Bath-sheba could have cleansed herself in private. But she chose to wash herself naked in the open. She probably knew that the king would observe her nakedness. She could have desired him to lust after her. She succeeded.

King David could have obtained anyone he desired. But he behaved like a common thief. Did Bath-sheba orchestrate a cunning trap for the king? Did she deliberately expose herself in plain sight? Did she non-verbally seduce the king? Did David get tricked into temptation?

Carnality will not respect proper codes of conduct. Seduction will bring integrity to its knees. Being blessed with power and influence is unimportant. Status and prestige is irrelevant. Lustful pleasure will always override logic. Our flesh can be extremely persuasive.

Any one of us could end being damaged just like David. Clandestine activities cannot stay hidden indefinitely. Decorative paint jobs will eventually peel away. But wrongful indulgence is still a moral crime. Ethical abuse can destroy us. We could create irreversible damage by sidestepping our obligations.Bath-sheba afterwards became David's wife. But God did not authorize this first born. He imposed harsh consequences on the parents. The son they produced died shortly after birth. God reclaimed this innocent soul. A blameless child returned to his Maker. Sinful gratification by his parents caused this problem.

King David made numerous serious blunders. Reckless and deadly sins created far reaching calamities for this leader. He habitually strayed off course. But his heart was always firmly fixed on his God. There were periods when God had to sternly chastise David. But David never rebelled against the will of his Maker.

There are times when we are our worse enemy. "The devil made me do this" is never an appropriate excuse in the sight of God. We delude ourselves when we resort to this comment. Those whom we hurt will not be amused. Wrong choice reasoning is always problematic.

Everyone will experience periods of sudden turbulences. But poor choice reasoning will always lead us astray. Yielding to run away emotions is a poignant example. Bad decisions will put us at risk for a fall. But we are flesh and blood human beings. And humans tend to behave in strange and peculiar ways under pressure.

We could jump in the wrong direction. Activating bad choices will always damage us. Sometimes the freight train of life will steam roll us. There could be times when we could barely miss the third rail. These are the realities of life and living.

We should never blame Satan for all our dubious blunders. Sometimes we are our own devil. Satan will be observing us from the sidelines. He could initially scratch his head in disbelief. Then he will begin laughing at us.

Chapter Thirty-One
Obsession Can Destroy

THE INEPTITUDE of some human beings could temporarily confuse a multitude of wise men. There are times when humankind logic and reasoning can defy the laws of reality. The book of Ester is an important documented example.

Reckless stiff headedness can get us killed. One vile person can be exceptional good at being bad. Doing what is right is never their central theme. A tyrant is routinely an expert at orchestrating fear through intimidation.

A man named Haman is a vivid example of bizarre behaviors. Blind rage caused him to target a group of people for extinction. He was professionally diabolically wicked. Hard core arrogance resulted in revenge seeking vendettas.

His pride took un-forgiveness to a new dimension. He became obsessed with a mindset of dominance. But he interfered with the wrong families. They were God's set aside generation. Haman was doomed from the start.

King Ahasuerus was the supreme ruler of Persia. His domain stretched over one hundred and seventy seven provinces. Haman was deputy ruler of this vast empire. He was in fact the prime minister. This man was not from the tribe of Israel.

Then there was Jew named Mordecai. He was an official in the king's government. He was a descendant of the tribe of

Benjamin. Mordecai had a cousin named Ester. She was his uncle's daughter. Her parents had died. Mordecai raised Ester as his daughter. Ester was a beautiful young woman.

The king was in the third year of his reign. He celebrated great feasts with his people. During the celebrations, he summoned his wife queen Vashti. But she refused to join him. The king felt disrespected. This was not a good example for the other women in his kingdom. He consulted with his inner circle. The decision was made to exile his wife. This is what he did.

He then began searching for a virgin. She would replace queen Vashti. Mordecai encouraged Ester to enter the race. Virgin Ester was sent to the king's house. She was highly favored. The king took her as his queen.

Haman received a new title shortly after the festivities. The king decreed that all servants at his gate should bow before Haman. Self importance immediately dominated Haman. Arrogance took hold of his senses. He got obsessed with the importance his job. He became an egoist.

Mordecai refused to bow before Haman. Mordecai was a dedicated servant of his God. He bowed only to his Maker. This infuriated Haman. He was embarrassed and enraged to boiling point. He decided to exterminate the Jews in all the provinces. He conferred with the king. He lied to this king.

He complained about some uncooperative people. They were scattered throughout the provinces. They refused to obey the laws of the land. These people only followed their customs. Haman said that the country did not need them. The king agreed with him. The king gave Haman sweeping powers. This put the Jews at Haman's mercy.

He quickly started preparation to wipe out a nation. He even built a gallows to hang Mordecai. Mordecai sent a message to the queen about Haman's plot. Queen Ester responded to her cousin's urgent plea.

The terrified Jews began praying. They all petitioned God for deliverance. They all fasted for three days. The queen then put a bold plan into action. She invited her husband and Haman to a feast.

Mordecai had previously saved the king's life. He had foiled an assassination attempt. The night before the banquet, the king was gravely distressed. He started reviewing previous events. He discovered that Mordecai had not been formally recognized for saving his life.

The king summoned Haman the next day. He asked Haman for suggestions for rewarding an outstanding man. Haman assumed he was this man. Then he answered the king.

"Let the royal apparel be brought which the king useeth to wear, and the horse that the king rideth upon, and the crown royal which is set upon his head:

"And let this apparel and horse be delivered to the hand of one the king's most noble princes, that they may array the man withal whom the king delighteth to honour, and bring him on horseback through the street of the city, and proclaim before him. Thus shall it be done to the man whom the king delighteth to honour" Ester 6 verses 8 to 9

The king then told Haman to bestow this high honour on Mordecai. A humiliated Haman had to comply with the king's orders. Haman returned home very upset. He was told he wouldn't prevail against Mordecai.

The queen's banquet got under way. Queen Ester explained the reason for the banquet. Haman was exposed for the wicked scheme he had tried to enforce. The king was exceedingly angry. Haman was hanged. This was on the gallows that he had built for Mordecai.

Mordecai emerged victorious. He received a well deserved promotion. The king installed him a deputy ruler of the empire. He was also given all of Haman's assets.

Haman became obsessed with his authority status. He embarked on an out of control vengeful vendetta. He tried to set himself superior to the God of all nations. His evil mindset got him executed.

Rational thinking can be absent when our life is in danger. Mordecai could have thought only of himself. He easily could have exiled himself to another country. Instead he petitioned his God for help and guidance. God gave Mordecai the courage to challenge a tyrant.

Positive turn of events change can begin with one person. Mordecai's faith encouraged him to stand firm. God put a fearless spirit in His ambassador. Queen Ester was God's anointed mediator. Evil was put to death. God granted deliverance for all His people.

There are multitudes of Haman roaming this planet. Power hungry people could instantly resort to murder. The fanatical force to be seen and heard is oftentimes compelling. This insane rush can result in wide scale massacre.

If we walk with a loaded gun, we will eventually use it. The laws of statistics tell us this. Anger is like a loaded gun. We could shoot to kill. We could exterminate the innocent. Many of us are extremely prejudicial. Some of us will hate others with unlike minds. We could become incensed. We could begin to plot their demise.

Some of us could broaden our horizon. We could include people who look different from us. They could behave differently from us. Their customs and practices could differ from our beliefs. This could pose huge problems for some. Many could feel trapped and powerless. Some could become insanely infuriated. Some could set out on a blind vendetta. But it is impossible to exterminate the world.

Many are quick to tag bigotry solely on race. There are different levels of bigotry. But there is one common denominator. This is undeniable. Bigotry is ignorance. Most will hate when they don't understand. A lot could resort to hurting others when they feel threatened.

Our world is all around diverse. All life forms are included. God designed it so. Everyone has to accept this fact. Some can kick and scream. But this is the way it is.

We all share the same atmosphere. Blood sustains life. Our blood comes from one Divine well. The color will never change. It is always red. We all bleed from a cut. All human beings are packaged with multi level emotions. Putting them in sequential order would be a no brainer.

Performing good deeds should be relatively easy. This gesture should invite an aura of peace and an air of tranquility. Evil thinking takes a lot of scheming and planning. Arrogance and pride are trigger happy relatives. Self importance is always the igniting lever.

Everyone should be treated with respect. But some of us can abuse this freedom of choice. Our mind and our brain could join in oneness. We could begin dictating how we should be treated. We could become resentful when our demands are ignored.

Intense anger could erupt deep within our bowels. We could get entombed in red hot fury. "Better than thou" attitudes can rapidly backfire. A dangerous un-forgiving spirit can easily endanger us. We can end up destroying ourselves.

When we encounter evil, we should take a stand. When the Spirit of God speaks, we should respond. Ignoring His call is like hiding completely exposed. He will always take care of us. He expects us to care for others. Sometimes this means putting our life on the line.

Wrong doing should always be confronted. Otherwise we are cowards. Believers don't have the luxury of being politically correct. Too often we are afraid of hurting, "other people's feelings." Double talk is a sin. The truth is rarely a popular topic. But it does not have an expiration date.

Public opinion told Mordecai to bow to Haman. Public opinion and God's opinion are never compatible. We need more people like Mordecai in this century. Saving our own hide should never be an option. Doing what is right should be our only recourse.

Our steps are directed by a Higher Power. We walk to the beat of God's drums. We should never remain silent to sinful activities. We should never be afraid to confront evil. We should never accept the status quo of the world. It is God who will lead us to victory.

Chapter Thirty-Two
Uncertainty Births Insecurity

AN EVIL VEIL OF UNCERTAINTY has begun to smother God's earth. Menacing dark clouds are hovering dangerously close. Dense fog is making visibility extremely difficult. And human beings are responsible for creating this crisis. We could be pushing ourselves towards extinction.

The population is experiencing nervousness and apprehension. Global financial institutions are still restructuring to rebound. Many world currencies are struggling to survive. Fear of another economic crash is a real threat. This is disturbing and frightening. Many are cursing their stock brokers.

Money markets could be on a collision course with an iceberg. This could be more powerful than the titanic disaster. We could drown and rot at the bottom of the ocean. The human barracudas could feast on our remains.

Prosperity for many has come to a virtual standstill. People are becoming increasingly insecure and scared. Many are fearful that austerity will help the rich and neglect the poor. Violence has erupted in many nations. Many have revolted against their leaders. Some have plundered and looted. Ordinary citizens have turned against their governments. Many turn to social media to vent their outrage. The rich and powerful have been put on the defensive. Infra structures in numerous regions have collapsed. The push for reforms has become an epidemic. And this is spreading.

Eventually reality will replace anger. Then we will need to access the consequences. Sometimes we could be swapping one evil for a greater evil. Change could bring us sorrow instead of joy. Disappointment could develop to despair. Rage could be re-kindled to greater proportions.

Nasty things occur when economies begin to crumble. Our finances could experience major turbulences. Life savings are usually the first to vanish. This could put excessive strain on many families. They could begin to disintegrate. Our new generation could suffer the backlash.

Human beings look forward to stability and predictability. Security gives us a feeling of protection. We could become furious if our way of life came under attack. We would employ all means to protect and preserve. Most could resort to drastic actions to defend their territory. Bigotry has been resurrected. This evil is again on the rise. In some cases it has peaked to unparallel levels. Some parents are re-indoctrinating the language of discrimination in their children. Ignorance is now controlling the minds of many.

Malice has taken up permanent residence in many of us. There are times when we can't even verbalize why we ceased to communicate and dialogue. Envy is at an all time high. Bickering and strife have carved out new guidelines. Deadly force vengeance is now the new and improved rule book.

Hate crimes are on the rise. And this is gaining momentum. Groups are being targeted because of the shades of their skin texture. Some are attacked for their core beliefs. We are supposed to be a civilized society. But humans are converting God's planet into a blood sport.

Dishonesty has become more daring. Murder has increased in many communities. Anarchy could quickly gain speed. Lawlessness could saturate many cultures. It could begin to thrive. The overall synopsis of our society looks pretty bleak.

Our legitimate choices are being infringed on. Our old ways of doing business could change forever. Many folks are walking around in a daze. Most are disillusioned. Some are scared stiff. "What is next," is the preoccupation of many. The multitude is increasingly becoming insecure because of worldwide uncertainty.

Poverty is on the rise. Simply making ends meet is sometimes a full time job. Life has become disastrously disturbing. The plundering by the rich has defied logical reasoning. Most citizens are in disarray on this planet that we call home. It is supposed to be our safe haven. But there is an eerie feeling in the land.Human beings are sometimes turning against each other like savages. The wicked elite are more aggressively trampling on the poor and the needy. The greedy and the gluttonous are aggressively lining their pockets. Hoarding by some individuals has become more widespread.Minor differences of opinions can quickly reach boiling point. Insignificant arguments can become violent clashes. This can result in vicious confrontations. These explosive settings could pinnacle into dense forests of un-forgiving spirits.

Husbands are cheating on their wives. Wives are cheating on their husbands. Our children young and old are running rampantly out of control. Misery and depression is at an all time high. A host of family values have virtually vanished.

Basic trust is now hard to find. Mistrust is on the rise. Life is menacingly presenting itself as being highly unmanageable. Society is functioning in chaos and confusion. Our population could become a casualty because of reckless behaviors.

We have poured slime over God's green earth. Moral integrity should to be our bullet proof vest. Unshakable ethical standards should always reflect our moral values. We could lose control when we stray or bypass our core beliefs. It is disheartening when we start doubting our spiritual leaders.

Some are earnestly praying for God to return. Some believe that God is on a slow descent to re-claim His world. Some say He has taken a pit stop. He could be giving humanity one final change. Getting our act together would be His goal.

Some of our sins are beyond vile. We should be relieved that God doesn't respond as humans do. We should be grateful that God is patient and compassionate. We should be thankful the He doesn't treat us with impunity. All humans would be wiped from the face of the earth, if Jesus were not our intercessor.

God constructed three foundational pillars, to mold and guild us and our children. Some refer to them as God's first three institutions. God designed these priceless structures to compliment and support each other. A collapse will be inevitable if any one of these protected walls, suffered structural damage.

A family is God's greatest gift to humanity. This is His first pillar. We are expected to mold and guide our children. We should be instilling in them highest calibre training. We should be influencing them by our positive examples. We should be instrumental in leading them to Christ.

The security of the home should be our children's comfort zone. Parents should be their defender and protector. This should instill confidence and trust in our offspring. Our children should feel comfortable to discuss any issue with us.

Worship should enforce healthy family values. This is God's second pillar. Our children should learn by observing us obey Godly principles. They should realize that there is someone more powerful than their parents. They should understand that they are also accountable to God for their choices. Worship should teach them to obey God's instruction manual and guidelines.

The home of God is where they should explore their spirituality. They should learn that their outer self depend on their inner self. Their behaviour should reflect how they feel. This is important. Children should understand that the church is an extension of their immediate family.

God's tabernacle is not solely for adults. We are not the only ones in need of healing and comfort. Children also are important people. But their needs are different. Many are beginner learners about the ways of God. Some are confused regarding Godly expectations. They could easily make wrong choice blunders.

They could be ashamed or embarrassed, to report everything to their parents. They could need an impartial listener. They could feel more comfortable confiding in their pastor. They could speak to a wise elder. An independent body could act as a buffer. This should make dialogue easier with offspring and parents.   These examples are some guidelines that God carved out for parents. But for many, family values are on the decline. Some parents try to recapture their youth. Some compete with their offspring. Some parents interact with their children as peers.

 The family institution that Almighty God designed is being defiled. Some have made a mockery of God's expectations. We are the parents. We are not our children's peers. Their friends are their peers. We confuse our children when we behave as juveniles. They could begin to feel insecure interacting with us. Inappropriate behaviours could encourage instability in their lives.

Religions come and go. Spirituality will last into eternity. But religion is waging a war against spirituality. And religious doctrine appears determined to overthrow spiritual indwelling. This has birthed major upheavals for many.

A lot of people are deserting their faith. Some encourage us to always live for the moment. Many say that God will never return to reclaim earth. Some contend that the rapture is a manipulative ploy. Our children could get caught in this deadly crossfire.Some of our bad leaders are in joint venture affiliations with the world. The in bad standing preachers have become cult driven. They have diluted and muddied God's verifiable words. They twist and distort our Savior's simple message. Spiritualism is being replaced by emotionalism.

Sometimes we sit in His home perplexed. Gallivanting in a night club could better describe this mayhem. Some leaders will encourage their followers to become fanatically emotional. Emotionalism is a mind propelled expression. Even Satan can get emotional to confuse our minds.

It is the responsibility of every parent, to encourage their child to excel and succeed. For this they need and earthly education. God established all learning institutions. He imputed wisdom in humans. This is God's third pillar. A good education is the most important tool for our children. Our education system is in a mess. Most teaching curriculums lay in shambles. God based instructions have been deleted from most learning institutions. Most sanctuaries are mute on this important issue. Some have even become silent partners with the heathen society.

Some religious leaders behave as if they are ashamed of the Cross. They disgrace themselves when they abandon Godly principles. They disrespect the One who controls their breath. It should be considered blasphemous when children are denied moral and ethical exposure.

Most parents practice high standards in their homes. They strive to abide by Godly guidelines. They instill in their children the need to live upright lives. Godly values are re-enforced in their children in God's home. But it is prohibited to discuss God in some schools.

Every offspring will suffer bumpy rides during their in-between years. This is called the perils of youth. Youngsters love to flaunt their independence during these periods. But performing in an independent manner requires maturity. Most children still struggle to bridge that gap. Sometimes we should hold their hands as they make transitions.

Children need guidance and support, when they wrestle with complex issues. Parents should be compassionate and understanding. They should always listen attentively. Reacting in frustration or anger can alienate our children from us. Parents should remind themselves, that they too created problems while growing up.

It is the duty of every parent, to encourage their children to communicate and dialogue with them. They should demonstrate empathy and patience. It is sad when some parents refuse to listen, and converse with their offspring. Screaming and yelling matches are counterproductive. Power struggles will usually end in gridlock.

Most children will become rebellious when their hormones begin to control them. This can be a time of major upheavals for the family. But our children should not be subjected to corporal punishment. Many will dig their heels in and become more uncontrollable.

Divorce and death are devastating and frightening for any child. Most children can be left feeling alienated and lonely. The death of a parent can leave children feeling abandoned. Grief can oftentimes turn into anger. Despair could encourage rebellion. Out of control behaviors could pose a problem.

Divorce carries the same feelings of emotional distress as a death. The breakup of a common law union usually will carry the same side effects. Both groups could experience similar rage. The only difference is that with divorce, both parents are still alive. Many children experience difficulty adjusting to a new relationship. A lot of blame could be focused at the biological parent. This could inhibit development of a positive bond with step parent. The new relationship could be healthy and stable for the couple. But the offspring could choose to function as an outsider. Acting out behaviors could get progressively worse.

There are predominately four places where youngsters deposit their hostilities. It is in their home. It is in the church. It is in their school. It is in their communities.

Adolescence is a period when most children refuse to listen to their parents. Some will wage outrageous wars against all authority, including the church.

Academic performance is usually the first to deteriorate, when children are experiencing difficulty coping. Disruptive behavior could quickly become cause for concern. Some children are expelled from school, because of low academic performance and behavioural problems.

This could infuriate most parents. They could become heavy handed and punitive. Situations can become more explosive. This could result in total dialogue shutdown. A battle of wills oftentimes can end in a stalemate. Deviant behaviors could eventually become a problem in the community.

Some could turn to other disturbed peers to fill a void. Kids of like minds tend to stick together. Negative peer pressure can be very destructive. The wrong crowd can effectively persuade some to resort to evil indulgences. This volatile environment can be more powerful than parental influences.

Satan uses adolescence as a weapon against parents. The devil is responsible for grooming some youths to become dangerously defiant, and menacingly antagonistic. He is an expert at substituting positive values with hard core rebellion. Many youngsters get inducted in gangs because of negative peer indoctrination. Gangs are usually formed when unruly youngsters of like mind band together.

It is always problematic when children refuse to obey parental rules and standards. Oftentimes parents are unfairly targeted. Not all children emerge from broken homes. Some are from very stable environments. But peer pressure can be very compelling. Mingling with the wrong crowd can be potentially problematic.

Society categorizes children as younger versions of parents. Many parents get blamed for every wrong choice that their offspring make. This is not always the case. These assessments could be completely inaccurate. But public opinion can oftentimes blame parents, as being the root of the problem. Many could condemn parents as having failed in their personal lives.

The general public could conclude that "bad parents" had also failed the children. This family could be viewed as being problematic. Some could reason that they were a burden to society. Some could even say that they had shamed God. These comments will always enrage affected parents.

This could result in an angry standoff between parents and the community. Decent parents can become vengeful monsters when provoked. No one likes to be convicted without a trial. Most accusers will not even agree to a hearing. Many persecutors rarely reflect that they too have children.

Parents should never give up on their children. Caring adults should always be available to lend a helping hand. Society should understand that every wayward child needs rescuing. Casting blame is never the solution when a child is at risk. Sometimes parents need empathy and support. The same applies to every child.

The alternatives are grim. The law is very heavy handed. It rarely is kind and compassionate. Those who prosecute are not known to be merciful. Their job is to rigorously uphold the law. Their duty is to crush all acts of unlawful behaviors. The penal institutions could become the guardians of our children. Our generation is not yet extinct. Our new generation is not yet fully in charge. They still have a far way to go. They need to learn from our positive examples. It might be a long and hard road to reverse negative behaviours, in some youngsters. But we should never exile them to the undertaker. Some of our children are stubborn as mules. Many temporarily become evil minded imbeciles. But we should never cease to pray for them. We should put them in the hands of Father God. And we should leave them there. Change will begin when the Spirit of God begins to re-mold them.

Jehovah is the only one who can calm their rebellious nature. Our God will never allow them to drown. He will calm their turbulent billowing waves. He will keep them safe amidst their rising tides. He will return them to the safety of our home.

Chapter Thirty-Three
We killed the Messenger

GOD PRESENTED TO HUMANITY His most important Person. He introduced His only begotten Son Jesus to the world. This was in accordance with the predictions of His chosen prophets of old. The long awaited Savior was now on earth. His assignment was to re- teach the population to obey their Maker.

Jesus was sent to earth because of moral and ethical decay. And God's chosen nation was primarily responsible for this widespread immorality. Jesus transformed Himself to reflect earthly features. Jesus became a flesh and blood human being.

Jesus made His debut in a unique and unusual way. This was in accordance to His Father's will. The population likely assumed that their Messiah would arrive on earth in royal splendor. But this was not the way events unfolded.

Father God selected a young virgin named Mary. She was chosen to be the carrier of His only Son. God dispatched His angel Gabriel to earth. His assignment was to present the good news to Mary. Gabriel told Mary not to be afraid. Mary was told that she was highly favoured by God.

The angel explained that God wanted her, to be the mother of His Son Jesus. Gabriel told Mary that the Holy Ghost would come upon her. And that she would conceive.

God's messenger informed Mary she would bring forth a male child. God's Son would be named Jesus.

Mary would have been humbled and excited receiving this news. She would have been delighted and honoured that God was pleased with her. But this young virgin could have been also terrified. She was engaged to a young man named Joseph. She was unsure how Joseph would react when she told him about her pregnancy.

News of Mary's pregnancy stunned Joseph. He responded as any man would. He didn't believe her explanation surrounding her pregnancy. Her tale sounded too bizarre and far-fetched. Impregnation without his input was absolutely impossible. He would have concluded that his bride to be had cheated on him.

A breakup would be inevitable. This would have been life threatening for Mary. She could have been stoned to death for infidelity. But Joseph was a young man of high integrity. He didn't want to expose Mary to embarrassment. He had no desire to humiliate her. He decided to quietly break off their engagement.

God quickly put an end to Joseph's sorrow and disappointment. He had an angel visit Joseph via a dream. The angel assured Joseph that Mary was telling the truth. God's messenger explained Mary's pregnancy in vivid details. (Matthew1 verses 20-21)

Joseph awoke from his dream. He was undoubtedly relieved that Mary had been faithful to him. He would have been overjoyed that God had selected Mary, to earthly birth His Son. Joseph took Mary as his wife. He did not consummate their relationship until after the birth of Jesus.

Caesar Augustus decreed a law that the people should be taxed. Everyone had to travel to Nazareth in Bethlehem to pay taxes. This included a very pregnant Mary. She took the long journey to Bethlehem with husband Joseph.

Mary went in labor while in Bethlehem. There was no accommodation for them at the inn. They had to look elsewhere for lodging. They had to settle for a stable. Mary brought forth her first born Son, and laid Him in a manger. (Luke 2 verse 7.)

A manger is a box or trough in a barn or stable. It was built against a wall for cattle or horses to feed from. There was a divider to shut out the flow of water. The Son of God's first earthly bed was a feeding trough. God chose the humblest environment to introduce His Son to the world.

God decides when and where we make our earthly debut. Some of us enter this world in the humblest of surroundings. We should never feel embarrassed or ashamed of our origins. We should never grow up feeling inferior.

How we entered this planet is irrelevant. It should have nothing to do with our potentials. We can all fulfill our predestined purpose in life. We can rise to greatness. We can sit in the highest places of honour. We can become world leaders.

God designed the cycle of life. Every living organism must have a beginning,. All species must begin with infancy. God could have made an exception with His Son. An adult Jesus could have arrived on earth ready to conduct His Father's business. But God chose His established human protocol to send His Son to earth.

The Messiah was no ordinary child. But He was still a baby. His needs would have been the same as any new born. Mother Mary would have had to tend to all baby Jesus' needs. Jesus would have required love and nurturing like any infant. Earthly parents were now Jesus' caretakers. Their assignment was to guide the Son of God through His tender years.

Mary was an inexperienced young mother. She would have been lacking the fundamental essentials of child rearing. But the Spirit of God guided and trained her to be a well balanced mother. All children need positive influences during their early years. This is the most precious gift we can give to our children.

God did not exempt His Son from undergoing formative years training. This is the most important period for healthy growth and development. God expects us to mold and groom our children wisely. It will forever be our sacred duty to instill positive values in our children.

There are some distinct differences between our birth and those of Jesus. We must have an earthly biological father. Our mother cannot conceive and reproduce otherwise. Jesus had no earthly biological father. The Holy Ghost was Jesus' Father. Mary's womb was God's chosen vessel to bring Jesus to earth.

We arrive on earth pure and innocent. But our blood line is polluted. We inherited tainted genes from Eve and Adam. Our sin nature will become pronounced as we grow and mature. Jesus' bloodline will never be polluted. Jesus is God in flesh form. Jesus is the unblemished Lamb of God. It is only Jesus who can purge our sins away.

Jesus was oftentimes categorized as the son of a carpenter. But He was remarkably exceptionally different. His wisdom exceeded His years. At age twelve He marveled the intellects with His superior knowledge. They were puzzled that an uneducated boy could be so well learned.

Some adults will avoid interacting with above average intelligent children. Some label super smart kids as opinionated brats. Sometimes their resentment could be verbalized in their family environment. Their children could overhear these negative comments. They could endorse their parents' frustration. Bright and gifted children are sometimes subjected to ridicule among their peers. Oftentimes their reasoning ability could outpace those of their peers. Various groups could feel intimidated and embarrassed. Some could secretly yearn to be on par with them. Insecurity could begin to breed resentment in some. This could create a volatile climate.

Some children are just outright mean. Some could begin unfairly targeting above average children. Some could quickly get branded as nerds. Some groups could resort to indulge in nasty pranks. The affected child could be left feeling ostracized. Some ignorant children could engage in bullying tactics.

Bullying is an indication of an inferior complex. Bullies mask their feelings of inadequacy feelings by acting tough. Their dominating attitude gives them a false sense of superiority. They oftentimes will prey on the presumed more vulnerable in their environment.

Any form of harassment is a crime against humanity. Society will routinely respond forcefully to visible acts of intimidation. But this is only surface level reaction. This crisis tunnels much deeper. And it is extremely flammable. Sometimes these poisonous venoms of hate are birthed in the home environment.Bullying is a dangerous progressive disease. And it can quickly become contagious. Many lives have been ruined because of the insensitive actions of some evil individuals. Some have committed suicide because they could not live with embarrassment and humiliation.

Strong arm tactics is an emotional sickness. It should be treated with the same urgency as a physical disease. We need to attack this problem by educating our youth. Always blaming "bad parents," will never produce solutions. Sometimes we will need to intervene.

Knowledge is a powerful weapon. It should give wisdom the opportunity to grow and mature. Understanding is an effective anger manager. Our youth need to be enlightened on the dangers of indulging in amoral behaviours. Tackling this problem will encounter numerous stumbling blocks. But we will have failed if we do nothing.Jesus was a prime example of bullying tactics. He was targeted for ridicule practically everywhere He went. Jesus was not the "macho man" typecast. He was labeled ever vile name on earth and in hell. Scorn and disdain were His close associates. But He never caved in under pressure.

John the Baptist was Jesus' first cousin. Some could reason that John was the opposite of Jesus. He was a rough and rugged man. He lived outdoors. His diet consisted of locusts and wild honey. He was always preaching repentance. No bully would have dared to mess with John.

Cousin John was the first human who formally told the world who Jesus was. He paved the way for Jesus' ministry. He proclaimed these words as Jesus came forth to be baptised: "Behold the Lamb of God which taketh away the sin of the world." John 1 verse 29 part B.

Jesus came to earth on official business. God had become extremely angry with the descendants of Abraham, Isaac, and Jacob. He was utterly fed up with their lifestyles. Their antagonistic behaviours deeply disturbed God. Jehovah deemed it necessary to resort to drastic measures.

God was determined to demonstrate to His cantankerous people, that he was still in charge of their lives. He dispatched Jesus to restructure His out of control nation. Jesus' assignment was to teach this rebellious generation a healthier lifestyle. His task was to encourage a problematic people, to begin practicing spiritually healthier lifestyles.

Jesus presented to humanity new and different approaches to obeying God. His aim was to lead them back to their Maker. His message was simple yet profound. "Turn away from evil, and behave in accordance to the will of God."

John wrote: "He came unto His own, and His own received Him not." John 1 verse11

Bigger problems than bullying challenged our Messiah, from the onset of His Ministry. Jesus did not fit the humanistic "God image" mold. Some viewed Him basically as a non entity.

He was mistrusted from the beginning. The people immediately branded Him an imposter. Most of the population perceived him as a no good person. They despised and hated the Redeemer. Some labeled Him the devil.

Jesus encountered massive resistance from the rich and powerful. Nothing about Jesus made sense to the religious leaders. Self righteous attitudes overshadowed their deplorable behaviours. They could not be convinced that He was the long awaited Messiah. Their deliverer should have overthrown the Romans.

Our Messiah spent three years leading by example. God Jesus exhausted countless hours, encouraging this out of control nation to turn from their wicked ways. The harder Jesus tried, the more rebellious they became.

They were firmly set in their ungodly ways. They were contented with themselves. They didn't need any help managing their affairs. They just wanted to be left alone. But Jesus continued His mission undeterred.

The multitude tried aggressively to intimidate Him. They all failed miserably. Jesus never stopped showing compassion. There were times when He had to sternly admonish His bickering flock. Sometimes He had to severely chastise them.

Jesus tried to teach the people how to be kind and compassionate. They invoked the laws of Moses against Him. They told Jesus that it was their right to retaliate. Our Savior demonstrated the necessity to be kind a considerate to the poor and needy.

Oftentimes they scorned and ridiculed the less fortunate. Most treated the underprivileged as misfits. Many viewed them as a hindrance to society. Some did not believe that the downtrodden, was worthy of God's grace and mercy.

God's Messenger focused on the topic of genuine forgiveness. He instructed the population on the necessity to forgive their enemies. Many considered forgiving as a weakness. He told them to love their enemies. They were accustomed to be at war with their enemies.

Jesus told His people they should endure persecution without retaliation. They would have loved to overthrow and persecute the Romans. They instead turned on Jesus. They consistently and relentlessly persecuted the Son of God.

The religious elite reacted in unbelievable shock, when told that the meek would inherit the earth. These words could have temporarily paralyzed the minds of many. For too long, arrogance had been the daily bread for most. Many had become extremely comfortable projecting an attitude of superiority.

Meekness meant humility. Humility meant total surrender to the will of God. Some probably had forgotten how to approach God with a contrite heart. Many had grown accustomed to demanding their wants from God. Many likely were never satisfied with God's promises, to richly supply all their needs.

The sanctimonious religious leaders should have listened to Jesus, when He delivered His sermon on the mount. They should have internalized His words of wisdom. (Matthew 5 verses 1-12.) They should have grasped the core essence of why Jesus came to earth. They should have realized that God was not interested in exterior grandeur.

Listening and understanding encourages action. The descendants from the tribes of Israel should have begun to examine themselves. They should have reasoned that their corrupt hearts needed purging. They should have realized that God expected pure heart honesty. They should have gladly accepted Jesus as their Messiah. They should have made a determined resolve to faithfully serve their God.

They should have begun to accept and obey Jesus as their Saviour. The Spirit of God would have completely transformed their lives. They would turn from their wicked ways. Embracing change should not be as difficult as they had envisioned. They should have discovered that meekness did not mean weakness.

They should have learned that it takes inner strength and courage to live genuine humility. Love should replace hate. Peace should supersede war. Their aloof attitude towards the less fortunate should have undergone a drastic change. They should have memorized the fact that God created and made all people equal.

They should have understood that obeying Godly principles would make them, easy targets for ridicule and persecution. They should have learned to wholeheartedly forgive their enemies. Forgiveness should free them from the restraints of bitterness and anger. But they were bent on listening to their carnal mind.

Perception rarely tells the whole story. Humans tend to rely heavily on their personal assessments. Oftentimes it is in line with their interpretation of a sometimes inaccurate diagnosis. Sometimes they rush to form opinions without ascertaining all the relevant information. Inaccurate assumptions created serious conflicts in Jesus' era.

Haughty attitudes and superiority complexes placed the majority on rickety egotistic stools. Fanaticism birthed dictatorial behaviors in many. Spiritualism was muffed by aggressive emotionalism. The multitude incited against the God who controls our breath. They cursed and demonized Jesus for speaking the truth.Jesus journeyed with the population. He taught and encouraged them nonstop. But many would not even listen to the message. The Son of God anguished with the people. At times He wept over them. But they just wouldn't take heed. They finally ganged up against the messenger.

They eventually resorted to murdering the Son of God. Humankind executed Jesus because they couldn't silence Him. The Son of God departed from earth many centuries ago. Now He sits at the right hand of His Father. And He is keeping watchful eyes on all humanity.

God is still telling the population to turn from their evil ways, and seek His face. And Jesus is still available to intercede on our behalf, when we transgress from His Father's will. But entrenched barriers are blocking direct access to the Throne of Grace. These restrictions range from doubt to unforgiveness.

Modern technology has blanketed the globe from corner to corner. Most of society is now heavily relying on electronic devices, to supervise and monitor their activities. Many steadfastly depend on their stationary and portable machines to ask questions and get answers. This practice is greatly disturbing. We will stray from the will of God when we get addicted to human designed substitutes.

God has never stopped reminding humanity that He is still in charge. But most human beings are as stubborn as mules. Many still struggle with truly believing that Jesus is Lord. They will resort to every imaginable humanistic indulgence to avoid dealing with God's truth. But the hand writing is on the wall.

The virgin birth of Jesus is an era long gone. And this miracle will never return. When Jesus returns to earth, He will descend to righteously judge humanity. Those who have been faithful to Him will sit with Him in glory. The unfaithful will be thrown into the fiery bowels of hell.

Many firmly believe that God has returned to His original blueprint for all humanity. There are some instructions and guidelines that have to be constantly stressed and repeated: We were made to be an extension of the God of the universe. We became a living soul when He breathed life into us. He installed within us freedom of choice. But we are expected to make wise decisions.

The Word of God is not complicated. It is simple and realistic. It is our responsibility to trust and obey God under all conditions. We are participating in idol worship, when we begin to indulge in things that do not reflect Godly standards. We will suffer harsh consequences when we live by our own rules and regulations.

The bible speaks of the remnant. This is a broad demographic spectrum. This includes all cultures, creeds, and nationalities. No longer will there be this sect, or that sect. We are all one people. And we are all included in God's plans for humanity. Some are fighting this reality tooth and nail. But no longer can they ignore this truth.

The unfathomable wisdom of God is dismantling formal organized religion. Humankind conjured up the grossly misleading word. God has reintroduced to the world the need to embrace a Spiritual connection to Him. The greater population is now yearning to experience the benefits of being spiritually connected to Almighty God. Many are embracing Spiritual indwelling and disbanding religion.

This dramatic turnaround is very heart warming. Jehovah never said He is a religion. Jesus never endorsed any religion. He never encouraged compliance to denominational principles and traditions. He taught the importance of having an honest relationship, with the Spirit of our God of the universe. Jesus emphasised the necessity to trust and exercise our faith in God.

Religion could be compared to politics. Human beings tend to be highly opinionated in their beliefs. Sometimes attitudes of unforgiveness begin in the church, and gush out to other areas. Oftentimes we encounter strong resistance when we truthfully proclaim the gospel. Many could hate us for speaking the truth. Some could literally harm us to avoid examining themselves.

We do not need religious indoctrination. We need the Spirit of God to lead and direct our paths. Some confuse spiritualism with emotionalism. Many still struggle because of the lack of knowledge. God is not an ideology. God's Word should never be categorized as merely analogies.

Apostle John further wrote: "But as many as received him, to them gave he power to become the sons (daughters) of God, even to them that believe on his name." John 1 verses 11 to 12.

Everyone should believe that Jesus is the Son of God. We should always internalize that Jesus' death and resurrection freed us from the shackles of sin. We should always rely wholeheartedly on God. Belief and trust should encourage us to exercise our faith in God.

Faith is savoring God's blessings, before He manifest His promises into reality. But double mindedness will impede our blessings. Doubt can kill our dreams and sabotage our faith. Unforgiveness will keep us in limbo. Satan and his crew are always eager to activate our unbelief button. Many have been denied kingdom entry because the devil tricked them.

Jesus said: "And I will pray the Father, and He shall give you another Comforter, that He may abide with you forever;

"Even the Spirit of truth; whom the world cannot receive, because it seeth him not, neither knoweth him: but ye know him; for he dwelleth with you, and shall be in you." John 14 verses 16-17.

The Holy Spirit is our permanent companion. He lives within us 24/7. He is our comforter and our guide. He will encourage us when we are in alignment with God. He will admonish us when we stray. We should always prayerfully reflect on the life of Jesus. We should rely on Him as our exemplary role model.

The Spirit will instill bold confidence within us. We will fearlessly proclaim the name of Jesus. Our lives will take on new meaning when we begin living by His examples. Jesus came to earth to re-introduce God to the population. Our commission is to steer the population back to God. Jesus lived among the people. We also live among the people. Negative attitudes became a way of life for Jesus, because He was different. Ridicule and scorn dwarfed positive teachings. We are also now different. When we are different, we will attract attention. We also will be exposed to hardcore negativity. We also could be ridiculed for our beliefs and standards. There will be times when our best is never good enough.

Once we were ordinary. But that was then. The Holy Ghost converted us to reflect Godly principles. Jesus amazed the population because He would not cave in under pressure. Sometimes we will be amazed when God begins to work through us. But we should always stand firm. We should never be a fence rider.

Jesus forgave the angry mod who wrongly sentenced Him to death. Jesus forgave His murderers in the midst of being severely tortured to death. He had compassion on the convicted thief who was also enduring crucifixion. He gave this vile felon a pardon into heaven. Our Saviour will forgive the worst offender who truly repents of their sins.

Jesus completed one hundred percent of His assignment. He unwaveringly represented His Father. He performed His duties in an upright dignified Godly manner. We should always reflect Jesus' high standards in our service for God. But many struggle needlessly to reach God's half way mark.Too often we get sidetracked by negative bombardments. Personal issues can suddenly resurface to confuse and torment. We can automatically lose focus when our heart is overwhelmed and overburdened. Our vision can become severely restricted, when conflicts block the windows to our soul. This could put enormous strain on our ability to concentrate and function effectively.

Satan's job is to encourage us to keep the Holy Spirit at bay. But we should fight back with determination and resolve. God will empower us with strength to overpower Satan. The Spirit will remind us, that we should never surrender to the demons of our emotions.A God focused heart will always keep us safely grounded. This is His promise. This is our bought and paid for birthright. These are inheritances worth fighting for. We should claim ownership to them. We should embrace these highly favored statuses. These are our eternal and everlasting gift.

Unforgiveness will forever be a volatile topic. But forgiveness will defuse all pent up rage. We cannot perpetually wallow in misery and self pity. Constantly feeling victimized will always encourage depression. We all need freedom and deliverance.

At some point we should leave all our bitterness and suffering behind. We should bury them in a designated Spirit filled location. This area should be called the shore of forgiveness. God will bury all our pain and suffering in the deepest part of the ocean.Over time, we should remember our hurts no more. We should be finally free from Satan's grasp. We should reconnect in harmony with the Spirit of the living God. Our spirit and soul should be at peace. We should now begin to enjoy life. There is no greater comfort and joy than a Spirit filed torment free heart.

Genuine forgiveness is not futile wish. Internal wholeness is not an elusive dream. A torment free mind is not a whimsical fantasy. But everyone will battle stormy periods in their lives. This is called the hardships of life. No one will escape this reality.

Jesus promised that after our hurricanes, we should expect His calm to prevail in our hearts. He demonstrated His promise by paving the way for us. He suffered. He bled. And He died so that His blood will cover and protect us, through all our trials and tribulations.

The grave could not hold our Saviour captive. Jesus walked out of that tomb on the first day of the week. His resurrection should give us bold confidence that He died to set us free, from all demonic bombardments. This includes breaking the chains of the barricading yoke of unforgiveness.

www.ingramcontent.com/pod-product-compliance
Lightning Source LLC
Chambersburg PA
CBHW060458090426
42735CB00011B/2028